THE
MAN
&
THE
BUSINESS

GRAHAM SHARPE
with Mihir Bose

RACING POST

Dedicated to everyone who knew William Hill
and everyone who has worked for the company.

Copyright © William Hill Organization Ltd and Graham Sharpe 2014

The right of the William Hill Organization Ltd and Graham Sharpe to be identified as the authors of this work has been asserted by them in accordance with the Copyright, Designs and Patents Act 1988.

Paperback edition published in 2015 by Racing Post Books
27 Kingfisher Court, Hambridge Road, Newbury, Berkshire, RG14 5SJ

First published in Great Britain in 2014

10 9 8 7 6 5 4 3 2 1

A catalogue record for this book is available from the British Library.

ISBN 978-1-910498-01-9

Cover designed by Mike Smith.
Designed and typeset by J. Schwartz & Co.

Printed and bound in the UK by CPI Group (UK) Ltd, Croydon, CR0 4YY

Every effort has been made to fulfil requirements with regard to copyright material. The author and publisher will be glad to rectify any omissions at the earliest opportunity.

www.racingpost.com/shop

Front cover: Hill's boards stand out as Brighton rocks at the races.

Backcover images (clockwise from top): Welcoming customers to William Hill; One of the earliest William Hill betting shop frontages, from the mid-1960s; a video wall in a flagship betting shop; one of William's proudest moments as he hands a trophy to the Queen; the William Hill mobile app – downloaded over 2,000,000 times; runners flash past the company logo.

CONTENTS

PREFACE
by James Henderson

James Henderson became CEO of William Hill on 1 August 2014, just as the original version of this book went to press. Here he outlines where he believes the company stands today, and the exciting times ahead for the Group:

I'm fortunate to have worked in almost every part of the Group in the last 30 years. The pace of change in the gambling sector – and at William Hill specifically – has accelerated hugely in the last decade.

Digital has really broadened our horizons and we've gone from being a land-based UK-centric business, to one of the world's leading betting and gaming companies.

International opportunities are particularly interesting. We've been very focused on strengthening online, then moving onto the US, Italy, Spain, and Australia, and in the process increasing our international revenues to around 18% as at the end of 2014. To increase them further we need both flexibility in our technology and to have a team of experts continually looking for those right opportunities. Technology is the foundation on which everything else sits. We are already successfully differentiating our customer offering through product expansion and our high-quality user experience. By optimising the mix of in-house and third-party technology we can differentiate further and bring customers an exclusive William Hill experience, whether on their smartphone or tablet, online or in-shop.

William Hill stands out as a rare example of a land-based market leader that has successfully transitioned into digital market leadership while maintaining that market leadership in retail. You can't overstate the enormity of the change that happened in the Group to achieve that.

Whether it is through acquisitions or organically, we've got a strong record of generating value – from the Stanley acquisition to creating William Hill US, to gaining a top three position in both Italy and Spain.

William Hill Australia is now properly equipped to compete in a very attractive market, having undergone significant change in terms of its management, operations, marketing, user experience and product range to increase its competitiveness. Commencing rebranding as William Hill in 2015 was another key step.

When you're looking to change, adapt and innovate as quickly as we are, you need a culture that doesn't stand in the way, but actively supports and encourages it. You can't do that dictating from the top. You've got to be collaborative, you've got to trust people and you've got to be prepared to fail. If you're not failing often enough, you're probably not pushing far enough.

Regulatory change is always our biggest opportunity and our biggest threat. Managing this is about having the right approach to responsible gambling and an open, proactive and collaborative way of engaging with governments, regulators, the wider industry and anyone concerned about what we do and how we do it. We've always been a responsible company and that ethos sits at the heart of our operations. If there's one criticism I have of us and the industry, it's that a lot of the good work we've done has gone unnoticed. I've made improving communication a priority for William Hill.

Gambling is a basic human instinct. The advantage of having a regulated industry is the transparency and control it gives to government, and through them, to society. What we all want is to be able to make decisions on the basis of good quality data. That's why research such as that reported on by the Responsible Gambling Trust is so important, because it takes the whole debate forward in a productive manner to enable us to make changes – based on facts, not opinion.

James Henderson
CEO, William Hill PLC, April 2015

FOREWORD
by Gareth Davis

I have never been what one would call a great reader. My dalliances with fiction have been largely confined to summer holiday reading. But I do have a passion for books about sport and business.

My fascination for books about sport began on Christmas Day 1958 as an excited little boy. That morning, I rose early and started tearing into the pile of presents that Santa had delivered. As a budding future England goalkeeper, I was delighted to find a bright green knitted goalkeeper's jersey, a 'Casey' football with a proper lace, and best of all, the autobiography of my great hero, Jack Kelsey, the Arsenal and Wales goalkeeper.

I was besotted with Kelsey and followed his career avidly. I even called my pet rabbit Kelsey. I spent most of that Christmas Day and quite a few subsequent days engrossed in Kelsey's book *Over the Bar.* My obsession with Kelsey faded when he declined to autograph said book in the car park at a snowy Gigg Lane, just before a Bury versus Arsenal third round FA Cup tie. However, my passion for sports books has never waned and I have assembled a great collection.

Understandably, my interest in business books developed rather later in life but I have still managed to read and collect a large number so far. My collection consists of titles by both distinguished business academics and celebrity entrepreneurs.

It gives me particular pleasure to introduce this book written by Graham Sharpe which combines both of my favoured subjects. It tells the story of the 80-year history of the William Hill Organization and its transformation from very modest beginnings to the global business that is William Hill today.

Graham's encyclopaedic knowledge of sport, sports betting and William Hill has been combined to provide a cracking good read that will entertain anyone with an interest in sport and how a business can develop by additional involvement in sporting activity.

Like many employees of William Hill, Graham has been working for the company for many years and his commitment to the business and its people can be seen throughout this book.

I've been very lucky during my time as chairman to work with Ralph Topping. It has been a great experience, and I wish him well in his thoroughly deserved retirement.

I'm looking forward to an equally rewarding working relationship with Ralph's successor, James Henderson, who has all the necessary attributes to take the company forward into the future.

It is particularly apt that this title is being delivered in William Hill's 80th year. In those 80 years some amazing people have contributed to building what is 'the Home of Betting' and I am sure that you will find Graham's account a fascinating read. Enjoy!

Gareth Davis
Chairman, William Hill PLC

INTRODUCTION
by Graham Sharpe

This is the story of a barely educated boy, one of 13 siblings, born in the early days of the 20th century in the backstreets of an obscure Birmingham suburb, who would, virtually single-handedly, reclaim and enhance the reputation of a much-maligned business which at the time of his birth was, as viewers of the BBC's acclaimed drama series *Peaky Blinders* will know only too well, literally in the gutter.

Bookmaking in those days was conducted in a manner more akin to the lawless cowboy towns of the American Wild West. Honesty and integrity were in short supply amongst those who took bets at the racecourse from those who came to watch horses run in races whose outcomes were often pre-determined. Those objecting to what they saw as at best bad practice and at worst downright crookedness could find themselves subject to threats and violence. With bookmaking carried out by individuals and gangs on the fringes of the law, disputes were frequently settled by fists and weapons. There were no legal betting shops, although it was not difficult to get a bet on with a bookie's runner who might visit your pub of choice, operate on the shop floor of your factory, or in the alleyways and shady corners of your street.

It could be a little difficult to get hold of your winnings.

Almost by accident, William Hill would enter this colourful but dangerous world and, after immersing himself in it to learn all there was to know about how it worked, set about transforming it, to the extent that today the company bearing his name ranks amongst the most respected and influential not just in Britain, but, increasingly, throughout the world, having re-entered the ranks of the FTSE 100 during 2013. It wasn't easy. Along the way William may well have had to indulge in the worst excesses of bookmaking's darker days himself, in order to understand how best to drag the art from the shadows where it had been lurking, protesting all the while, into the harsh light of respectability where it stands today.

This book examines every aspect of William Hill's life and times. He was no irreproachable paragon of virtue either in private or public – some might say he was often guilty of hypocrisy in both. It also continues the story of the company he created beyond the day in October 1971 when he died at the age of 68, showing how it expanded over the next forty-plus years into a world-ranked business working across, at the time of writing, nine countries and nineteen time zones while doing business via the internet with customers in over 120 countries.

I joined William Hill in March 1972 and, as the company celebrated its 80th anniversary in 2014, was proud to be able to say I had worked for it for over half of its existence. I hope I have done the founder and his company justice.

Graham Sharpe
Media Relations Director

PART ONE

Three months before his death, William Hill presents the Gold Trophy to Her Majesty The Queen, owner of the winning horse, Charlton, at Doncaster on 17 July 1971.

CHAPTER 1
EARLY DAYS

A run-of-the-mill bookie might have decided not to bother with the Rufford Abbey Handicap. It was, after all, the last, and perhaps least, of the races at Doncaster that September day in 1952. The card had been dominated by the oldest of the five annual 'Classic' races, the St Leger, which had been won earlier by the odds-on favourite, the Derby winner Tulyar, whose success delighted the crowd but dismayed the layers. Many in the crowd had already headed for home, counting their winnings en route to their cars, buses or trains. The two-and-a-quarter mile, nine-runner Rufford was, to most racegoers, an irrelevance. William Hill's racecourse team even suggested to their boss that they give it a miss to make sure of catching the 4.30 train back to London – the next one wasn't for another two hours.

William was approaching 50, and already sensing that the heyday of racecourse betting had passed. A tall, well-built man, an imposing presence, who always wore a white silk shirt with wide red braces and used a huge silk handkerchief, he was now only regularly standing on course on Saturdays and big race days. He was inclined to agree with the lads: little point hanging about for the last. 'Let's go.' Even as they were packing up, however, he was approached by the secretary to a lady owner with a runner in the race. Not one of the best-known female punters of the day, though, and an apparently unfancied horse. Could she back it for her employer? How much? Ten thousand pounds, please. At a conservative estimate, that amount of money would today equate to a six-figure sum, perhaps in excess of £200,000.

The veteran journalist Geoffrey Hamlyn told racing writer Jamie Reid what happened next. 'Hill accepted the bet instantly, turned his staff round and marched them back to the rails. He climbed back on to his stool and within a matter of minutes had laid four other horses to take out a similar sum as the secretary's boss's runner.' 'Hill's roar when it comes, is heard far above the muffled chattering of the track,' was how another contemporary writer, Robert Jackson, recalled the time he'd spent on course with William just months earlier, 'as he offers prices on a grand scale. You never hear "Ten to one" from Hill's lips; always "A thousand to a hundred."' William showed little emotion as the Rufford was then won by a 9/1 outsider called Barnacle, though the name would have struck a chord – as a youngster he'd lived in a village of that name. William had just turned a profit for his book, it is said, of as much as £50,000.

Now at last it was time to depart the racecourse. To add to his satisfied mood, at Doncaster Station the 4.30 train turned out to have been delayed by signal failure, so 'they settled down for dinner in the dining car and Hill travelled back south a happy and wealthier man.' Maybe the figures became inflated as the story was told and retold. Perhaps his actions were a little over-confident, reckless even – a throwback to the days before he had become the head of a large organisation employing hundreds of people, when he was the only one responsible for his actions. But it was days like this that had led a member of a rival bookmaking firm, according to the author Richard Sasuly, to say of William Hill that 'he played with numbers like a great pianist', and why he'd come to be lionised as 'King of the (betting) Ring'.

William Hill was born on 16 July 1903, at the family home, according to his birth certificate, in the Aston (though some would say Small Heath) suburb of Birmingham. Two years earlier the National Census of 1901 shows his father not to have been the greatest fan of prying officialdom, perhaps also giving a clue to where his son would get his characteristic bluntness from: to the question, 'Where Born?' comes the less than revealing response: 'England'.

William Hill senior was a 'general enameller and japanner' (japanning is a method of varnishing a surface, such as wood, metal, or glass, to obtain a durable, lustrous finish) for the Daimler Car Company. 'Our father was not only a painter of coaches,' explained his youngest son, Joe Ward Hill, 'but was responsible for the complicated heraldic designs and crests with which all horse-drawn coaches were then adorned.' This artistic flair would subsequently appear in William junior and other family members. Then 29 years old, Hill senior was living at 32 Henshaw Road, a small terraced house, with his wife Lavinia, 26, whom he had married five years earlier. At the time, they had two children, two-year-old Ethel and one-year-old Thomas (known as Fred) – possibly named after the couple's boarder, printer's compositor Thomas Gill. Their third, Cissy, arrived in December 1901. The couple's first-born child, Lavinia, had died the year she was born.

By the 1911 Census, William junior, now seven, had three more siblings: Walter (known as Dick), born in 1905; Ida (known as Molly or Fanny), born in 1906, and baby Grace, just three months old. Grace's twin, George, had died in infancy. William and Walter apparently looked so alike they could almost have been mistaken for twins. Four more children would be born: Mary, on Christmas Day 1912; Elizabeth in 1914; Jesse on Boxing Day 1915, and the last, Joe Ward Hill, in 1922. The family was now living in Malmesbury Road, Aston, according to the youngest son Joe 'one of the less savoury districts' of Birmingham, and although 'there is no evidence [William] ever went to bed hungry, all around him there were children who did so'. This, Joe suggested, was the genesis of William's lifelong left-wing views.

'Lavinia was by all accounts a big, warm personality,' says Chris Foott, 'our' William's great-nephew, who has become the family's unofficial archivist, 'while also being someone you simply didn't want to mess with!

'But she must have been very strong-willed, as she managed to raise her 11 surviving children to adulthood in some semblance of order. She kept the family together and instilled strong ethics, and she learned a trade (hairdressing) which she made sure that all of her children mastered. (William adored her, says his nephew Sandy Brown, and would regularly send her cases of champagne and, at Christmas, a chauffeur delivered turkey. William's nephew, Chris Harper, recalls him saying she was so well organised that had she been a man, she'd have become an Army General.)

Betty Booth [née Elizabeth Hill] often proudly reminded us that she had done Mrs Thatcher's hair – although God only knows if that's true! On the downside, many members of the family have been a bit too fond of drink, many have been stubborn and obstinate (often beyond the point of reason), and several had a seriously nasty streak.'

William junior was a 'sickly' child, in and out of hospital – although he would eventually grow to touching six feet tall with broad shoulders. There is a record of him attending school briefly in June 1908, but he seems not to have gone regularly until 1911. 'He was so backward that he could not keep pace with his contemporaries,' remembered Joe. William showed a talent not only for drawing and painting – even having a section of a school exhibition devoted to his work, said his brother – but also for 'flogging' his drawings for up to £1 a time. He would later use this artistic bent to good effect when he designed a poster to publicise his first venture into fixed-odds football coupon betting. However, the brevity of his school career would later come back to haunt him: 'I had to teach him how to write letters,' his great friend Phil Bull later wrote, 'and deal with lots of other things where his lack of formal education was a handicap.'

In 1912 young William's father was enrolled as a founder member of the South Birmingham Social and Flying Club, promoting amongst other things pigeon racing. He had his own pigeon loft, and was a regular exhibitor at the Bingley Hall pigeon show in Birmingham. It seems probable that the young Hill children would also have been introduced to the delights of this sport, which had its own gambling element.

Sixty-five years later in 1977, the William Hill link to the Club was marked as the company sponsored the William Hill Memorial pigeon race and donated a trophy to mark the opening of its new clubhouse.

The Derby may first have registered with young William when, in 1913, protesting suffragette, Emily Wilding Davison, rushed on to the Epsom course and was fatally injured as she brought down the King's horse, Anmer.

In 1915 William's family moved again, Daimler having been taken over several years earlier by the Birmingham Small Arms Company, BSA, a major industrial conglomerate which manufactured everything from firearms to motorcycles and buses. Their new home was in the village of Barnacle, near Coventry, where his mother had been brought up – possibly, now the First World War was under way, to avoid the bombing of Small Heath factories by Zeppelin airships. From there William was expected to walk to school, but after a short while he declined to do so any longer. William's nephew, Chris Harper, offers an interesting postscript:

'William once drove me up to Barnacle – he had agreed to give some money towards creating a sports field and clubhouse there and was to officially open it. On the way up he told me I didn't know how lucky I was, and that as a kid he'd had to walk across those fields on his three-mile trip to school. When we got there we re-traced his steps – it was about half a mile!'

Nevertheless, at this point William's conventional education was effectively curtailed. 'Grandpa William Hill wanted all three of his older sons [Fred, William and Walter] to do apprenticeships and study for formal qualifications at technical college,' believes Walter's son, Neil Hill. 'Fred and Walter did so, but not William. His major interest was making money *now*, not studying for further technical qualifications.' At the age of 12, William now started his full-time working life as a farmer's boy, at the princely salary of 2/- (10p) a week. His duties included attending Nuneaton market on a Tuesday and driving any cattle purchased there back to the farm as well as touring local villages in a horse and trap, taking meat orders. He took to the work, which gave him an enduring fondness for the country life. He would later tell an interviewer that it was around this time that he 'lost the first few shillings I ever saved in a flutter on a horse'. The instinct to gamble and take risks would inform both his private and working lives from this time onwards.

But how did that gambling gene turn up so definitively in this Brummie lad with a coach-painter dad? 'I never heard any reference about his father, William senior, being involved in gambling,' says William's nephew Neil Hill, who has researched the family background. There is a suggestion within the Hill family, consequently, that, unlike the horses which William would painstakingly and lovingly breed when he became the owner of two stud farms, there is a potential problem with his pedigree. An unexpected and undocumented bloodline in his and his siblings' backgrounds might just have been responsible for the injection of calculated risk-taking without which William and at least one other of his brothers and sisters could not have made a living from gambling. It could also have introduced the love of horses which manifests itself in many parts of the family. (Joe Ward Hill's grandson, Ben Newton, inherited both, being expelled from school for gambling, then owning and breeding racehorses.) In short, there is no doubt that William Hill senior's mother was Sarah Hill – but considerable doubt that her husband Samuel was his father.

Since by the time of the 1861 census Samuel and Sarah were already living apart just a few years after having wed, and William senior was not born – in the village of Lostock Gralam in Cheshire – until 1870, it seems unlikely that Samuel was William senior's biological father. According to Christopher Foott, who has done as much research as anyone into his extended family, William senior used to talk about his actual father being the 'lord of the manor':

> It seems entirely possible that 'Grandpa' made up the story of the 'lord of the manor' to mask the truth of his mother's unhappy death and his father's neglect. But on the other hand, it also seems entirely possible that he was not Samuel's son, which leaves open the possibility of being the illegitimate son of the lord of the manor – as he himself implied.

In 1918, at the age of 14, William was taken away from the job as a farmer's boy he had come to enjoy so much. His father had set up his own workshop as a coach painter, while still working for BSA, and now, relocated for war work to BSA's Birmingham works, which took him away from his workshop, he put his son in charge and let him run the business, including overseeing several older workers. William's role earned him £25 per week, an extraordinary amount of money for that time, if we can believe his brother Joe's recollection – equivalent to £1,000 nowadays. His father soon had second thoughts, however, and had William apprenticed to BSA as a tool maker, shrinking his wages immediately to 7/6d per week, of which his mother commandeered 5/- for his keep. Perhaps it was at this time that William's father is supposed to have said, 'It's time you took your coat off and got down to business.'

Responded the son, 'Any bloody fool can take his coat off!'

At its peak, BSA was the largest motorcycle producer in the world. However, William did not take to engineering – Neil Hill was told by his parents that William had been less than enthusiastic about his father's wish that he develop a trade: 'The low rates of pay offered to an apprentice and consequent lifestyle were not for William. But opportunities for a 16-year-old in 1919–20 to make significant amounts of money were very limited in and around Birmingham.' During his two years at BSA, therefore, William came up with the idea of acting as unofficial bookie to his work-mates – in a 1970 interview he was to boast that the 3d and 6d bets he'd taken off his workmates had 'shown a handsome profit', which at the time was planned to go towards a farm of his own. Meanwhile the family had moved to Acocks Green, a new, fashion-able, developing suburb of Birmingham – William Hill senior was a well-established and skilled artisan with his work, so could afford a larger house. As William junior's income had taken something of a hit, he also started to arrange and promote, via self-designed print-ed posters, a weekly dance at the local village hall. He also learned ballroom dancing, something he would always remain fond of. Ice cream sales during the interval brought in more cash! 'In William's early years "flogging" was a way of life,' brother Joe recalled: 'every object appraised on how much it would fetch – he had a persuasive tongue and could strike a hard bargain.'

Former Birmingham bookmaker Don Butler, whose own father worked at BSA before himself going into bookmaking, believes that William started gambling more seriously as a 16-year-old when he was part of the local 'Woolf Gang'. This would have been around the time Birmingham racecourse, at Bromford Bridge, reopened in 1919 after the end of the First World War, a year after a 'one-off fix-ture' the previous Easter had seen the legendary Steve Donoghue ride a winner in the first meeting for three years. There were about seven of them in the gang, including Jack Woolf himself, who became a well-known Birmingham bookmaker, and his brother, Solly, Joe Tittle (possibly Tickle), Tommy Turner and Ted Revel. They were a group of relative youngsters in their teens, but very shrewd and street-wise, and William was very much one of them.

Ron Pollard, who worked for William for many years, says Tommy Turner was 'the son of a race-gang leader who protected Bill in Birmingham in his younger days and had a job for life as a result'. 'Tommy Turner was with William from the outset,' remembers John Smurthwaite, who started with William Hill in the mid-1960s, when Turner was working on the racecourses in the south. In 1976 Jeffrey Bernard, the hard-drinking and gambling *Sporting Life* and *Spectator* columnist, bon viveur, and later subject of the stage play *Jeffrey Bernard Is Unwell*, wrote this:

> Tommy Turner used to stand up on the rails for William Hill in the old days. Tommy is typical of the older generation of racing professional. Under his soft brown hat there is a face that looks as ripe as a windfall. I once saw him make a book at Worcester races while at the same time, between races, he managed to consume an entire bottle of Courvoisier in the Members' Bar. I hasten to add that it was an accurate book which showed the old firm a profit.

In his will William would leave £2,000 to a Thomas Turner.

Before long, William began his move into serious bookmaking, at a time of racecourse protection gangs and attacks on rival illegal betting shops, depicted in 2013 by the popular BBC2 drama *Peaky Blinders*. 'It was quite common knowledge amongst bookmaking families in Birmingham,' says Professor Carl Chinn, whose own family was one such, 'that William Hill started up in Tyseley and Greet, areas of Birmingham close to Small Heath, where he came from, and where, I think, he had runners [men collecting bets for him] at one or two of them.' One veteran Birmingham bookmaker suggests that William's departure from BSA might have had as much to do with him not settling some of the winning bets he had laid to workmates as his dislike of the actual factory work.

CHAPTER 2
BLACK AND TANS

Of one of the least-known, riskiest and most surprising episodes in
William Hill's life there appears not a word in later company-en-
dorsed publications like *The Hill Story*. For in 1921, around a year
after leaving BSA, William joined the Royal Irish Constabulary.
According to many interpretations, that meant he became a member of the controversial 'Black and Tans'.

During the Irish War of Independence, following the Easter
Rising in 1916, thousands of British men, many of them First World
War veterans, answered the British Government's call for recruits
to join the RIC as Temporary Constables to help maintain order
and fight the Irish Republican Army, the IRA. Their nickname
arose from a shortage of RIC uniforms that meant they had to
manage with mismatched trousers and tunics from the RIC, British
Army and British Police. A later Auxiliary Force, recruited by Lloyd
George, who became infamous for their attacks on civilians and
civilian property in revenge for IRA actions, are also often referred
to as the 'Black and Tans', but some historians maintain that at the
time they were actually known as 'Auxies'.

William's younger brother Joe Ward Hill, in his 'racing biography' of him, stresses that he 'knew little or nothing about the
Irish "Troubles"'. One Irish account suggests an 'indiscretion' back
in England prompted the flight to Ireland, but nephew, Neil Hill,
heard from his parents that William answered an advertisement by
the British Government calling for volunteers 'to face a rough and
dangerous task', in return for free board and lodging, and a good
rate of pay – according to Joe Ward Hill – '£500 on enlistment, plus
a further £500 on retirement'. The roll call of deceased officers in
the previous six months published in *The Royal Irish Constabulary*

List & Directory 1920, issued when the RIC had some two years' existence left, was evidence of one of the most dangerous occupations in the world, and men were leaving the service in droves. This was reflected in the rates of pay outlined in the Directory: the starting salary for a constable with less than six months' service had risen from £39 a year in 1889 to £80 in January 1920, with some RIC recruits reportedly paid 10/- a day – a generous wage after the First World War – others as much as £1. What is incontrovertible is that William, then only 17, lied about his age to get in: the records of the Royal Irish Constabulary show that he signed up at Birmingham recruiting office on 24 February 1921 as his three-years-older brother Fred (Christian name Thomas). There are no specific details of his service, other than that it took place in Cork, nor of any involvement in the Auxiliary Force.

William trained at Gormanston and was posted to Mallow, County Cork, where, according to Finbarr Slattery in his book *Following the Horses*, he spent a lot of his spare time in Moss Foley's pub in the town. 'Mrs Foley took a liking to him. The fact that he was so young brought out the mother in the woman and she kept a watchful eye on the youngster.'

Apparently that watchful eye gazed at the British commanding officer when Hill was deployed to guard a 'big house a few miles out in the country, owned by the gentry'.

Fearing that 'somebody might take a "potshot" at the lad, [she] made an appeal for him to stay in town: the request was granted'. Years later William, 'driving a big car and with all the trappings of a wealthy man', returned to Mallow to pay a surprise visit to the Foleys' pub and show his gratitude to Mrs Foley, calling for 'Drink for the house on me', and subsequently becoming a regular visitor when in the vicinity. It also seems very possible that William met the popular British actor Stanley Holloway during his time in the Royal Irish Constabulary – Holloway had joined in 1920, and left shortly before its disbandment in 1922; William's granddaughter

Caroline remembers Holloway singing 'Get me to the Church on Time' around the swimming pool at her grandfather's house in Jamaica, much to the merriment of William.

As to William's conduct and reputation during his spell with the controversial Black and Tans, an unlikely testimonial comes in the later reminiscences of IRA commander Tom Barry, who was clear not only that Hill *was* a Black and Tan, but also that he was a 'good' Black and Tan. 'The Black and Tans,' he wrote, 'included good and bad, like every armed force you meet, and quite a number of them were rather decent men.

'One of them was a fellow named William Hill. Well, William Hill and Co. are now the biggest turf accountant in the world, I suppose. At that time Hill was stationed in Mallow and he was a very good fellow and a very jolly fellow. He'd come in and have a pint and he never insulted anyone or did anything to anyone.

He's now a millionaire many times over, of course, but at that time he was there simply because there was no work to be found in Britain. I understand that he got on very well with the IRA up in that district.'

Possibly not everyone agreed with Tom Barry. The former Ladbrokes managing director Berjis Daver recalled a visit to Cork on business when he was mistaken for a William Hill man and 'subjected to a most unpleasant approach'.

A letter to the *Irish Examiner* newspaper in June 2007 from Dr Brian Murphy, Murroe, County Limerick, points out a further historical irony, noting the placing of a successful bet by the racehorse owner J.P. McManus that Bertie Ahern would be returned in that year's General Election as Taoiseach – with William Hill. 'At a time when events of historical significance have recently taken place,' reflects Dr Murphy,

– the power sharing at Stormont, the accord of Unionists and Republicans at the site of the battle of the Boyne and Mr Ahern's address to the British Houses of Parliament – it may be worth an historical footnote that a company founded by a Black and Tan was associated with the FF [Fianna Fáil] election success! J.P. is to be congratulated not only for winning his bet, as seems probable, but also for selecting a 'good Black and Tan' company with which to do business.

William (and the RIC itself) was 'disbanded' a year after he joined, on 6 February 1922, with an annual pension of £46 16/s, and William's younger brother Edward (also known as Dick) was adamant that 'Brother Bill' came out of the RIC with around £1,000, telling his son Neil, 'I don't know how much was daily pay and how much was "contract completion bonus."' Back home, he would soon have a family to support.

William began taking bets from punters in pubs in and around the Acocks Green area – 'chugging around' (as he would later put it) proudly on the secondhand motorbike he may well have bought from BSA. Less than two months after he returned from Ireland a probably unplanned, very much younger brother for William was born: Joseph.

The gratuity from the RIC seems to have been put towards a small office – more than likely just a room – in Pershore Street, Birmingham, where he based his fledgling turf accountancy business, collecting bets from around the local area personally and probably also from 'runners' working for him on commission and bringing them to the office for settling along with those being phoned in. *The Hill Story* relates that 'he was quick to prove his reliability and aptitude for the job, but things in the office were a bit too slow for his taste, not enough business was coming in to satisfy an agile, ambitious mind like his.'

So William decided that the real opportunity was to be found on the racecourse. Off he went, 'with a stand and a satchel', to 'do battle at Uttoxeter racecourse'. This was in some ways an excellent time to be starting out as a racecourse bookie, but in others, a desperately dangerous time to do so. 'Soldiers returning from the First World War, and the families they returned to, had money and were in a mood to spend it,' writes the *Racing Post*'s David Ashforth:

> During the brief post-war boom, racecourse attendances reached record levels. Bookmakers' satchels bulged, and so did the eyes of the criminals who preyed on bookmakers and punters alike, at railway stations and racecourse car parks, on the race trains and at the racetracks, where pickpockets, card sharps and three-card tricksters plied their cheating trade, and race gangs terrorised the ring, and each other.

William lasted just one day before he was relieved of his 'monkey' capital of £500. Undaunted, he regrouped, refinanced and tried again, and this time lasted three weeks. He was serving a tough apprenticeship. 'I tried to run before I could walk,' he admitted later. 'I thought I could reach the top of the ladder before I'd got my feet properly on the bottom rungs.' Instead of launching his on-course career in a modest way, amongst the lesser bookies and smaller-staking punters, he'd risked his hard-earned nest egg in 'a big splash in Tattersalls (the race enclosure where high-rolling, well informed gamblers would congregate), where a fool and his money could be only too quickly parted'. William's younger brother Dick, confirmed that 'Bill' quickly lost about half of the £1,000 he'd amassed this time. 'I do remember my mother telling me,' says William's nephew, Sandy Brown, 'that she once hid William under a kitchen table, due to the fact that he had to leave Warwick races in rather a hurry!'

One of these incidents involved the decent amateur rider Mr W. H. Blandford, who rode at the first ever Cheltenham Festival in 1911. Once he'd finished his riding career he enjoyed regular trips to the races at Midlands courses like Stratford, Uttoxeter, and Warwick. His grandson Mark Blandford, who founded Sportingbet (part of which would later be taken over by William Hill), recalls his father telling him that his grandfather used to bet with the young William Hill and one afternoon was fortunate enough to land a good win. 'It was such a good win that William asked for time to pay. I believe he did eventually pay up, but it is a family joke that grandfather might have asked for a cut of William's fledgling business instead – who knows how much that might have been worth today!'

The inexperienced William had been a novice ready to be fleeced amongst the big-time bookies of the day and the far-better-informed racegoers of the inner ring. 'Bookmaking is an art', Hill told his long-standing racing journalist friend, Peter Campling of the *Sun* in 1970: 'You don't just stand up on a racecourse and shout the odds and take anybody's money and hope for the best. I did that once as a youngster, and I finished up walking home. That was my first lesson in bookmaking.'

It was one that he took to heart. There followed six months of determined study of horse racing. He later told Campling that his 'bible was the form book'. He had served his apprenticeship and learned from his mistakes. There would still be ups and downs, but the former began to outnumber the latter, and he was on an upward curve. As soon as possible he was back on the course, but this time outside in the smaller betting rings. Now, according to Campling, 'He soon found he kept more money than he paid out.'

CHAPTER 3

MARRIAGE AND LONDON

William undoubtedly had an eye for the ladies from an early age and, despite living at home with Mum and Dad, had found a neat way of enjoying some private time with his latest flame. 'William used to carry his girlfriend upstairs,' recalled his friend Richard Baerlein, the racing journalist, 'so that his father only heard one set of footsteps going to bed.'

But in November 1923, at the age of 20, when he was living at 74 Bath Row, Birmingham, William got married. His bride was Ivy Burley from Small Heath, also 20, the daughter of a metal merchant. 'They were both very keen on ballroom dancing,' says his nephew Neil. 'The West End Ballroom in Birmingham was *the* place to go in those days, and my understanding is that Bill and Ivy were so good that they gave demonstrations.' The groom described himself as a 'Commission Agent', which today generally means someone who passes bets to a bookmaker for a cut of the stake money. Whether William's parents were present at their son's wedding is unclear, as the witnesses are recorded as Constance and James Stanley Burley, Ivy's parents, but the wedding may well have had to be organised in some haste, as their only child was born just over three months later. In those days there was also no little stigma attached to pregnant brides. They would remain married for almost 48 years.

Despite the lengthy marriage William was not always faithful. He had at least two illegitimate children by different women, a daughter and a son, and rumours amongst family and friends put the total possibly as high as five. He did not seem to go to any great lengths to disguise his roving eye: 'William was convinced he was never going to die,' recalled his nephew Chris Harper: 'he used to say he wanted to be accused of still chasing after women at the age of 90 – and found guilty!' Such behaviour may have come down through the genes – Harper relates another family story about William's own parents:

Grandma Hill rang her husband, William, to tell him she was pregnant again – with the baby who would be Joe Ward Hill – some years after what they'd thought was their last child. 'You'll never believe it, I'm pregnant again,' she said. The reply came: 'Hello, who's speaking please?'

But it seems 'everyone who knew them agreed that Ivy was always the perfect wife,' said Joe Ward Hill. 'Blonde and beautiful, she combined charm with a shrewd appraisal of the character of others.'

On the marriage certificate Ivy is listed as 'Milliner', but according to Joe Ward Hill she was also a ladies' hairdresser, and opened a hairdressing salon which flourished to such an extent that at one point William closed down his Starting Price business (in which he would record and settle the bets he would take on the street, in factories and pubs and perhaps by telephone) to concentrate on the on-course side of bookmaking. Was this the start of an anti-betting shop attitude, one wonders? Whether William ever wielded a razor and scissors, or left such hands-on involvement to Ivy, who may have been trained up by his mother, is not clear.

William and Ivy's only child, Kathleen Lavinia, was born on 10 February 1924. At the time the couple were living at 126 Pershore Road, Edgbaston but, in a forerunner of the mysteries that would surround her life, Kathleen's birth certificate says she was born at number 300. Possibly a relative lived at that address. The couple's pet-name for her was 'Bubbles' – 'The Guv'nor named one of his horses after his daughter,' remembers Bert Arnold, who worked for William Hill from 1948, 'calling it "Lovely Bubbles."' By general consensus she was an indulged child – 'completely spoiled', felt family members and friends.

Between 1925 and 1928, as his daughter began to leave infancy, William was gaining enough on-course experience and confidence to prepare himself for a move to the capital, at whose racetracks he hoped to establish himself as a real player in the world of book-making. Hopes that he would become a little more financially circumspect now he had another mouth to feed appear to have been a little optimistic. William seems to have been using up a great deal of goodwill from family members during these early years. 'My understanding is that William bummed a lot of free meals etc. from his sisters when he was young and often down and out,' says Christopher Foott:

> They weren't an especially warm, loving bunch of women, so I think they gave him a lot of grief for it. But when he made it, they were all lining up to be his favourite sister, and there were arguments about who he liked best, and so on. I think he got pretty sick of it all – the Hill women could be a very petty and vindictive crew when they got into it. Bubbles was raised almost as another Hill sibling – she was only a couple of years younger than Joe Ward Hill, and I think she spent a lot of time with her grandparents. William was probably so sick of his sisters' bickering that he [eventually] kept himself and his family at arm's length.

It seems he had to be bailed out again at this time. Carl Chinn's impression is that when Hill went to London in 1929, his (Carl's) grandfather, who had struggled as a bookmaker until 1928 when Tipperary Tim won the Grand National as a 100/1 shot, having never laid the horse to a shilling, lent him the money – '£10 or £20, quite a lot of money in those days. I also spoke with another couple of bookies who told me that their fathers had done the same.' Chris

Harper says his father, a butcher, also once loaned William £500 to get him back on his feet.

There are rumours within the family that the fledgling Hill marriage was in danger of splitting asunder. Joe Ward Hill, who started out as a hairdresser but began his move into bookmaking by taking bets from customers from his position 'behind the chair', which he laid off with William if necessary, wrote that William 'hardly conformed to most people's idea of a perfect husband'. 'Ivy took off, possibly with someone else,' says Peggy Evans, daughter of William's three-years-younger sister, Ida (also known as Molly). 'They were apart for a while. Then one day, when Bubbles was being looked after by William's mother, there was a knock on the door. Lavinia and Bubbles both headed for the door. When it was opened, there stood Ivy, who scooped up her daughter and ran off.' When William found out, he was desperate to discover where mother and toddler had gone – 'he did everything he could to find the child, to no avail,' recalled Peggy. 'Then he began to make money. Lo and behold, Ivy turned up and begged to be taken back. William took them back.' There is a school of thought, however, which suggests that but for Ivy's goodwill, William's bookmaking career might never have got off the ground – she would later tell the people working for her that she funded him out of, and to the detriment of, her own hairdressing business. One source has it that she went as far as to sell her successful salon.

Hill arrived in the capital 'full of ruthless ambition and drive,' says *The Hill Story*. One wonders whether he had had to use those qualities to survive in what was, and remained for some years, potentially a very perilous working environment for bookies. 'The divide between honest bookie and race gang villain was often a thin one,' explains Robert Murphy, chronicler of the underworld of this era. 'It was also to the bookie's advantage if his clerk (who recorded the bets) and tic-tac man (who checked out odds changes amongst rival bookies) could double up as his bodyguards.' And, adds Murphy, 'It was the ambition of every clerk and tic-tac man, whether or not he was a member of a gang, to erect a stand and become a bookie in his own right.'

The most notorious racecourse gang of this time were the Sabinis. Darby Sabini was a contemporary of William's, born four years before him, and said to be the inspiration for the gangster character Colleoni in Graham Greene's famous novel *Brighton Rock*. With his brothers Harry, Joseph, Fred and George, along with other disreputable types, he ran a protection racket at racecourses during the 1920s and 1930s, extorting cash from bookmakers. Amongst their activities were driving legitimate bookmakers from their pitches and hiring them out to others who were in their pockets; 'selling' bookies lists of runners, which cost less than one penny to produce, for at least ten times as much; 'hiring' them the stools on which they stood; charging them well over the odds for 'services' such as chalk to write with on their boards, and sponges to wash the boards down with. Sabini and his cohorts would use razors, guns and other weapons. Complaints or resistance would frequently be met with extreme violence – sometimes gang members would simply stop would-be punters from approaching the bookie, or would wipe off the displayed odds before betting on a race was finished. One victimised bookie, Hymie Davis, enlisted London underworld figure Arthur Harding's gang to fight off the Sabinis at Kempton Park. Harding sent along 60 men. The police had been tipped off and ambushed the gangsters, resulting in a pitched – and pitch – battle.

'The racecourse business was a profitable one,' Harding later confessed: 'When a gang went to a racecourse like Brighton, they could clear £4,000 or £5,000 easy. At Epsom on Derby day it could be £15,000 or £20,000.' Also involved in racecourse warfare at this time were the 'Brummagem Boys' from the Birmingham area, and therefore surely known to William, who were led by a bookie called Billy Kimber, also depicted in *Peaky Blinders* (the name of another genuine gang of racecourse and betting shop villains). Kimber's lengthy feud with the Sabinis saw him team up with a Leeds mob to take them on in a showdown at the 1921 Derby meeting, only for the two gangs inadvertently to set about each other. Eventually 23 of 28 Birmingham gang members arrested were found guilty of various crimes, and sentenced to varying terms of imprisonment from nine months to three years. The Home Secretary of the day, Sir William Joynson-Hicks, vowed to crack down on the gangs, and matters came to a head at Lewes racecourse on 8 June 1936 when a gang of up to 30 men attacked bookmakers. Hammers, iron bars, jemmies, knuckledusters and broken billiard cues were scattered around the ring. Sixteen gang members were found guilty of malicious wounding, assault, and riotous assembly, and sentences were handed down totalling over 53 years. We know that William paid attention to what went on, for as he moved through the ranks he made sure he had 'minders' around to deter any threatening heavies.

William began to feel his way and find his feet, bookmaking at London's greyhound tracks, first in the cheap ring at White City. Peter MacMurray, a William Hill client to this day, recalls that at Wembley Stadium, where greyhound racing had begun in 1927, William did not always have enough money to pay all the bets he'd taken if the favourite won the first race, so Peter's father, a regular attendee, on one or two occasions 'loaned Bill – as my father called him – "a fifty" – a huge sum in those days'. William was appropriately grateful, attending the christening of Peter's elder brother, who was named William in tribute. At Harringay dogs he could take more than 1,000 bets a night.

William then set up to bet in the cheap rings at what he called the 'festival meetings', at the likes of Ascot, Epsom and Goodwood. As Charles Sidney explains in *The Art of Legging*, racecourse bookmakers operated then, as now, to a ranking system. At the top were the rails bookmakers, operating predominantly on credit and usually with higher-rolling clients already known to them. They were located in the Tattersalls, or Tatts, area of the course, usually in front of the grandstand. They would not usually display any odds (known as 'betting off the card') – 'the rails bookmaker does his business either by inquiry for a price or by screaming aloud his terms of business.' The lower-ranked layers would show their prices on a board.

Below Tattersalls was the Silver Ring enclosure – presumably because its patrons bet in shillings rather than sovereigns. According to the racing journalist Geoffrey Hamlyn, who first met William in 1933, he did not bet in Tattersalls' ring until 1941, when he moved to the bigger tracks, where he would attend in person until 1955. 'He could do double the business in half the time of any other layer you cared to name.'

William began to command wider attention at Northolt, famous for the pony (as opposed to thoroughbred) racing held on its splendid one-and-a-half-mile racecourse constructed by Sir William Bass and Viscount Lascelles, which had opened in 1929 and closed in June 1940 when the land was taken over for a prisoner-of-war camp. William bet on the rails at Northolt between 1933 and 1939. He is also said to have stood at Portsmouth Park (or Paulsgrove) pony races, and at Greenford Park, near Northolt, whose trotting racing was described by one jockey as 'great fun and, I suspect, very crooked'. 'When William went down south he made his money on the trotting,' Joe Ward Hill told Carl Chinn.

CHAPTER 4

GOING UP AGAINST
THE BIG BOYS

What William Hill observed of the bookies he was up against in London did not impress him: 'So these were the *big* boys,' he reminisced many years later, according to his obituary in the *Bloodstock Breeders' Review*. 'I watched them and I thought, "My God! I could beat you lot with one hand tied up behind me."' He began trading on course 'on the boards' as – for reasons that remain obscure – Albert (Buck) Carr, before moving on to the rails. He was keen to live up to the slogan on his betting board: 'Courtesy, civility and integrity', to ensure he stood out at a time when it was not unknown for bookmakers to intimidate winning punters by refusing to pay out, or claiming that they had bet on a different horse from the one they knew they'd backed. William was always well turned out, to look the part of a prosperous layer, made a point of getting to know all of his clients, and would pay up with a smile, in the knowledge that winning punters would then return, and give him the opportunity to get his cash back – with interest. Ever the perfectionist, he always read the influential Augur column in *The Sporting Life*, which pinpointed many long-odds winners – including, between 1936 and 1939, three out of four winners of that most difficult of handicaps, the Cambridgeshire – and would even consider hedging any outstanding bets he held on Augur's tips. Today, bookmakers are equally respectful of tips by the *Racing Post*'s 'Pricewise' column.

William also began a lucrative if illegal sideline running a book at the Coventry Club in London's Denman Street, although other sources suggest it was the Pelican Club in Soho. It might easily have been both. Runners and riders' details were chalked up on the state-of-the-art technology of the day, a blackboard, on to which the results were written as they came in via ticker tape. He was basically operating a betting shop, years ahead of its time. He soon had a thriving business, but it only lasted a year before it came to the attention of the authorities, who closed him down in a dramatic raid. William was reportedly fined.

By now he seems to have become familiar with many of London's clubs; at the Old Vaudeville in Old Compton Street he had, in the late 1920s, met the biggest music hall star of the day, Chesney Allen and his wife Aleta – 'and from that day he and his wife Ivy became our greatest friends,' Allen later told William's brother Joe. 'Ivy was an inspiration to him, and in those early days she worked in his office.' He also recalled them playing snooker 'for a shilling a game' with stars like the Crazy Gang and comedian Will Hay, along with jockey Charlie Smirke. It was as a result of his friendship with Allen that William joined the charitable Saints and Sinners Club, donating at least £2,000 a year for 30 years and sponsoring races in the name of the club, a gesture he wanted to remain secret, but that was 'leaked' by brother Joe.

On 26 July 1933 the William Hill Organization Limited was incorporated as a limited liability company ('s' and 'z' would be interchangeable in 'Organization' over the years). Now William's risk was limited to the capital he had invested in it. The following year he opened his first London office, at the prestigious address of 97 Jermyn Street, SW1, a street occupied in the late 17th century by Sir Isaac Newton, and at the same time as William, at number 93, by occultist Aleister Crowley, where it sat above the premises of Walter Barnard & Son, a well-established but now seemingly defunct hat makers. It was 'a starting price office', he later told journalist Peter Campling, opened 'for the convenience of race-course clients', presumably allowing them to telephone their bets in to him, as it was strictly speaking illegal for customers to come in and bet with cash, or even to post their wagers and stakes. This is not to discount the possibility, or even probability, that one or both methods were in use when the authorities weren't looking.

The entire staff of the William Hill Organization housed in this one-room office comprised William and a young clerk by the name of George Cortesi, who must have been well thought-of as he was still with the company 20 years later, by which time he was legendary for his superstitious hatred of the colour green. Cortesi once lost his temper big-time, insisting that a young employee remove his green jumper immediately, and then grabbing it and throwing it out of a window into the traffic below. Another story has it that he suffered from piles, and was less than pleased when his favourite cushion was removed and replaced with a green one. The future managing director John Brown first met Cortesi in 1959, and professes himself baffled by the pathology – 'but to this day I still don't wear green.'

There was another George Cortesi in the racing and betting business, however: someone 20 years older with a lengthy criminal record, and a member of the 'Cortesi Gang' who regularly did battle with the Sabini Gang. This led to rumours that William was employing racecourse gang members. Both George Cortesis apparently lived at the same address; the older man was not the clerk's father but his uncle. At one point the house in Holloway hosted eleven Cortesis; one of the clan, Albert, a bootmaker, had a shop proudly proclaiming his supply of bespoke shoes for royalty as 'Cobblers to the King'. William's will left £2,500 to George Cortesi of Holloway 'in appreciation of loyal support at all times', but by the time of William's death the younger man had been dead for three years, although it seems unlikely William would not have been aware of his passing. Therefore, as no amendment was made to the will and the older George was still alive and still, as far as can be told, living at the same address, it appears likely that *he* would have received the bequest!

William was at last on his way to the big time, and now had a clear ambition. Racing at Northolt, whose average crowd was some 3,500 and where he was now the owner himself of a few

William Hill's first London office opened in Jermyn Street, in 1934, above a hat shop.

horses, had stirred something which went back to his boyhood days – a love of the country and the dream of possessing a farm with its own stud and racing stables. 'I decided to go into the bookmaking business in a big way – make enough to buy a farm and then retire,' he told *The Hill Story*. From this point forward he became intensely ambitious and competitive, taking on rivals who, through inheritance or long standing, were controlling the big-money betting markets. In 1937 there were estimated to be 20,000 bookmakers in England and Scotland.

Soon the Jermyn Street office was unable to contain the volume of business it was attracting. There were now half a dozen clerks, together with a racecourse staff. In 1939 the company moved in to new premises not far away, in one of the capital's best known streets, Park Lane, at the same time as William Hill (Park Lane) Ltd was registered by Companies House, with nominal capital of £10,000. William later admitted he 'had sunk almost everything he had in this new venture': as managing director he was entitled to a salary of £1,250 per annum, almost £70,000 in today's money, plus a further £1,000 (£55,000) to cover all his expenses. He was also allotted £5,000 of 5% preference shares, and entitled to two months' holiday a year.

The premises at 32 Park Lane, the stately former residence of Lord Inchcape, were equipped lavishly to accommodate the 30 staff who would work there, and William began to advertise to potential clients on a large scale. He was clearly very serious about dining at the top table. It appears to have been Sam Seeman, a shrewd marketing man and the boss of Classic Cinemas Ltd, who convinced William just how important advertising was in the promotion of a growing business. Perhaps hedging his bets a little, William was listed at the time as a director of Cinema Centres, and Joe Ward Hill believed that Seeman had a 20% interest in William Hill (Park Lane). Before the Second World War broke out William began to revolutionise ante-post betting by offering his own independent prices months ahead for races he thought would interest his clients. Now, William was promoting these ante-post odds for the big events, such as the Lincolnshire Handicap, the Grand National

Hills moved to an even more prestigious Park Lane address from Jermyn Street, in 1939, stretching William's financial resources in the process. Photo taken from the Curzon Place side of the building.

and the Derby. The policy brought him into conflict with the die-hards who held as sacrosanct the accepted system of odds 'call-overs' held at the Victoria Club, the foremost London gambling

William with his long-standing client (Sir) Peter O'Sullevan, who opened his Hill's account in 1939. The pair are hoping for a tip from Irish trainer Con Collins (left), another pal of the founder.

club formed in 1860 where bookmakers and their clients would gather to hear the latest odds for big races announced. They would then back horses and lay bets between themselves, and the odds set there would govern the ante-post market. The public's response, however, fully endorsed William's progressive move.

William was now no longer often seen at the greyhound tracks, although he retained his interest in racing at Northolt Park, where the betting market was as strong as that of some Jockey Club-authorised meetings. Sir Peter O'Sullevan, who opened an account with him on 3 July 1939, and would still have one 75 years later, was betting with William here, as he had been 'in the shilling ring' at White City greyhounds. It was here, too, that Chesney Allen fell under the spell of pony racing. Allen 'could often be seen mingling with the huge crowds there', said Bill Marshall, who trained for Allen, and later for William, and was left Allen's unique 'Crazy Quilt' racing colours when he died. Allen 'frequently only made it back to the Victoria Palace Theatre' (where he played to sell-out crowds with fellow Crazy Gang member Bud Flanagan) 'with minutes to spare before the curtain rose'. Another of William's friends, racing writer Richard Baerlein opined that at Northolt, William 'had a lot of help, as he was in close contact with Tommy Carey, the leading rider who was retained by Miss Dorothy Paget, the leading owner'. This comment leaves itself open to more than one interpretation. The retired trainer Barry Hills, himself no stranger to the occasional gamble, offers one:

> It has been suggested that William's system at Northolt Park in the early days was quite simple: he laid heavy gambler Dorothy Paget on her horses, then ridden by her jockey Tommy Carey, who was retained – but the good news for [William] was that [Carey] was stopping them for him – but not so good for Miss P, as she was called.
>
> Everyone started somewhere.

At least two other, very well informed, long-serving racecourse figures have maintained that at least one jockey riding for Dorothy Paget, who arrived as a major owner at Northolt with her string of runners in 1935, was heard to suggest that they were not always ridden on their merits – to both his and William Hill's advantage.

Such stories could well be apocryphal, however, and there are few figures who rise to the top in any business without being accused of unsavoury practices during their elevation. But in 1939 another kind of sharp practice was alleged against William when he became embroiled in a 'serious row' with his friend Geoffrey Hamlyn, the racing journalist. More pertinently, Hamlyn was also the starting-price returner for *The Sporting Life*, and he took great exception to William having 'knocked out' (extended the odds of) a pony of his own, Win Over, at Northolt from 5/2 to 10/3 – in Hamlyn's opinion (since Hill was the only bookmaker offering 10/3 and the *Life* returned it at 5/2), a case of deliberately extending the odds of a horse at the course for the benefit of people placing bets off course, which would be settled at the odds prevailing at the track.

Nigel Spencer, who followed in the footsteps of his father Leslie in standing at racecourses for William Hill, takes up the story on Dorothy Paget – 'a huge punter in her day [who] had many battles with William,' he says – 'sometimes having up to £10,000 bets'. Eccentric, fabulously wealthy and lesbian, and indeed possibly the biggest owner and punter of all back then, Dorothy would often sleep during the day if she was not going racing, rising in the evening to work overnight, and William told Nigel's father that he used to let her place bets on races which had already been run that afternoon. The reason might have been that he knew that, as a consistent backer of losers, and honest with it, she would be very likely to lose, despite the outcome already being known. In fact, Ms Paget's betting methods – she'd sometimes stake in pounds the same number as that of the last telephone number she had called or received a call from – make it unlikely that any bookmaker would need to 'fix' races her horses were running in, as it was extremely unlikely that she could ever have made her punting profitable.

The June day of the 1939 Northolt Derby, a race which attracted crowds of some 10,000, when William's previously mentioned pony, Win Over, dead-heated for second place, is usually taken to be the first occasion on which William and the two-years-younger Paget met. The race was won by Ms Paget's unbeaten Scottish Rifle, a son of Epsom Derby winner Cameronian, and she was there to accompany her horse back to the winner's enclosure. But a tale of the two meeting many years before, shortly after the First World War, when William was just starting out, chimes with other family memories that he did occasionally welsh on his bets at low-profile meetings. 'He made his mark, legend has it, at Hawthorn Hill races [in Berkshire] one day by taking a chance', wrote Chris Pitt in the bookmaking industry magazine, *BOS*:

Dorothy Paget only used to bet with one famous firm, and then only by credit. She never carried money with her. On this particular day the firm didn't turn up and Hill was the only man to offer her credit facilities. It was a grand bluff, for he couldn't have afforded to pay her out if the horses had won. Luckily for Hill, they didn't.

Perhaps this is why he had headed for Ireland not long after!

CHAPTER 5

WILLIAM HILL AT WAR

On 3 September 1939, the British Prime Minister Neville Chamberlain reacted to the invasion of Poland by declaring war against Germany. William was not called up, judged unfit for military service 'owing to his poor record of health during his youth', wrote his brother Joe. Racing would continue during the war, albeit on a reduced scale and so William, whose father had died that June, threw himself into his business 'as though the war did not exist', and made a book on the rails at every principal meeting throughout the conflict. Several of William's major competitors – companies like J. John, James Maclean, David Cope, Douglas Stuart and Scotland & Co – had responded to war's prospect of cancelled race meetings, for horses and greyhounds alike, by cutting down on their advertising outlay, resulting in a rapid downturn in business. William, though, had started advertising in a big way, concentrating on the *Greyhound Express* and *The Sporting Life*, and with his own business depending on maintaining, if not increasing, turnover, he risked the wrath of the other companies by continuing to promote his firm through the media. It was a brave, and the right, thing to do, and by the end of the hostilities William had emerged, wrote his brother, Joe, as 'probably the leading advertising bookmaker'.

It might have been around this time that William, in an echo of racecourse retreats of years earlier, was reduced to 'hiding in a cupboard in Park Lane'. 'Although his business was completely solvent, William was desperately short of ready cash to meet his commitments, the most pressing being the heavy rental of his Park Lane office,' recalled Joe Ward Hill. Now he was visited by the rather intimidating figure of Charlie 'the Hammer' Maskey, the bodyguard of Bill Chandler, the founder of the Chandler bookmaking empire. Greyhound racing was a big deal at the time: an estimated 92,000 spectators were at White City for the 1939 Greyhound Derby Final, and Chandler was number one bookie at the track, where he controlled 20 of the 200 bookmaking pitches (and where William Hill, on first doing business there, had created something of a sartorial stir by turning up wearing plus-fours). The story told by the then head of Chandlers, Victor, who, in May 2014, sold his interest as major shareholder as Michael Tabor assumed control, involves William owing Bill 'a bit of money'.

The Hammer, whose nickname was apparently earned during his days as a blacksmith, was dispatched to collect the debt, only to discover that William didn't seem to be on the premises. Who shopped William as having popped into a small cupboard to collect some stationery is lost in the mists of time, but 'he paid in the end,' believes Victor. Clearly there was no lasting ill feeling as Victor's father, Victor senior (who took over as boss from Bill) subsequently used to stay with William at his holiday home in Jamaica.

The Derby of 1940 was switched to Newmarket's July Course as Epsom had been commandeered by the military, and William had finally arrived in the big-time bookmaking world when he bet there on the rails for the first time. He first set up where the bookmakers had traditionally taken the smaller wagers of a quid or two, but his arrival soon resulted in the higher-rolling punters moving down to bet with him.

'His personal métier was the rails,' concluded *The Sporting Life* – during the war William was now leaving his SP business largely to his staff. 'Four- or even five-figure bets were nothing unusual. He could stand horses in the big ante-post races for £100,000 or more' – today that kind of sum would amount to considerably more than a million pounds. Perhaps the 'Who knows what tomorrow may hold?' attitude of the times accounted for the gambling of such huge sums.

From 7 September 1940 London was bombed by the Luftwaffe for 57 consecutive nights. Up to a million houses were eventually destroyed or damaged, and over 20,000 civilians killed. In March 1941 Joe Ward Hill narrowly avoided death when 34 people died in the bombing of a Soho nightclub he was visiting. William's daughter, Kathleen, who'd been at school in London, was evacuated to Roedean School in Sussex (in its records William has himself down as 'Accountant'), and then to Keswick in the Lake District. The Blitz went on until May 1941, and when things got a little too close for comfort in the capital William and Ivy retreated from 13 Embankment Gardens, SW3, where they were living, to a caravan in Taplow – 'knowing the old man, he probably thought it was safe, and not on the flight-path of the Junkers!' joked his nephew Sandy.

By 1942 William was 'the acknowledged leader of the betting ring', according to Joe Ward Hill, and that year's Derby proved to be the race that showed William's mettle. The odds-on favourite Big Game had been backed as though defeat was out of the question – as much because he was owned by King George VI as for his breeding and form, both of which suggested he was unlikely to get the trip, despite having won the shorter 2,000 Guineas in good style. 'William was so convinced that Big Game would not stay,' observed Richard Baerlein, 'that he laid the colt till the cows came home' – to the extent that the chairman of Ladbrokes, Arthur Bendir, was reportedly of the opinion that 'If Big Game had won the Derby, William would have been unable to settle.' This may have been true as, around this time, someone had 'lent him £5,000 or £6,000 to tide him over when the bank wouldn't accommodate him any further'. To his relief, William's judgement was spot on, and the 4/6 chance finished out of the first three as the horse he had beaten three times before over shorter trips, including the 2,000 Guineas, the 6/1 third favourite Watling Street, ran on strongly to win. William could breathe – and spend – again.

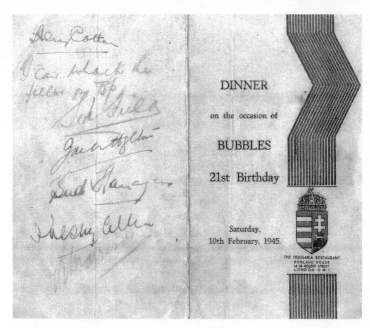

William and Ivy's daughter Kathleen's 21st was celebrated with a bash at a plush Hungarian restaurant – guests Henry Cotton (top golfer); band leader Jack Hylton; music hall stars Bud Flanagan and Chesney Allen, and comedian Sid Field all signed the programme.

When William and Ivy's daughter Bubbles turned 21 in 1945, her birthday was celebrated with a lavish dinner at the Hungaria restaurant in Regent Street, with guests including the Open Championship-winning golfer Henry Cotton, band leader Jack Hylton, comedians Sid Field and Will Hay, and William's Crazy Gang friends Bud Flanagan and Chesney Allen, all of whom would seem to have been her father's, rather than her, invitees!

It was early in the war when William first encountered the man who would become his longest-standing friend. Such was the fractious, disputatious friendship that evolved from an initial meeting over a betting dispute that William Hill and Phil Bull, working on opposite sides of the eternal contest between bookie and punter, could easily have starred in their own prequel to the Jack Lemmon and Walter Matthau movie as 'The Odds Couple'.

Bull would go on to found the highly-regarded *Timeform* racehorse annuals and rating service in 1948, but at the time he was working as a teacher, and under the *nom de plume* of 'William K. Temple BSc' had created a betting system called the Temple Racetime Analysis, a weekly list of horses he recommended backing based on their time performances, which he was selling to clients, many of whom then used it to bet with William Hill. 'For some time Hill had been perplexed by a fairly large number of winning accounts which normally would not be showing a profit,' wrote Geoffrey Hamlyn in his unpublished biography of the bookmaker. The system involved backing horses at Tote odds, and William, feeling it depended on occasional quirky long-odds dividends, therefore decided to accept such bets only at starting-price odds.

Never backward in coming forward, Bull risked blowing his schoolmasterly cover by ringing Hill to complain – and found himself invited to visit him at his Park Lane headquarters. Hill welcomed into his office 'a man of about 30, with flaming red hair and a beard of similar colour, in a cheap sports jacket and a pair of flannel trousers several inches too short for him'. Instead of the expected brief discussion degenerating into an argument, an intense conversation ensued, lasting several hours, which continued on and off for the next 30 years until William's death. 'The friendship was immediate and real,' Bull would later write: 'a two-way exchange of affection and help and advice and ideas and assistance.' Hill offered Bull a job as 'personal assistant and general factotum in the business,' which Bull accepted with alacrity – he had had enough of teaching. 'I don't think I ever paid him a penny,' reflected William in 1970. 'He was frank about wanting to see how the "enemy" worked and what he had to beat – I found his ideas stimulating and valuable.'

Bull's duties in Park Lane initially included arranging the company's advertising, discussing ante-post odds, and accompanying the boss to the races. He would go on to become William's racing manager and bloodstock adviser. He was also the man who loaned him that '£5,000 or £6,000' when the bank was being awkward.

During 1943 a 17-year-old named Ron Pollard saw an advertisement in the *Greyhound Express*, and applied for a job with Hills as a 'ledger clerk'. Ron caught a number 36 bus from the family home in Peckham up to Hill's West End office:

Here was the bookmaking firm reputed to be the world's biggest, yet there were only about five people working in the offices. Still slightly puzzled, I found myself being ushered into one of those big Park Lane rooms once lived in by the aristocracy, with a huge desk in the middle.

On a couch in the room, remembered Pollard, sat two men. 'One was called Bill Stratton. And beside him was the famous Welsh boxer, former British heavyweight champion Tommy Farr.' These were Hill's 'minders'.

Pollard got the job. He started working for William Hill in July, and his wages were 'the princely salary of £3 10/- a week'. This was still a time when many punters preferred to bet by telegram, which came with a built-in guarantee of posting (whereas letters stuffed with cash might fail to reach their bookie). It was the world of a 'Glasgow' – the code word William Hill would use to indicate a bet of five shillings (25p) – a 'Jarrow' (12/6d) and a 'Ramsgate' (£3 10/-). Pollard would go on to have a high-profile career in the world of bookmaking, in which, through his skill as a public relations man, he would one day become the public face of Ladbrokes. But Pollard soon discovered that behind the scenes at the company all was not quite as it seemed.

There was racing on only two days a week, and we were handling cash betting. This was totally illegal. In those days the only place you could bet with cash was actually on the racecourse. All other transactions were required to be on credit terms.

To my further astonishment, the police would ring up to say they were coming round to raid us – would we please make sure there was some money about.

When the police did arrive, the thousands and thousands of pounds that would normally be lying about were not to be seen. I was locked in a cupboard with all that money, and a small amount was left on the table for the police to see. The police would duly arrive, they would pick up the money and then they would charge us. The day before the court hearing, Hill's lawyer would ring to say he had been advised by the police how much we would be fined and would we please write out a cheque for that amount ... God knows what William Hill paid to be informed of police raids, tip-offs which allowed him to protect very large amounts of money indeed.

Still, Pollard's innocence was not lost cheaply. 'A few days before Christmas, Mr Hill called me into his office and said that he thought I was doing very well and that he was increasing my salary.' He also handed the young employee an envelope containing his annual bonus, which he did for all staff each year, reportedly putting some 20% of profits aside for it. 'The cheque inside was for £64' – some 20 weeks' wages.

Two years later, one summer's afternoon in 1945, the war against Japan not yet over, a skinny young lad from Cardiff got his first glimpse of a city dreadfully damaged by Hitler's bombs as he came up to London to apply for a job at Park Lane as a settler. Sixty-six years later Angus Dalrymple, who would go on to write for *The Sporting Life* and later for CBC-TV News in Toronto, looked back on that day:

'Can you settle?' Henry 'Nick' Nicholls, Hill's bluff and hearty staff manager, gave a bemused look as he gazed down at my slight figure – in less than two years I would tower over him. He took me into the phone room and gave me a very tricky settling test; £5 each-way doubles, trebles and an accumulator on four winners including, I shudder even now to recall, a 100/7 shot and one at 8/13 in a dead heat. I set to work and after many minutes gave my completed paper to Nick. He took it to a man with a pronounced limp, who was walking near a desk. This was Don Hart, Hill's communist racing manager; the Soviets, of course, were our allies then. He had been crippled when stabbed in the leg during a clash with Fascists in Hyde Park in the thirties. Don took a paper from the desk and gave it to Nick. I then saw them shake their heads as they compared my returns with theirs.

Nick, frowning, came back over. 'Your doubles are wrong, lad – and so are your trebles. Your accumulator's adrift, too. So I'm afraid it's no-go.' He saw my face fall. 'Look, son, we'll take care of your fare up from Cardiff.'

I was just going out to head for home, when I heard Hart's deep voice suddenly call out, 'Hold it, Nick'. Don was again looking at my answers, but now with a slight smile. The two whispered for a second. Then Nick, also smiling now, came over. 'Our racing manager's just noticed something. Tell me, have you ever settled bets on a credit basis before?'

'Never, sir, I've only worked on cash letters and street stuff from our runners.'

'That accounts for it. You've included the stakes in your returns; we don't do that because all bets with us are on credit. Congratulations. Would you like to meet Mr Hill?'

I was shown into a private office ... I was looking at a dynamic, well-dressed, dark-haired man in his early forties with a genial smile and twinkling eyes. 'Sit down, son. Cigarette?' His mellow Midlands accent rolled over me like syrup. I couldn't believe the firm's founder was lighting me up.

Hill asked how much Angus was then earning as a settler with Sherman's in Cardiff, and was told £2 per week. '"What I can give you is £5 a week basic and an extra pound every time you work a dog night. You can do that five times a week if you want." Mr Hill put down his pen and smiled. I was in. I joined the firm on Monday, 30 July 1945.'

Every morning, Angus and his colleagues finished settling greyhound business from the night before; 'then came the settling of thousands of postal bets,' before they calculated ante-post bets and wrote out vouchers for the clients. After stuffing promotion leaflets into envelopes it was dealing with the afternoon dog and horse racing, whose runners and results 'were shouted to us in a strong northern accent by "Willie" Williams from the phone room's doorway. Then came his bawling of the "weighed-in" signal, followed by his equally clamorous delivery of the Tote dividends.' Having once answered the phone with his own slogan, 'William Hill of Park Lane at your service', Angus was told by Don Hart, 'Go to the cashier and tell him you're getting an increase in pay of a pound a week – that was Mr Hill you just put through. He said to tell you he liked the way you answer the phone.'

Dalrymple recalls William's reaction when dozens of black plastic ashtrays with gleaming chrome tops fitted to the new, polished tables in the settling room vanished within a week: 'Well,' Hill remarked to 'Nick' Nicholls, 'at least we've still got the tables.' 'I never saw William Hill in a bad temper,' he says. Here was a man who loved to tell jokes in the settling room and would often repeat them, forgetting, or not caring, that his staff had heard them before. One slightly off-colour story was about Dorothy Paget, his best client, and how a new announcer at Chepstow races got the sack on his first day. 'Attention, please!' his voice sang out over the loudspeakers. 'The stewards have informed me that Miss Dorothy Paget's Fanny has just been scratched. In the paddock.' Then came the extra information that cost him his job: 'May I have your attention again, please. The stewards now inform me that to the best of their knowledge and belief, Miss Dorothy Paget's Fanny has never even been entered!'

William's good humour deserted him, however, Angus Dalrymple found, when his staff fell short of professionalism. When he was robbed by his own staff, he always prosecuted:

I remember Bill Bentley, manager of the settling room, suddenly making a mad dive at a settler entering the adjoining men's room. Bill had spotted a tell-tale flash of white and pink paper in the settler's hand which indicated he was holding the white original and pink copy of a telephone wager. Bill grabbed the settler a second before a £200 losing bet was flushed down the toilet. The settler got three months in jail.

And in 1945, Gus Dalrymple recalls William instantly dismissing a settler called 'Barney' Barnet purely because he didn't approve of a message he'd been stamping on letters sent out to clients, which William felt made the company look 'common and cheap'.

Dalrymple recalled how William 'encouraged' clients to settle their debts (unrecoverable by law) by creating The London and Provincial Trade Recovery Service, which then wrote to late-paying customers advising them that their debt had been referred to LPTRS for collection. 'The letter said that unless the debt was settled the Pools Promoters Association would be informed. At that time pool bets had to be placed on credit and the threat, although untrue, duped punters into thinking that if they ever won the pools they wouldn't be paid.'

When the war in the Far East finally ended the William Hill offices provided a great view of the Victory Parade, but as Christmas approached Angus Dalrymple received two invitations. 'One was from the government telling me to report for military service in January; the other was from William Hill asking me to go to his first ever staff party.' The parties would become annual staff highlights for many years, along with regular trips to William's Whitsbury Stud. Dalrymple's apprehension at joining the military, and his disappointment at giving up his well-paid employment, were tempered, though, when William Hill said that 'while I was away doing my service in the army he was arranging for me to be paid my salary in full every week. What a man.'

CHAPTER 6

A GROWING FAMILY

'Bubbles' – William's daughter Kathleen – met her first husband during the war when she was working as a secretary at the American Embassy for the army law branch of the US military. Family stories suggest she won an award for her bravery in helping those wounded by bombing in London. At the time she was living at William's London address in Albion Gate in Bayswater. She and US Army Judge Advocate Lieutenant Matthew Leary from Vermont were married in Marylebone in November 1945. Her father was photographed smiling at the ceremony, although he felt two good reasons, says his niece Peggy Evans, for being unhappy about his daughter's choice of husband: 'He was an American and he was Catholic. William was very upset over that – he didn't like either.' Kathleen had been baptised into the Catholic church four days before the wedding.

The relationship was not to last. Bubbles emigrated to Burlington, Vermont with her new husband, but soon found her lifestyle had to change. Her husband discouraged her from drinking and wearing make-up, and 'she was made to cover her arms, wear long skirts and a hat when she went out,' says Kathleen's cousin Chris Harper. In August 1946 William and Ivy became grandparents for the first time when Kathleen gave birth to a son, Timothy James, but the marriage foundered not long after the arrival of a second child, Linda Jane, in 1947.

'I know from what my father told me,' says William's nephew Neil,

that Matthew Leary, a highly principled army lawyer, was determined his children would be brought up as normal, middle-class US citizens, without any significant monetary influence from Grandpa Bill – whether the grandkids would like it or not! Unfortunately, the same reasoning applied to his wife Bubbles, and my understanding is that it all became just too much for her to handle. Bubbles had always been able to have anything she wanted, so to suddenly deny her that right soon became unacceptable for her.

Kathleen had become effectively excommunicated from her family. She returned to England but was forbidden to see the children, who were never allowed to come to England. When she did go back to visit them access was very restricted, to little more than watching them walking to school. William tried to intervene, but despite hiring Sir Hartley Shawcross, the barrister and Attorney-General who had been lead British prosecutor at the Nuremberg War Crimes tribunal, and despite him and Ivy going to the States to plead their case, they were unable to persuade the court to grant his daughter custody. Angus Dalrymple remembered reading about the case. 'The opposing lawyer began by asking, "What do you do for a living, Mr Hill?" and when he answered, "I am a bookmaker," the lawyer told the judge, "No more questions," and sat down.' In the States, bookmaking was a much-vilified occupation. For Bubbles, who genuinely seems to have had only very sporadic access to her son and daughter, the whole situation must have been traumatic. 'She was allowed to have the children for a period and took a house,' says her cousin Peggy Evans, 'but when the time came to hand them back, it broke her heart, and she could not bring herself to put herself through that experience again.' Bubbles' marriage was over but she would remarry.

By the end of the war, William was into his early forties, and his health was already declining. He was overweight, and possibly through overwork and stress his stomach was playing him up. But he wasn't letting it affect his appetite for work. 'With a bottle of milk under his arm and a satchel containing £4,000 in his hand,

Mr William Hill arrived at Newmarket from his Park Lane office to do another day's work amongst the big men of racing,' the *Evening Telegraph* informed its readers in 1945. 'He gets up at 7 a.m. and is sometimes still working at midnight.' The milk, it added, 'was part of a diet he has been put on'.

William's respect for those who had served in the military was demonstrated several times shortly after the war. The Press Association's Alan Goddard told present day bookie and writer, Simon Nott, the tale of a now-dead racecourse character known to all as 'Johnny RAF'.

When asked how he got his name he'd tell the story. It was soon after the Second World War had ended, and he used to go to the races in his RAF blazer – gatemen were often ex-forces, so he'd more than likely get waved in free. This particular day he tried to get a bet on with a bookmaker, but was told that he'd missed the price and wasn't on. William Hill, betting next door, overheard the conversation and shouted, 'This man has been fighting for his country! It is a disgrace that he should be bluffed out of a bet. He can have that bet, and any in future at the top price with me.' William told the man he was on, and didn't need a ticket, asked his first name, was told, Johnny, then instructed his clerk to put the name down to 'Johnny RAF' – and the name stuck.

Roy Sutterlin was a 25-year-old veteran of Bomber and Coastal Commands who joined Hills as a telephonist in Park Lane, and tackled virtually every aspect of the company's business, from ledger work and field book clerking to making the tea – 'We would often work from 9am to 11pm.' He eventually became the first employee to work right through to board level as Credit Director. Towards the end of his career Roy remembered William as 'a very, very hard but fair man'.

We once had an extremely bad day in credit, when we lost more than I ever recall doing before or since. I was waiting for Mr Hill to come in the next morning, and I was most worried about what he might say. He asked for the Field Book and went through it, looking at every entry on every page for every race. When he turned over the final page he turned to me and said, 'I don't know what you're worried about – I wouldn't have done any different myself.' If William had come into the business today he would still make a mark: he was a giant.

Probably the only person to be employed by William Hill as a result of a letter from Burma was Major Peter Hand-Blackwell, from the family which owned the Crosse & Blackwell company. Whilst serving abroad during the War in India, Ceylon and Burma he had channelled bets from fellow officers back to Hill, and followed this up by writing from Burma to ask William for a job. He was eventually taken on and told to start on course at Goodwood the next day, earning '£25 a week and a dollar (25p) in the pound commission. I lost £6,000 on the day, took a "sharp" bet for some each-way doubles which cost £3,500, and at the end of the day William said, "God almighty, it's a wonder they didn't have the braces off you as well."' Blackwell thought that his career had started and finished on the same day, but William reassured him, 'They'll give it back.'

Blackwell soon discovered that William's social skills were perhaps not fully formed. He'd invite his racecourse team for a drink in top London clubs like Scott's or the Carlton after racing – 'This was expensive', declared Peter, 'he never had any money on him so we bought the drinks and he also usually borrowed a fiver for his cab home.'

A bizarre military connection was revealed only after a record-breaking win in May 1952 – when Monty Parker from Windsor

Major Peter Blackwell successfully applied for a job with William Hill – from Burma, becoming a trusted lieutenant of the Guv'nor.

won £25,348 (c.£635,000 today) from his £1 each-way Tote odds double on two horses at Ludlow. There was an internal inquiry into why the bet was never hedged after its first part had won. It transpired the settler responsible was a former British military hangman in Palestine. When William was asked whether he should be fired, he showed his magnanimity and nose for publicity: 'Keep him on – he's given us our best advertisement for years.'

Being the biggest bookmaker standing at the biggest meetings meant William was now in a high-stakes game. Another day, at Royal Ascot, Blackwell recalled William facing a damaging £85,000 loss on the day after four races, only to bet on the last two races 'as if there was no such thing as settling day. Rank outsiders won the last two races and William went home a winner. As he got into his car he uttered two words: "Thank. God."' The only other time Blackwell would see William show any emotion at results was when Nimbus, the horse he bred, won the Derby.

Five years after the Big Game gamble, there were again rumours that William would not have been able to settle had Tudor Minstrel won the 1947 Derby. 'Ru' King, probably the biggest bookmaker and commission agent in the Midlands, had struck a hefty £25,000 to £3,000 bet with William on Tudor Minstrel – after the horse's victory as favourite in the 2,000 Guineas his odds had shrunk to 6/4. However, Hill was one of the few to know that Tudor Minstrel's trainer Fred Darling's real Derby hope was Blue Train, revealed Richard Baerlein in the 1980s, and the trainer himself was one of those on Blue Train at 10/1. Gordon Richards, the superstar jockey of the day, was left considering which of the two horses to ride in the Derby only for Blue Train to break down less than a fortnight before. William decided to back his judgement, based on his knowledge of breeding, that Tudor Minstrel would not stay, and laid the horse to lose him in excess of £175,000. (MeasuringWorth. com estimates today's value of a 1947 £1 to be at least £30, making £175,000 worth £5,250,000 today). Tudor Minstrel eventually finished a disappointing fourth. Had the horse won, Baerlein wrote, 'William could not have settled at once. That might have been the last we would have heard of William Hill.' William himself once told his nephew Chris Harper, '[I] would have gone down.'

Instead, 'he never looked back, that set him on the road to riches, and he was able as a result, to found the company's next HQ, Hill House, in Piccadilly, on his winnings,' added Baerlein.

The near miss with Tudor Minstrel came two years after a less well-known brush with financial disaster at hare coursing's Blue Riband event, the Waterloo Cup, now outlawed, which was run at Altcar near Liverpool. It was an event that attracted enormous crowds, many of whom loved a serious wager on the outcome – Hill's company took £60,000 on the 1946 running, and £100,000 a year later – and William went regularly to stand in person. In the 1945 Cup much of the money had been gambled on a greyhound called Joint Command, owned by another Birmingham bookmaker and former gang colleague, Jack Woolf, who backed his dog at 100/7 so heavily with his old Brummie acquaintance that, Woolf later revealed, 'Billy Hill told me he wouldn't be able to pay if my dog won. "Don't worry", I said. "You've got till tomorrow!"' Joint Command reached the final but only after such a testing semi-final that it seemed impossible for him to recover to beat Bryn Tritoma, who had gone off at 200/1. But, relates the Waterloo Cup's official history, 'William Hill's heart must have stopped when … the exhausted Joint Command came back from the dead to lead Bryn Tritoma two lengths. The hare broke back and Bryn Tritoma was in, but when Joint Command eventually killed he can only have been a single point adrift.' William retained his support for coursing, and the veteran bookmaker Stephen Little remembers meeting up with him at Newmarket races around the end of the 1960s, and finding him quite happy to sign a petition on behalf of coursing to be sent to Parliament.

Interestingly, in Waterloo Cup betting advertisements of those days, William was boasting that his business had been 'established in 1922'. At this time, William had as 'an associate' a bookie called Fred Charles, who was a coursing form expert. The two would later fall out via an acrimonious split over money, with Fred claiming he was owed a substantial sum.

With business expanding quickly the staff at Park Lane had grown from 30 to 100. It was clearly necessary to acquire larger premises, and in September 1945 William had signed a lease on 225 Piccadilly, formerly the Winston Hotel, a huge seven-storey building at the corner of the Haymarket opposite the London Pavilion and within yards of the globally famous statue of Eros. He was now operating from the very heart of London. The property required a great deal of reorganisation, which William set about with his customary gusto; it was renamed Hill House and in 1947 William Hill again moved offices.

Opposite: Traffic was stopped to allow removal of the William Hill Piccadilly office safe when the company moved on to Blackfriars Road.

CHAPTER 7

THE CIRCUS MOVES TO PICCADILLY

'Out of warren-like rooms and corridors of what had formerly been a luxury hotel Hill began to fashion his new headquarters,' enthused *The Hill Story*. 'The windows looked out on the changing sights and lights of the world's most famous roundabout.' Angus Dalrymple helped on the day with the move, and remembers Leslie Marrison, William's general manager, coming up to him in the afternoon with a parcel.

He said, 'Just before we left Park Lane, our mail supervisor ran out with this registered parcel marked "Urgent" which had just arrived from your mother in Cardiff. He asked Mr Hill if he'd mind taking it to you at the new office. Mr Hill remarked to me on the way, "Don't let this get around, Leslie, but if I'm supposed to be one of Britain's most successful businessmen, what the hell am I doing with Angus's laundry on my lap?"'

The staff had to cope with an immense rush of business in barely furnished and improvised quarters. Two hundred telephone lines ('It is quite simple to place a bet merely by dialling Whitehall 3422') were installed, along with a battery of calculating and adding machines, together with a split-second system of checking and recording every bet received. This 'great nerve-centre of the nation's credit betting' had to be created in the face of post-war shortages and restrictions – but that did not prevent new turnover records being set week by week. Soon William's business was receiving 50,000 letters and 100,000 telephone calls a week.

William gets down to shirt-sleeve order to check the bets with field book boss Willie Alsford (standing) and colleague Keith Morgan.

'William's wife, Ivy, was in charge of the cleaning staff, and often helped them,' says Bert Arnold, who joined as a young lad in 1948. 'Sometimes the Guv'nor – we called him the Guv'nor, but always addressed him as Mr Hill – would ring from the course to invite us to join him for drinks and snacks in a pub called Rayners in the Haymarket, almost next door to the office.' The Christmas dinner dance used to take place at the Connaught Rooms, and Bert recalled chatting at one of them to the comedian Tommy Trinder, and a very young Shirley Bassey being at another. 'The staff entrance was around the corner at 40 Haymarket, where there was a huge time-clock for the staff to clock in,' remembered Angus Dalrymple. By the early 1950s 'I was settler number 38 in a field of 115, but ... the total number of time cards was 469.'

Keith Morgan joined the company in 1950 and ended up working in the Trade Room, where he remembers William being 'very phlegmatic with bad results – when there was a succession of good results for us, he'd say, "I don't like this – it's better to give 'em something back. We need to lose."' And woe betide anyone if the field book, which contained liabilities for any particular race, had any prices out of order:

> On one occasion when I was looking after the field book he came down and lost his temper over something. He had put his cigar in an ashtray on my desk but when he threw the book down it hit the ashtray, spilling the ash and the cigar into his lap. He brushed himself down grumpily while I stood there trying not to laugh!

Morgan also soon encountered William's famous inability to praise: the most he ever received 'was when the Old Man once said to me, "Thank you, Morgan" – a rare accolade.' Phil Bull reflected on this contradiction in William's character, and the reason for it:

> The real truth is that he is a person very much concerned for other people and he has a very highly developed social conscience. What he doesn't have is a capacity in the ordinary way to translate this into proper relations with individuals. He is too much of a perfectionist that whenever anyone is doing work for him, the moment they make a mistake he pounces on it and tears the person off a strip. But he is quite incapable of patting anybody on the back and saying, 'That's a jolly fine job of work you've done . . .'
>
> The result of this is that people who work for him feel that he is a carper and a critic, and not an appreciative person – and I must tell you that when I was with him this is what I felt. If, when I was doing something for him, I made a mess of it, he was highly critical. And the whole of the time there, though I know I did an enormous number of things that pleased him, he never once patted me on the back.

Many people who work for him can't take this. They become discouraged after a time. It took a little time to understand that it wasn't really that he didn't appreciate what you did, it was that he was constitutionally unable to tell you so. So you had to learn this if you were to appreciate him properly.

He is still unable to build up a person's self-confidence and get the best out of them by making them feel they are worthwhile. He never will be able to do it ... This derives from his rough early days in Birmingham, the struggle for existence and self-assertion, and this has been ironed into his character throughout his early life. It's a deplorable shortcoming, a deplorable development of his character, but it is something easily understood. It is a thing that has happened all his life.

A *Racing Review* feature from 1951 paints a nice picture of what it was like for 'Mr Britain' to ring the switchboard at Hill House, 'manned' by intelligent and courteous ladies who are 'on the alert' at all times, and request, 'Horses, please.'

'Mr Britain' is immediately put through to the Horse Telephone Room, where a hundred operators give service. These telephonists sit in rows of ten, all facing an enormous blackboard, 25 feet wide, on which are chalked up complete results from all meetings, runners, betting from the course, and every other scrap of information likely to assist a client in his or her effort to defeat the book. From before the commencement of racing, to the 'weighed in' on the last race, a clerk 'lives' on the 'Blower'; meanwhile, an assistant watches the 'Tape', and tears off messages as they arrive, and fixes them on a 'Gripper Board', showing runners, jockeys, betting changes, and after each race, full starting prices ...

Now, to return to 'Mr Britain', who has asked for and received all possible information about his fancy. He now decides to have half a crown [12.5p] each-way on Gentleman's Relish. No backer should think that all the betting 'dope' is only willingly given to the client who bets in ponies, monkeys or grands. The William Hill Organization attends with the same courteous service to all. Mr Hill understands and appreciates the needs of a racing man, and as a result has 'built' a service known at all points of the compass. 'Mr Britain', having had his wager, waits to hear his bet called back by the telephonist so that there can be no mistake when he receives his statement.

Every bet is taken down in duplicate. Both copies are handed to junior clerks for immediate independent 'timing'. Sizeable wagers are recorded in the field book by a wizard of rapid calculations. Consider for a moment, three or four meetings, with bets arriving in shoals, and only a few seconds to straighten out the book's position before the 'off'. Doubles, trebles and all other accumulative bets have to be quickly dissected, but the job is accomplished without anyone getting out of his stride. In a mammoth betting organisation such as this, at times, quite naturally, liabilities become enormous. A 'No Limit' business with many thousands of clients must show up a 'red letter day' for someone. Towards the end of the programme accumulative bets often give the bookmaker five-figure liabilities. If the position begins to look top-heavy, arrangements to adjust the SP books are made through the 'Blower' with the course representative.

The telephone room near the 'off' is activity itself, and although 100 telephone operators are taking down bets and messengers flying round the room with bets to be timed under the clock, there is little noise. Red lights show up on the telephone banks and being immediately answered become green; there is no buzzing, no ringing. The telephonists confirm wagers quietly, efficiently and without fuss. There is a supervisor at every row to help with any problem which might arise or give a decision when needed.

'They're off.'

'The money's on the way.'

'Mr Britain's' bet has been dispatched to the Settling Room. This department is divided in what we can call two sides – Whites and Pinks. You remember every bet taken by telephone is in duplicate. The top sheet is white, the underneath copy pink; these wagers are always kept apart and arrive into the Settling Room by different 'collections'. Over thirty clerks are fed with 'whites' and a like number with 'pinks'. The same bet is worked out by two independent 'settlers', who rarely fail to arrive at the same answer no matter how intricate the betting problem. If figures disagree, the bets are re-checked, perhaps by a third party, but you can be quite certain the right answer is found before the 'all right' is given. Settling is a hard life in a busy firm. A warm summer's afternoon, with most of the hot favourites placed, makes the settling of innumerable place doubles, trebles and accumulators at awkward odds and perhaps a dead-heat or two for third place, anything but a Sport of Kings. Ready reckoners are unheard of in Hill House. A first-class settler can work far quicker without such aid.

September 1947 had produced another Hill innovation with the first ever edition of the monthly *Racing Review* magazine, priced at 2/6d but complimentary to clients. It was the only illustrated racing periodical at the time, was also available by subscription, and would survive until 1955. William Hill were also sponsoring a racing-themed programme on Radio Luxembourg, which could be picked up in Britain, even though the signal was notorious for fading in and out of earshot. Racing journalist Geoffrey Gilbey took part in one: 'Mr Hill's only instructions were, "Give as many win-ners as you can, and give backers all possible help." I remember how delighted he was when over the air I tipped Master Vote who won the [1947] Hunt Cup at 25/1.'

'At the end of each week we ledger clerks had to make out cheques for the winners and take their handwritten statements to the Guv'nor, who signed the cheques,' says Bert Arnold. 'He would ask questions about the client's account if that account had a win-ning balance – and we had to be alert as we always had to know if the winnings were due to ante-post bets.' On the final day of the 1947 Flat season one of William's clients had won a total of £20,657 for £28-worth of bets.

'We take a great many bets which run into a possible win for the punter of thousands of pounds,' said William in a 1949 interview that gives a fascinating insight into his thought processes.

I shall always remember the case of the 'dour Scotsman' who invested a £6 double on Jockey Treble in the Lincoln of 1947 and Double Sam in the Grand National of the same year. The price I laid him was 50,000/1, and when Mr Oxenham's five-year-old came storming through to win his Lincoln liter-ally on the post we, who make our living at racing, had one more example of a small betting man apparently knowing more than we do.

Now, at this time, or should I say at ten minutes past three on that Wednesday afternoon, Double Sam was a 500/1 chance for the Grand National, but immediately Jockey Treble proved victorious ... Mr S.D. Clark's 11-year-old 'lepper' automatically became one of our 'bogeys'. I therefore instructed one of my staff to approach the holder of this £300,000 to £6 double and see whether he would be interested in hedging part of his wager to ensure his being on a winner no matter what the result of the National, and also to reduce our liability. This small punter, a dour Scotsman he certainly turned out to be, was also an exceedingly clever businessman, and after much persuasion, in which I personally took a hand, he agreed to lay us £150,000 to £1,500 Double Sam, thereby reducing our liability by half, and at the same time ensuring his winning at least £1,494, even if his second nomination should not be returned the winner of the Grand National. Double Sam met his doom at the 28th fence and our client, although backing a losing double, had still won £1,494 for a £6 investment.

This was an early example of the principle behind the now increasingly common 'Cash In My Bet' facility offered to clients who can close bets out en route to their conclusion.

William began campaigning for bookmaking to run according to 'a set of rules acceptable to all in general principle'. It's very likely he was the author of a piece on 'Standardising Betting' in the William Hill-published *Racing Review* in 1949:

The flat racing season of 1948 was reported to have been a disastrous one for bookmakers, and if the advertisement columns of the sporting newspapers are any guide, the list of Starting Price offices for sale would bear out such a contention.

The small bookmaker was the worst sufferer, because his variety of wagers was not sufficient to enable him to make a reasonably varied book, and his only alternatives were either to lay off his wagers, or to turn gambler and take the risk of holding them all. The backer, too, has had his problems, which were concerned chiefly with the variety of rules in operation by different bookmakers.

The article criticised bookmakers who would only accept win bets in races with sufficient runners for each-way terms, and pointed out that 'Limits for doubles, trebles, accumulators and the like vary with different firms, and unless a backer is absolutely conversant with all applications of every rule, his temper is likely to become frayed on occasion.'

The laws of betting, too, need some form of standardisation. At present they are unfair, complex and in some instances, even ridiculous. As the law stands today it is illegal to give a bookmaker a betting slip, either with or without money, but the Post Office will undertake to transmit your wager by telephone, telegram or letter.

The Gaming Act is another bone of contention. Under certain provisions, both bookmakers and backers can plead it as a means of evading liabilities, with the important exception that the backer can find ways of betting again, but the bookmaker's business is brought to an end.

Then again, at this point in the story there are plenty of people willing to testify that for William rules were there to be broken. Ron Pollard had reported back to work after protracted war service – to discover that in his absence William Hill had been sending his mother £1 a week on his behalf, which she in turn had fed into his Post Office savings book – as 'a junior ledger clerk ... learning the game from the bottom and, if need be, running the odd errand.' One such errand saw him dispatched during 1949 to the Dorchester on Park Lane with the small matter of £2,500 in cash – 'worth more than £100,000 today, I suppose,' he estimated when interviewed for this book. He was to deliver the readies to Fred Harkus, 'a personal friend of William Hill, who also happened to be agent to many of the top jockeys'. At this time, wrote Pollard in his autobiography, it was not uncommon for all the big bookies

– William Hill, Bill Chandler, Willie Preston, Percy Thompson – to have one of the top jockeys on their payroll: 'most often, a jockey would be riding to trainer's orders; sometimes, however, he would be riding to a bookmaker's orders. His fee for doing so, which they called "the usual", would be £100 on the winner of the race involved, at whatever price it was returned.'

Pollard believed the particular rider for whom the two-and-a-half grand was intended had been aboard a hot favourite at 'Glorious Goodwood', where it had been beaten by one other runner, a 25/1 outsider, hence the £2,500 payout. Sixty-plus years after the event in 2013 Ron Pollard couldn't remember the name of the horse but stood by his account. But the problem is that in all the results for the entire 1949 Glorious Goodwood meeting there is no 25/1 winner. However, the biggest betting race of that meeting would probably have been the Stewards Cup, and in 1949 the 4/1 clear favourite – five points shorter in the market than the two joint second favourites – was Luminary, ridden by Charlie Elliott, who rode 14 domestic Classic winners. In the event, its backers were given what appeared to be a tremendous run for their money but at the winning post Elliott's mount was just half a length behind 20/1 runner-up Spartan Sacrifice, who was in turn a mere short head down on the 33/1 winner, The Bite. There is little doubt that William Hill – and many other bookies – would have been very pleased to see Luminary narrowly beaten and save on a substantial payout. It may be significant that Fred Harkus was described to the author as 'a putter-on for [jockeys] Charlie Smirke and Charlie Elliott' by a respected observer of the racing scene of the 1940s and 1950s. Pollard said he lost his 'innocence' at this time and 'would learn not to be surprised at anything'. Of Hill he says, 'I was never blind to his shortcomings, but I owed him much and he was for me the original likeable rogue.'

Pollard has more. During the same year, he clerked for William for the first time, at Salisbury. 'I was filled with enormous trepidation,' wrote Pollard, 'yet we had a quiet start and everything seemed to be going along serenely when Bill leaned down and said, "Get ready, then. We are going to have a go at this favourite. A real go – just get every bet down in your book."' The short-priced favourite belonged to a leading owner of the day: 'Bill did not seem particularly perturbed about any liabilities,' recalled Pollard – 'he was betting like a man who didn't expect to have any.' Quoted at even money elsewhere, Hill was shouting, 'I'll go 5/4, I'll go 5/4.' 'Need I say that the favourite did not win?' wrote Pollard. 'The favourite was not going to win – Bill had seen to that. He, or more likely a distant someone, had had words with the jockey, who would have collected "the usual" – £100 on the winner at whatever price it came in at.'

William Hill cleaned up around £20,000 on that race. Pollard says he was given a 'pony' (£25) by Hill's other clerk, the loyal Tommy Turner. From race results and betting patterns in a number of Salisbury meetings that year, it's not difficult to identify a number of candidates for the race Pollard refers to – one in particular featuring an extremely 'leading' owner's horse ridden by a high-profile jockey with connections to William Hill, which returned a starting price of 11/10. Pollard even alleges that Dorothy Paget was the victim of just such a sting, 'and I fear that I was the distant "someone" who played his part,' claiming that he was at Taunton where Paget had placed a 'large bet' on a favourite. 'A message came down the line for me to give a certain jockey £100: "He knows what it is for. He will be parting company," I was told from Hill's London office. The horse did not win, for the jockey did indeed part company from his mount.'

Ms Paget features in further rumours about a couple of races in 1948 where William allegedly had the favourite stopped, according to a reliable and well-informed source who wishes to remain anonymous. 'On each occasion the stopped horse was owned by Dorothy Paget and ridden by Bryan Marshall. And each time she had gone for a "double banco".' Ms Paget would risk tens of thousands of pounds a time on her 'banco' and 'double banco' bets – confident tips from her trainers – her standing instruction being to bet enough to make her a profit of £20,000 per bet. This caused a sensation once, when she took it into her head to back a horse which went off at 1/8 odds – meaning she had to risk £160,000 to make her twenty grand. At Wye on 13 September, Cracker, whose odds drifted from even money to 11-8, finished ten lengths second to a 13-2 shot called Borneo ridden by an amateur, in a race where Marshall, allegedly, went from the weighing room to the paddock via the rails to ask William Hill what he wanted him to do that day. Then at Sandown on 26 November Marshall rode Prince of Denmark, a horse that had won his previous two races at Liverpool and Worcester and started at 4-11, but was beaten a length by a 100-8 chance called Land Baby. But there were no enquiries about either race and, claims our source, William Hill and one or two others cleaned up.

However, perhaps it wasn't all one way traffic. In his biography of Dorothy Paget, Quintin Gilbey detailed an occasion when she cooperated with trainer Fulke Walwyn to dupe bookies and punters by permitting Marshall to ride her hot favourite, knowing full well that Walwyn's other runner, with an unknown riding, was much better fancied and duly won. 'The public don't pay my training bills and bookmakers are quite capable of looking after themselves.'

William disliked the feeling of having been the victim of a manipulated result and believed that 'If ever a horse was doped, that horse was Talma II.' The French-trained St Leger contender was heavily backed from 100/6 on course on the day of the 1951 race, in to 7/1 second favourite, with William laying the horse to lose £30,000. Before the race the horse was in a lather of sweat, and he won by over ten lengths. He never showed such form again, and there was no drugs test.

William reviled doping and in 1961 offered '£10,000 to catch the dopers and see them put behind iron bars' when a gang was 'nobbling' high profile runners – a story fully told in Jamie Reid's award-winning *Doped*.

In the spring of 1950 the rules were even broken on building work at Hill House, with the consequences threatening William's presence at the Cheltenham Festival. The company had been charged with carrying out work to a greater sum than that permitted – £100 – without a licence, and accused of hiding the fact that the work was happening by having it done at night and behind drawn curtains. The work was vital. William had been turning business away because the administrative offices were struggling to cope with an influx of new account holders. (Interestingly, it emerged during the case that William's salary, £1,250 a year, was the same as it had been ten years earlier, and equivalent by now to a modest £37,000 today.) The company pleaded guilty, but there was laughter in court when the judge said he needed time to consider the appropriate fine, and it was pointed out that William needed to be at Cheltenham races for the next two days. 'Hill was released on bail,' smirked the *Daily Mirror*, and the delay seemed to work in William's favour, because the fine he received was just £500 with £50 costs.

CHAPTER 8

FOOTBALL FIXED-ODDS

Fixed-odds betting on football began before the turn of the 20th century. In *Athletic News* in 1889 Mr Brook of Rose Cottage, Dewsbury was advertising '£2 2/- given for having four winners in the Third Round. Send selections and six penny stamps by 2 March.' It soon became more sophisticated, to the extent that in 1915 it was responsible for the first authenticated fixed football match, a vital First Division game between Manchester United and Liverpool in which a number of players had bet on the correct score.

William Hill launched his first fixed-odds betting coupon in September 1939, even brushing up on his schooldays' artistic talents to design a promotional poster, but the turnover of just £6 18/6d from 28 returned coupons was not enough to cover the printing and postal expenses. 'With its meagre lists and poor prices … it doesn't stand comparison with our present coupon,' he reflected in hindsight, 'but it looked fine at the time – I was pretty proud of it.' He persisted, and in 1944, with business having grown so rapidly that the football turnover almost equalled racing, it was no longer possible to accommodate it in the Park Lane office, so William Hill (Football) Ltd became a separate company, in New Bridge Street near Ludgate Circus, and around the corner from the very heart of the newspaper business, Fleet Street, while a further new company, William Hill (Glasgow) Ltd was formed, according to *The Hill Story*, because 'William Hill was becoming a household word', and

he now found that he was receiving a lot of bets through the post, enclosing cash. As the betting laws stood it meant that all bets were void, and the money had to be returned to the

Hill's Postal Betting Offices in Glasgow. Here there are 400 employees handling 32,000 letter bets daily.

A presence in Scotland bestowed a slightly dubious legality on postal bets.

clients. This anomaly had twice resulted in William being prosecuted and a third proven offence could have resulted in his imprisonment. Apart from the loss of business involved, this situation threatened to damage his good name with people who didn't understand the law. Punters who had picked a loser would be pleased enough to find their stake money back in the next morning's post – but what about the ones who were already standing drinks all round on their supposed winnings?

'I could see they'd be writing me off as a welsher,' was Hill's own comment at the time. By setting up in Scotland, William 'did not attract so much attention from the authorities' and 'was able to set up a service for the cash-with-bet backer – a branch that was to grow into a tree nearly as mighty as its parent!' The MP turned author A.P. Herbert, however, was still musing in 1953 in his book *Pools Pilot* on the dubious legality of fixed-odds postal betting:

Messrs Z do football betting at fixed odds only. They have a large office in London, and another, it is said, in Scotland. If you send them a bet in London you must not send the money with it – that would be 'ready money' betting which (off the course) is illegal. You may send it next week, for then it will be credit betting, which is all right ... Exactly the same law, the Betting Act 1853, applies to Bonny Scotland. But, to put it mildly, it does not carry the same weight in those far parts...

Mr Blanket's bet on the Obvious Eight, with its humble shilling, is carried to Bonny Scotland by train. But it is not then hurried to Messrs Z's great Scottish office; for Messrs Z have no great Scottish office, though they have a small one. The sack of wagers is now transferred to an aircraft and conveyed back to London. Mr Blanket's little ready money bet is deemed to have acquired legality by its brief visit to Scotland. This, we think, is about the funniest thing that happens in this island, and it happens every week.

The fixed-odds football coupons were now being issued from both Glasgow (where William, unlike Messrs Z, did have a real office!)

WILLIAM HILL

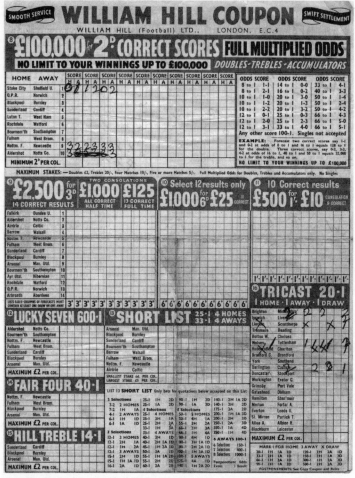

An early fixed-odds coupon.

and London, for the 1944–45 season at a price of a ha'penny per coupon (a compulsory charge imposed because of a government Control of Paper Order), with two issued per week: 'In order to save unnecessary work in these days of staff shortage,' came the request, 'we should appreciate clients paying a full season's fee in one amount.'

74

The coupon for 4 November 1944 ('Smooth Service, Swift Settlement') makes for intriguing reading. It features 55 matches, including Liverpool v Manchester United, Newcastle v Hull, Lovells v Bath and Aberaman v Cardiff. There were ten different sections, including a Triple Chance at 20,000/1 for finding the correct outcome of 13 games; a Lucky Seven at 300/1; Snip Six, 120/1 and a Trim Three (inspiration for a catchy name seems to have run out here!) at 10/1. Another section, a correct score on a selected game, in this instance Manchester City versus Everton, offered some intriguing prices, ranging from 12/1 for 1-0 and 0-1, to 100/1 for 4-4, but stipulating that 'in the event of the result being a score other than any of those priced above, all bets are lost.' From 1947 Hill's sponsored programme on Radio Luxembourg delivered all the English and Scottish football results and a summary of the day's matches every Saturday at 5.30pm.

The fixed-odds coupons were in direct competition with the already well-established pools companies, who offered a less sophisticated, but perhaps easier to understand product. Those taking part in the pools could win life-changing amounts of money by randomly selecting eight matches to end in a draw, thus claiming a percentage of the total amount staked that week, less deductions to ensure the company issuing the coupon was guaranteed a profit margin. For the promoters it was a 'no lose' proposition, unlike the fixed odds which guaranteed all winners at pre-determined payout odds. But then in 1948 a 10% Pools Betting Duty was introduced – and raised to 20% before the end of the year. By October of the following year it was 30%, and by 1951 only 42 of 231 pools firms were still in business, and feeling very unfairly treated in comparison with the fixed-odds businesses. At Hills, meanwhile, expansion was continuing apace, and a modern five-storey building in Finsbury was taken on in 1952 to serve as the new headquarters of this fast-growing arm of the company. In Glasgow the premises had soon been doubled in size and 400 staff (another 1,000 worked in London) were handling 32,000 letters daily.

Particular stress was now laid on security. All the staff entrusted with watching over the arrival and handling of mail, together with the resulting cash intake, were former police officers, whose job it was to supervise the collection of the massive coupon mail in locked and sealed bags of the company's own design. They ensured that the arrival of every single coupon and bet was duly recorded and that no unauthorised person touched or tampered with them. The company was so proud of its state-of-the-art technologies and systems to deal with fixed-odds bets that in 1954 it produced a booklet boasting about them. *Your Guide to Fixed Odds* enthused about the array of 'Totometers' which 'can count up postal orders, £1 notes and such like at roughly five a second, or 20,000 an hour'; marvelled at microfilming of coupons which 'snapped pictures so tiny that 6,000 go on a reel' at a speed of 6,000 an hour; paraded Postal Franking – 'at the rate of 10,000 an hour' – and goggled at Graphotype Machines which 'typewrite' your name and address on metal. The booklet also revealed how once an envelope machine had opened letters at the rate of 15,000 per hour, 'a girl' opened out the envelope with a deft slit at each end before stamping it for identification – but that coupon checking was carried out by 'hundreds of men – yes, all male – for some reason they seem better cut out for this work'.

On 1 December 1956 William Hill paid out £827,365 (over £17 million in today's money) – reportedly the largest sum of money ever paid out on one day's football matches, either by a fixed-odds or pools company – and underlining the appeal of fixed odds over pools: 'It was one of those days when matches ran true to form, and every one of the clients who had correctly foretold the results profited fully by his acumen,' declared Hill's *Sporting News Annual*, 'unaffected by the similar good fortune of thousands of fellow-backers'. A Mr Shipp of London received the biggest cheque – £56,000 for a 10/- stake, and over a million pounds today – from William Hill himself. By 1960, three million football coupons were being distributed every week by William Hill (Football) Ltd, and its annual profits had risen dramatically, from £145,179 in 1954 to £1,355,657 in 1960, with the total dividend paid out to shareholders over £600,000.

But fixed-odds betting was an extremely competitive business, and 1960 proved to be the high-water mark of Hill's business, even though the following year showed total national fixed-odds betting was up from £45 million to £50 million, whereas turnover on football pools was down year on year by 10% to £101 million (pools betting duty had now reached 33%). In 1961 all betting shop proprietors holding William Hill accounts became collecting agents for the company, entitled to distribute Hill Fixed-Odds coupons over the counter to their clients for a commission. Possibly in an effort to take on the popular football pools directly at their own game, William also launched Hill-Line, a new fixed-odds bet, offering punters odds of up to 800/1 to find six draws from a full list of games. On 11 March 1961 there were 20 (21 on some coupons) draws – so many that the main dividend on the pools, for which eight draws had to be found, was little more than a pound – but when the smoke had cleared Hills were left bemoaning a total payout of £500,000 to 137,000 winning clients.

In the heat of the battle to win a greater share of the market by competing layers, fixed-odds punters were able to take advantage of some extremely generous odds, but an increasing bone of contention amongst bookmakers was the ever-rising reward available for selecting three draws, which had been lengthening from 40/1 and was now widely offered at 66/1. But when a meeting of over 100 fixed-odds bookmakers at London's Connaught Rooms passed a resolution that the maximum odds for three draws should be 40/1, William dismissed it as 'the tail trying to wag the dog', and he and Ladbrokes' boss Cyril Stein – united for once – declared they had no intention whatsoever of adhering to it, as it would be tantamount to a cartel to deprive punters of generous odds. But the business was declining: in 1961 the net profit had more than halved to just over half a million pounds, and in September that year – four months after betting shops had appeared on the High Street – William Hill paid out over £1 million to fixed-odds punters for the first time. In the same week, to illustrate the scale of football business still being done, the company paid out just under £280,000 in winnings to racing punters.

Instead of arguing with the other bookmakers, therefore, in 1962 William Hill and Ladbrokes, who had only launched their own coupon in 1960, went head-to-head against each other in the High Court, when the former accused the latter of infringing the copyright of their fixed-odds coupon. The question was: is a William Hill football coupon a literary work on which the company could claim copyright? The case went all the way to the House of Lords. Ladbrokes' argument was that the skill, industry and experience did not lie in the production of the coupon but in the selection of bets: the coupons themselves were like a salesman's articles, and the choice for the punter was a business decision, not a copyright question.

But the Law Lords disagreed: in Lord Devlin's judgement

> Any selection, for an example an anthology, requires a process of decision between alternatives and I cannot see that it matters whether the decision is made on literary or on business grounds. An anthology of saleable poems is as much entitled to protection as an anthology of beautiful poems. It is pointed out, quite rightly, that an anthology is different from a list that is descriptive of articles for sale, since the anthology is itself the thing that is to be offered for sale. But if this distinction was a good one, there could never be a copyright in a catalogue of goods.

Lord Pearce went on to praise William Hill for the way they had always produced their football coupons:

The plaintiffs have been pioneers in this field and had invented various bets and nomenclatures some of which have
been adopted by their rivals. A study of the coupons of 23
principal firms engaged in the fixed odds betting business
shows that a large proportion of the bets in the plaintiffs'
coupon are also offered by their rivals, and much similar-
ity of language, arrangement and substance will be found in
their coupons. It emerges clearly that the arrangement and
contents of the coupons are the central point of the business – what one witness called the heart of the business. The
coupon must contain an assorted selection of bets that will
attract a customer and induce him to fill up the coupon in
preference to rival coupons. To this end, the plaintiffs have
devoted much work and money and ingenuity. Out of the
vast number of bets that can be offered, they select and de-
vise those which, while being profitable to them, will fill the
coupon with the greatest allure.

William Hill were awarded damages of £1 – all they had sought
in trying to establish the principle – and the two giants continued to battle for supremacy. That year Hill's fixed-odds record was
smashed again in October as 26 draws turned up on the coupons
and they paid out £1,312,810, but annual profits were transformed
into a net loss of £80,049. Ron Pollard, who had moved from
Hill to Ladbrokes, claimed that after one fortnight of bad results
Ladbrokes lost today's equivalent of £3.5 million – 'It was touch
and go whether they would survive.' The next two years saw the
competition to offer ever more generous fixed odds become almost
suicidal: in October 1963 Hill offered 100,000/1 for nine draws
for a minimum of 1d and maximum £1 stake, and even though
fixed odds had built up, incredibly, five million clients sending in
two million coupons a week, and made up a third of a total annual turnover approaching £50 million, over-generous odds and

frequent draw gluts meant it was now a loss leader. In June 1963, the Football company reported a deficit on trading of £579,197 – reduced by some creative accountancy to a net loss of £315,197

Then in the Budget of 1964 the Chancellor of the Exchequer Reginald Maudling introduced a tax of 25% on fixed-odds football betting, reducing pools duty to the same level. Ten footballers had recently been charged with having deliberately thrown matches for betting purposes, so a desire to nip corruption in the bud might have been partly behind the measure – or just a convenient excuse. 'I think the Conservative government knew it was their last Budget,' William reflected later. 'Maudling estimated that fixed-odds turnover was £50 million a year and that he would get £12.5 million out of that. I told him he'd get 25% of nothing. That's exactly what happened.'

The effect was immediate: odds were trimmed to cover the tax burden, but the betting war meant not by enough to protect profits. And although an initial slump in consumption after the imposition of a tax on a product, e.g. alcohol and tobacco, has often been followed by a gradual return to previous levels, this did not happen with fixed-odds betting, and the decline proved long-lived: industry turnover on fixed odds fell steadily from around £65 million in 1963 to £15 million in 1965, £7 million in 1967, and £5 million in 1968; the pools stayed virtually level, at £128 million in 1967, £126 million in 1968. The new tax itself actually raised barely £4.5 million, over half of which, £2.5 million, was Hill's contribution.

William could never be swayed from his belief that the pools companies had lobbied for such a tax to be imposed, and even that money had changed hands – possibly into Conservative funds, or even to individuals – to ensure it. He also suspected a wider political agenda, the nationalisation of the whole betting industry, perhaps within five years. 'The Pools Promoters will be celebrating, and thanks to their lobbying they will be drinking wine mixed with blood – bookmakers' blood,' he thundered. 'Fixed odds are finished.' But it was naïve to think the pools promoters could ever have been happy about the tax discrepancy, though according to Robert Sangster, the major horseracing owner who had once been head of Vernons pools, what they had actually been lobbying the Chancellor for was the tax exemption enjoyed by the fixed odds. 'William Hill always seemed to be very aggressive towards me after that,' remembered Sangster, 'as if he thought I was personally responsible for the imposition of tax on fixed odds!'

'In order to keep my staff, my plant and my offices occupied,' William went on,

> it will be necessary for my firm to enter the pools field. Only when we cannot lose will we be happy to pay 25% duty. For that reason, we shall direct all our energy into building up a pool. I shall carry on the fixed-odds business for a while to see if there is any hope, but I very much doubt whether we could manage to break level in a season.

In fact the company was soon laying off 40% of its regular football staff, and 50% of the 'casuals', though ironically in November 1964 Arthur Wyles, a British Rail welding inspector from Nottingham, won a world-record payout of £100,000 for just £1, after finding nine draws on Hill's coupon. 'The more money we take,' said the boss as he handed over the cheque, 'the more we lose.' The impact of the tax truly struck home in 1965 when it was revealed that William Hill (Football) Ltd had lost over £2.5 million in twelve months, entirely, said the company, due to the payment of fixed-odds betting duty. Both Hills and Ladbrokes inevitably announced they were scrapping fixed-odds football and though William Hill did make a brief move into the pools in 1965, the venture was not a success – by the November turnover was running at just £60,000 a week, £40,000 below break-even – and lasted only till the following year.

There was a half-hearted and ultimately doomed effort to resuscitate the fixed-odds game in 1966, but the coup de grâce was dealt to the terminally ill business in 1968 by the Labour Chancellor James Callaghan's Budget raising the duty again to 33.3%. (It would rise even higher to a farcical 42% in 1972, by which time fixed-odds was dead and buried.) 19 April 1969 saw William Hill's last postal fixed-odds coupon. 'In all, our turnover went down from £16 million to about £1.5 million so we had to give it up,' complained Hill. 'The criminal part was we had to start dispensing with more than 1,000 permanent staff and 20,000 part-time agents. The building we're in now [Hill House in Blackfriars Road] was a hive of industry and it became a morgue. Now we let a large part of it to the Post Office. All because of taxation.'

The heyday of fixed odds was over for good, but in 1974, three years after William Hill's death, it saw an unlikely revival. Individual Odds betting, as it was reincarnated, was largely thanks to the persistence of one man, albeit in collaboration with Hill's football betting guru Tommy Graham and other major bookmakers. John MacFarlane was the managing director of Queen Bookmakers, a Scottish betting shop chain that had formerly enjoyed a substantial fixed-odds turnover, who came up with a new-style coupon that quoted a separate, flexible price for each eventuality – home, away and draw. This would make it 'individual-odds' betting, no different from any other type of bet, and therefore qualified for general betting duty only, then at 7%. Queen Bookmakers won the case brought by Customs and Excise in Scotland's Court of Sessions, and within a few weeks Individual Odds football coupons appeared throughout the land. Odds-based football betting had risen from the dead, and would now thrive and expand. Boosted by the growth in televised live matches and the rapid expansion of internet betting, it now rivals horseracing as the most popular betting medium of all.

CHAPTER 9

WILLIAM'S WHIT AND WISDOM

'What a great moment for William Hill,' gushed his own publication, *The Hill Story*, 'as he surveyed those 1,500 acres of farmland and spacious gallops, and knew that at last his great ambition was realised.' The Whitsbury Manor Stud nestles secretively into the countryside near Fordingbridge in Hampshire; horses had been trained there since 1880, and it had come on the market when its owner Sir Charles Hyde, proprietor of the *Birmingham Post and Mail*, died en route whilst emigrating to the States in 1940, having become convinced that Hitler would win the war.

'I do remember going down with him and we walked round the place,' said William's friend Phil Bull, 'and I thought at the time, this is a peculiar place to go and buy a stud, way out here. I never had any idea that he might build it up into the substantial stud that he did – and really I don't suppose he had either!' William had always had a liking for the countryside, however, since his early days as a farmer's boy, and by the time he was bookmaking at Northolt he'd owned several horses. The stud came with 142 boxes, and as far as Bull remembered William had to pay £60,000 for it. Chris Harper thinks William got it for £40,000 at the 1943 auction in Salisbury by outwitting a local ring of would-be buyers. Whatever the actual price, Lionel Barber, William's business partner in later years, was to complain that the deal had caused the company 'financial indigestion'. But it would become one of the most ambitious and satisfying projects of William's life.

His arrival at Whitsbury did not, however, go down that well with all of his neighbours. The racing journalist Jamie Reid tells a story of a former Lord Mayor of London who had invited William to dinner and was somewhat put out by his robust approach to

Graham Sharpe and Chris Harper in front of the Whitsbury wall which Chris moved 'heaven and earth' to repair. 'Not straight' was William's grumpy reaction.

a whole Stilton, which he spooned straight into his mouth as though it were melon or ice cream. 'We don't do it that way here,' William was informed, 'whereupon he gave his host a quick lecture about the basic diet and eating habits of undernourished Brummies pre-1914.' He was a house-proud proprietor, according to a story told to the racing journalist Norman Pegg, spotting that the grass needed clipping on one of the greens during a walk around the stud one day. 'So he pepped up the groundsman. He did that immediately after a good lunch,' pondered Pegg's informant. 'What he'd have done if he'd been starving, I don't know'. Chris Harper in turn encountered William's congenital inability to praise anyone for their work. His uncle had insisted that he get a wall rebuilt before the arrival of some important visitors. Harper rushed to collect supplies and oversee toiling builders, finished in the nick of time and was particularly proud to hear William's VIP guests admiring the new wall. But the only comment he got when his uncle walked past him was, 'Not straight at the top.'

In his book *Farmer's Breakfast* Arthur Ling, a farmer and author of amusing 'semi-autobiographical fiction' somewhat in the vein of James Herriot, and often with a gambling theme, describes a trip to Whitsbury he undertook shortly after the war with fellow members of a committee allocating rationed supplies of agricultural fertiliser:

> Our generous hosts William and Ivy Hill brought our visit to a close. We were all thrilled by the excellence of the bloodstock we were shown at this stud.
>
> I was even more thrilled by some of my scientific colleagues who, while using such expressions as, 'Of course, I never bet,' 'It's a mug's game', 'Just have a bit on the Derby,' noted in their diaries with meticulous care the names of any horses that William hinted 'stands a chance at Newmarket', 'will be trying at Redcar', 'has been unlucky up to date but … '

At Whitsbury William launched into breeding on a grand scale. He was keen on French horses and imported a number of decent performers such as Whitsbury's founding stallion Sica Boy, Gyr and Taj Dewan. 'William was only really interested in breeding Classic winners,' declares Chris Harper, and it would take him just a few years to break his Classic duck. William had asked Phil Bull to buy him mares, and at Newmarket Bull had bought a grey named Kong, who had won Royal Ascot's historic sprint, the Wokingham Stakes, at odds of 33/1 in 1937, for 710 guineas. Kong would become the dam of the excellent sprinter Grey Sovereign, who in turn became an outstandingly successful sire, and also Nimbus who, together with Jai Hind, was amongst four yearlings William sent to the sales from Whitsbury in 1947. Nimbus sold for 5,000 guineas, Jai Hind, who went on to win three of his first four races, for twice as much. Hill had sent Kong to the Italian-bred Nearco (who William had also purchased), the sire of the 1945 Derby winner Dante, and though few were convinced that this pairing was likely to produce top-class offspring, William had done his homework well, confirmed Norman Pegg. 'He had followed the French idea of mating a tough mare and a high-class sire. That's the winning mixture. He may be uncertain and now and again quarrelsome but he is a deep and thorough student of anything he takes up.'

By the 1949 Derby, in which Jai Hind also ran, Nimbus had already won the 2,000 Guineas, and only the great multiple champion jockey Gordon Richards' mount Royal Forest was better fancied. A nervous William watched as Nimbus, ridden by Charlie Elliott (rider of that beaten Stewards Cup favourite at Glorious Goodwood in the same year) who had already twice won the Derby, jumped into the lead from the start, but with two furlongs to go, let William take up the story in his own words:

As they struck the rise to the winning post there were Nimbus and Swallow Tail locked together and staggering slightly like a couple of drunken sailors, arm in arm. And there was Amour Drake thundering up behind them.

Struggling up the hill, all but spent, Nimbus and Swallow Tail began to veer across to the right, away from the rails. Rae Johnstone on Amour Drake snatched up his horse quickly and switched him to the inside. The manoeuvre cost him a couple of lengths, but there he was, soon back in his stride and overhauling the other two horses fast. In the very last strides, Nimbus and Swallow Tail sort of bumped apart, and in one last effort, Charlie Elliott on Nimbus lifted his horse over the line. Even as he did so, Amour Drake came flashing past. There was a photo finish ... but I knew Nimbus had won. I vaulted the rails of the Members' enclosure and rushed to the unsaddling enclosure. I wanted to be with Nimbus and run my hand over the quarters of this game horse as a gesture of thanks for bringing me the thrill of breeding success.

Norman Pegg is sceptical about William's gymnastic feat – 'For one thing he was then in his forties, and by no means a lightweight' – but he does confirm that William had actually bet against the horse he bred, backing Amour Drake to win him £200,000 in private bets. 'I should be publicly horsewhipped for deserting home industries,' William admitted, but regarded it as 'the best fortune I ever lost!'

In tragic postscripts, Nimbus' pregnant dam, Kong, was kicked on the head and died, and Henry Glenister, who bought Nimbus for his wife Marion, committed suicide in 1952 for financial reasons.

Chanteur II was another excellent acquisition. William bought the French colt just before the horse won the Coronation Cup in 1947. He later denied reports that he'd paid £92,000 for him, but did admit to Norman Pegg to happily paying a record sum (probably around £70,000) for the hardy stayer as 'it's about time we had some tough sires at our studs.' He was also stung for £10,000 by the French Ministry of Agriculture before they would sanction the sale. Chanteur II, who stood at Banstead Manor and Highclere Studs, went on to become a champion sire – indeed, the leading sire in Great Britain and Ireland in 1953 – producing such Classic winners as the 1953 Derby winner Pinza (who cost Hill a reported £317,000 paid out to winning punters); Cantelo, who William bred and owned himself, and won the 1959 St Leger at 100/7 in William's maroon, pale blue and maroon hooped sleeves and quartered cap colours (a tribute to his favourite football team, Aston Villa), and Only For Life, who won the 2,000 Guineas.

Tony Morris, the *Racing Post*'s long-serving breeding expert, re-called William's inimitable presence at Newmarket:

> When I first came to Newmarket for the sales I shared digs with his chauffeur. In the Tatts arena, this fellow used to sit in the top row opposite the auctioneer hour after hour, and I was curious to know whether he was genuinely interested in the proceedings. Not at all, he told me. His role was to keep an eye on William, and when he saw him stub out his cigar, to bring him another. I soon got used to witnessing that routine, but was shocked when interviewing the great book-maker to find that while I was smoking a very nice Havana he was puffing away at a miserable Wills Panatella.

When William took over Whitsbury he employed Norman Scobie, who had been the private trainer for Sir Charles Hyde, to train about 25 horses for him and his friends, amongst them Chesney Allen and the bandleader Jack Hylton. But in January 1947 they ended up in the High Court, when Scobie sued him for slander for referring to him as an 'imposter and an Australian bush-ranger' in front of 'a score or more people'. It had all begun when Scobie had asked William to put £600 each-way on a horse called Vilmorin, and the horse had gone on and won at Salisbury at 25-1 in an attempted betting coup that included putting a little-known jockey on board to throw punters off the scent. William managed to place £500 each-way at 'starting price' but felt that to put any more on would have ruined the price and alerted the market. The Tattersalls Committee which ruled on betting disputes found in his favour. Scobie's counsel argued that the use of the epithet amount-ed to calling his client 'a thief and a robber'. William, giving evi-dence, conceded that 'I did call him a ponce.'

'What did you mean by ponce?' inquired Scobie's barrister.

'I meant he was a parasite and a sponger.'

Mr Justice Croom-Johnson found for William, with costs, and he soon engaged Monty Smyth as his trainer.

Two years after his purchase of Whitsbury, in 1945, William had acquired a second stud. Sezincote, at Moreton-in-Marsh in Gloucestershire, was smaller but more famous than Whitsbury. A Cotswold stone property with fine stud buildings and six state-of-the-art boxes, saddle room and stud groom's cottage, it came with over 200 acres of land, 50 of them woodland. It grew its own wheat, roots and linseed and made its own hay. Its paddocks were protected from the strong winds that blow across the top of the Cotswolds by lengthy rows of larch and fir. It was managed on much more 'formal' lines than the somewhat laid-back approach at Whitsbury. Its late owner John Hirst had, since its establishment in 1929, concentrated on breeding yearlings for sale – one of only half a dozen top-class studs at the time to do that. Hirst had also been one of the pioneers of breeding staying stock. The stud also boasted a herd of commercial, dis-horned Hereford Shorthorn bullocks that were bought in early summer and sold fat in the autumn.

In taking over Sezincote William's intention was 'not so much to extend Whitsbury, but rather to gain a place for his yearlings at the prestigious Doncaster sales,' explains the breeding expert Alan Yuill Walker in *Thoroughbred Studs of Great Britain*. 'In those days there was a "dead man's shoes" system which made it difficult to get one's horses into the best, most prominent Sales,' adds Chris Harper. The continuity of ownership required by Tattersalls was ensured by John Hirst's nephew Alan becoming a shareholder in the stud. William proceeded to develop Sezincote on the same progressive lines as Whitsbury, with Peter Parsons, one of William's closest confidants, as his stud manager, and the two properties became known as the William Hill Studs, housing some 15 mares each – Nimbus, foaled at Sezincote, was one of the first yearlings sold under that name. Sezincote's old mares were weeded out and replaced by mares of the highest class, and it was decided that in future none but the very best stallions would be used. At the Newmarket December Sales in 1948 William paid the then-record sum of 18,000 guineas for the seven-year-old brood mare Ferry Pool. Herself a winner, Ferry Pool produced several outstanding Nearco foals, including one bought for America at the 1951 Doncaster Sales for 8,000 guineas. Then at the Doncaster Sales in September 1954, top price on the first day was the 8,200 guineas paid for Indian Game, a bay filly by Big Game out of Iroquois II. By September 1949 things were progressing at Sezincote – the previous 12 months alone had returned over £22,300 for just five lots sold. When Peter Parsons retired in 1963 he was succeeded by Norman Lonsdale, who had started with Phil Bull and whose years at Sezincote produced good winners such as Gulf Pearl, Aegean Blue, Bracey Bridge, Khaleka and Credo Credo.

Whitsbury was already well on the way to becoming one of the most cutting-edge stud farms in the country. It hadn't been cheap – William joked that it had cost him 'ten fortunes'. A journalist who visited him there in early 1952 found him indulging another of his farming passions, his 100-strong, record-breaking herd of attested pedigree British Friesians, from foundation cows of the Terling, Monkton, Chaddersley and Clavering herds, which out of all Hampshire's 831 herds had become the record milk-producer with an average of 1,473 gallons – 150 ahead of its nearest challenger. But 'even there,' noted the journalist, 'Hill cannot resist the temptation to bet. "Give you 11/8 that the Friesian is going to have a bull calf," you hear him say to his farm manager, John Willett, as he goes on his rounds.' In the early 1960s William would join six other British Friesian breeders in the south-east of England (amongst them Charles Clore, who would later take over William Hill) to make their own expensive, top-quality bulls available for improving the breed as a whole through artificial insemination. The article was accompanied by a photograph of William riding out at either Whitsbury or Sezincote, still immaculately clad in suit, tie, white shirt and cuff-links, and a pair of what looked more like

Wellingtons than riding boots, and no riding helmet – looking completely at ease in the saddle.

Another report from the time of a typical Whitsbury weekend, by Robert Jackson in *Illustrated* magazine, paints a bucolic portrait of the former farm-boy, now country gent, at ease in surroundings a world away from Henshaw Road where he had been born almost 50 years earlier.

He has a country house of his own amongst the fine modern homes he has erected for his managers and staff. Here, in the midst of the countryside he loves so well, Hill is relaxed and at peace with himself. As he strolls around the farm, he will ask about the latest yield of Monkton Myrrh, champion milk producer of the county who gave 2,216 gallons in 305 days at 3.46% butter fat; or perhaps will take a proud look at Whitsbury Dilly Boy, the sturdy offspring of Terling Lady Dilly 58th RM, a magnificent pedigree cow in whom Hill invested 1,000 guineas. The onlooker can soon see that the present owner is no 'dude' farmer. In fact, much is owed to his shrewd knowledge of bloodstock and understanding of modern farming methods for the fine herd of cattle that Whitsbury now possesses, amongst them a second home-bred bull, Whitsbury Field Marshal RMP, and no less than five home-bred cows in the 2,000-gallon class.

Another hour of the day will find Hill taking the same expert interest in the work of the Whitsbury Stud, where equally progressive methods have been applied to horse breeding and training – and with equal success. As he inspects the foals with an appraising eye, Hill is perhaps looking for another Nimbus, numbered amongst the 23 winning horses that Whitsbury has produced in its comparatively few years as a stud farm. (It is worth noting that Nimbus was foaled at Sezincote.) It is unique in bloodstock history for a breeder to have produced a Derby winner within three years, as Hill did.

In the early 1950s Trevor Reeves was working at Whitsbury for William's trainer Monty Smyth, and remembers often seeing William's wife Ivy and daughter Bubbles walking through the yard together – 'their perfume could unsettle the colts'. He also remembers the mare Lovely Bubbles, who her namesake would turn out. One day Trevor was called up to the 'Big House' by Mrs Hill and asked to cut a branch from a tree which was overhanging the walled garden and allowing squirrels to find their way in there to pinch the fruit from the trees. 'She gave me two brand new £1 notes,' he says – 'I was earning two bob a week at the time! They were lovely people, but you wouldn't want to get on the wrong side of Mr Hill.' One who did, Trevor adds, was Brian Durr, a stable lad at the yard who deliberately concealed the talent of the two-year-old he was looking after, and then profited by tipping off one of his paying punters to back the filly at 20/1 when it won at Kempton. 'William gave Monty Smyth a bollocking – we all heard his voice reverberating round the yard, asking how she could have won when he'd been told she was backward – and, worse, complaining that one of his clients had landed a hefty each-way bet on her!'

Having completely renovated Whitsbury's Manor Yard from 1959–63, and in 1961 transferred both studs to his personal ownership, William opened a stallion yard in 1962. Up to the start of the Flat racing season that year, horses bred at Whitsbury and Sezincote had won 382 races and a total of £264,066 in prize money between them. Subsequently he would buy a 65-acre farm in Whitsbury village known as Majors Farm and, having demolished the farmyard buildings, build a 35-box yard which in 1968 Sir Gordon Richards was the first trainer to occupy (his subsequent decision to move out may have been down to his somewhat untidy way of doing things, which did not chime well with William's fastidious nature).

William's initial stallion purchases, however, were not a success. 'All failed to come up to expectations', said bloodstock expert Alan Yuill Walker. 'Sica Boy, the first one' – a bad-tempered yet brilliant French-trained winner of the Arc de Triomphe but a most disappointing sire – 'was a total flop,' said Chris Harper, 'as was his second, Celtic Ash. Taj Dewan was very good as a racehorse, but not a stallion, and Gyr was infertile. Only Ballymoss was quite successful.' Ballymoss had ended his fine career in 1958, shortly after winning the Arc de Triomphe, having also won the Irish Derby, the St Leger, the Coronation Cup, the Eclipse Stakes and the King George VI and Queen Elizabeth Stakes. His jockey Scobie Breasley called him 'quite the best horse I ever rode'. William became chairman of the Ballymoss syndicate that bought him from his American owner John McShain after negotiations to sell him to the Queen Mother had broken down, and it was agreed to send him to Banstead Manor Stud. But then, in 1964, says Chris Harper, 'William sent a horse box down to Banstead and took Ballymoss from under their noses, claiming that the horse had contracted an equine venereal disease while he was there. When he came to Whitsbury he was cured. Ballymoss, never a great stallion, sired Derby winner Royal Palace and was grandsire to Dunfermline' (the Queen's filly who won two Classics in 1977). He was best known as a top sire of broodmares and was the dam sire of top class animals such as Levmoss, Le Moss and Teenoso. In 1965 18 yearlings submitted to the October Sales by William had attracted what was claimed to be a record sum for a single vendor of 124,650 guineas.

However, 1968 was not a good year for Whitsbury. In March a mare at the Manor Stud, Alexi, broke her back in an accident, leaving a three-week-old filly foal, sired by the French stallion Klairon, without her mother. A local farmer answered the stud's appeal for a foster mother in the shape of a shaggy brown New Forest pony. The pony was worth some £80; her new charge £5,000. Worse was to come in July, when a freight aircraft landing at Heathrow from

Deauville skidded off the runway and crashed into two station-ary aircraft. Six brood mares and two foals died in the accident, together with the plane's three crew members and three of the five grooms accompanying the horses. Three of the mares and the two foals were William's, including Navan, who had a foal by the stal-lion Charlottesville with her, and Noorose, who had with her a foal by the Derby winner Santa Claus. Altogether their financial value was £80,000 (approx. £1.2m today). William became one of the Trustees of 'The Flying Grooms' Disaster Fund' set up for the dependants of those who had lost their lives, and within days a four-figure sum had been raised.

Bill Marshall was training just outside Basingstoke in the 1950s when he first met William Hill. 'My punting was going really badly at the time,' he explains, 'and I owed Hill £600.' But he had a cunning plan to run past the bookmaker: 'I was about to run two horses at the little jumping course of Wye in Kent. Being sure that both would win I went to see Hill and asked if I could have a bet on them. Hill said that was fine – but asked when I was going to pay him the £600. I told him I couldn't settle unless the two horses won at Wye.' Strangely enough, Hill did not immediately embrace the scheme.

'So, you want me to back them to get you out of trouble?'

'No,' said Marshall, 'I want to help myself and you too. I want £25 to win on each horse and a £25 win double.'

Hill agreed, said Bill, and he also 'cleverly pushed the starting prices of the two horses out to 4/1 and 9/2, when they both should have been 6/4 – and the two animals duly came home in front.' When they met up in the bar after racing, 'he paid me out in white fivers,' recalled Marshall, 'and did not deduct the £600 I owed him. He told me he'd forgotten that debt.'

Some years later, Hill approached Marshall about coming to Whitsbury to train for him. 'After several drinks he offered me £3,000 a month, a house, a car and a telephone,' said Marshall.

'Then came the catch – when he demanded the first £12,000 of my trainer's percentage of prize money.' Marshall left immediately. 'He called me later and said, "That was just my opening gambit".' Hill agreed to let him keep his full share of the prize money, and Marshall had the job at 'the finest place to train horses that I have ever seen.'

Marshall remembers his new boss as 'brilliant to work for' – but not always easy:

One day he was set to fly off to Jamaica when the Newmarket Sales were on. He asked me to buy a well-bred filly if I saw one. I liked a small filly that was from a good family and physically correct. Bought her for 6,000 guineas and rang Hill in Jamaica. He told me that he had been told that the filly was 'a weed', so I told him that if he didn't want it, 'don't bloody well have it,' and put the phone down on him. He rang me back three times that day, but I wouldn't speak to him. I was really mad. He eventually got hold of me and I told him I'd put the filly down in my name. He replied that I'd bought her for him and he was keeping her.

The filly, Miss Slip was a winner at Wolverhampton, beaten a short head at Royal Ascot, won Goodwood's Group 2 Molecomb Stakes – and 'was later sold for £325,000'.

William had great faith in young people, never demonstrated in more remarkable fashion than with his nephew Chris Harper. Back in 1963 'I was just a kid,' says Harper, when the phone went at home: 'It's Uncle William.'

He said, 'I hear you're into farming' – I had a degree in agriculture, but I'd been brought up on a small farm, peasant farming: he had a thousand acres. He asked me down to Whitsbury, showed me round and asked me what I thought

95

of the place. I said it was wonderful but was critical of some aspects – including the harvest being weeks behind, and ploughing not having been done. 'Would you care to manage it for me?' he asked. I was 22, with little experience, and I had arranged to go to Canada in the not too distant future. I said I'd have to think about it. He made it clear that if I didn't take it I wouldn't be asked again. 'There will be no concessions,' he told me: 'I want the show run properly. If you can't do it I'll get somebody who can.'

I rang him to say I would like to take the job.

'Right, you start on Monday.'

'But I have to give notice where I am.'

'What's more important to you – your past or your future?' Yesterday was of no interest to William: he was always looking ahead, only interested in tomorrow. What he did give me, though, was a chance in a million.

I came down on 2 October 1963. 'What do the staff think about this?' I asked my uncle.

'The staff don't know. We'll tell them in the morning.'

David Singleton was the current manager – a lecturer in animal husbandry. He'd been there ten years. William lined up the staff, asked them all to introduce themselves and say what they did. He then told David: 'As of today, my nephew is taking over from you. You will get six months' salary but I don't want you to put foot on this farm again.' David burst into tears.

'Phone me Friday,' William told me. 'Look at what needs doing; let me know what you want to do, give me a resumé.'

On Friday I phoned him. 'Uncle Bill, we need big, big changes.'

'I'm glad you said that. We've been losing too much money.' I told him the dairy had been badly designed.

'What? It cost me a fortune!'

'Well, the design wasn't right – I want the beef to go, it is too expensive; the chickens must go – I know nothing about them. I'll plough the land up and plant wheat. We'll need to buy a new tractor – it'll cost £5,900.'

Eventually William calmed down, and told me I'd have a year to prove myself, and by the way, he'd given four other members of the family jobs previously, and the longest any lasted was six months!

Some 50 years on, as this book went to press. Chris Harper was still living and working at Whitsbury.

Bob Urquhart had first arrived at Whitsbury in 1962 as a teen-ager, and subsequently became Yearling Manager when still only 25 years old. 'Since first meeting William Hill as a raw apprentice,' he says,

I understood he had 'mellowed' somewhat, yet I well re-member some of the advice he had imparted to me: 'I will always tolerate mistakes, we all make them, but I never expect them to be repeated.' This terrified me! He insisted on perfection, was fanatical about cleanliness, and when at Whitsbury we were alerted that he was coming for the week-end, every besom brush (rounded, rather than flat) on the premises was employed by the staff to sweep all the yards and drives, and to wash down all the 100-plus stables ac-commodating the horses.

I remember his advice to me on the subject of betting, and I have transmitted his words of wisdom many times since: 'Never bet in a race which includes a horse or horses which have never run before. Never bet for the sake of it, i.e. Grand National, Derby or a big competitive sprint, such as the Stewards Cup.'

Many of William's visits to Whitsbury seemed to coincide with shooting parties – the birds were reared on the farm, overseen by gamekeeper Bert Perks, a great character, according to Chris Harper. 'William enjoyed the shoot,' he remembers.

We had eight days shooting per year, two of which were after Christmas, and as William always left for Jamaica the day after Boxing Day I was lucky enough to have these days for my friends. It was fairly low-key, William was a very moderate shot but loved the days amongst his friends, who would come from all over and generally stayed the weekend. He had had made for himself a pair of 25-inch Churchill 12-bore guns. These were beautiful guns. He had a very strong right eye, and shot off the right shoulder, so the stocks had to be offset by 2 inches, which was quite strange to see. The top greyhound trainer Jack Harvey was one of his best friends and came regularly, being a very good shot.

Ada Johnson, one of the housekeepers, recalled the panic the staff felt after one of these parties when the guests had all departed the library, where drinks had been served, to troop in to the dining room for lunch. The staff were setting about clearing away the detritus left behind, including overflowing ashtrays and half-finished cigars, when the call came from the other room for William's cigar. Ada had to dive into the bin to retrieve what remained of it. 'Ivy just rolled her eyes.'

But although Whitsbury was a working farm, stud and training centre, it was also a home for William and Ivy, and as such the scene of many family gatherings. Their granddaughter Caroline has fond memories of a place of 'great warmth and love – Ivy playing the piano and singing in the music room at Whitsbury, and delicious food too – prepared by his Italian couple, Ida and Wolfrano. Grandpa loved Whitsbury, and was very connected to the land there,' she continues: when she and her sister Sarah visited,

> He would take us on many drives around the property in his jeep, often getting stuck in mud on small roads, visiting the dairy farm, the prize bulls and the calves, always stopping to get a fresh glass of milk at the dairy, and visiting the foals in the stables and following them very closely as they grew up.
>
> He was very involved in harvesting too, and loved it, warning us not to play in the giant vats of grain – which, of course, we did, and got caught by the farm manager at the time, which meant big trouble. But we were allowed to roam the land on our bicycles, and this gave us a huge sense of freedom and happiness. After being locked up in boarding schools and London flats with our father, Whitsbury was a total paradise for us.

Sarah feels the same:

> Many of my happiest memories are from times at Whitsbury. We could do no wrong when we were there – we could just take off on our bikes and disappear for hours on end. Nobody was ever worried that we'd get into any danger or trouble.
>
> I was once driven down to Whitsbury by Grandpa's chauffeur Smithy, who had a handlebar moustache. The car was immaculate with a tortoise-shell interior and it smelt of leather, but it was a two-and-a-half-hour drive and I frightened the life out of Smithy by announcing, 'I think I'm going to be sick'. We would go up to the church each Sunday and I would sometimes read the lesson.
>
> As soon as lunch was over, Grandpa would go into the TV room to watch the racing if it was on, and he'd sit in a big winged chair with his feet up watching the big old TV and

puffing away on his cigars while we would play around him – and sometimes after certain races, presumably when well-backed horses had won, he'd get on the phone and shout at someone. Caroline and I would argue about which one of us slept in Grandpa's room and which in Grandma's. We both wanted to sleep in Grandpa's because he snored very loudly once he was asleep – 'like a herd of roaring lions', said Caroline! I remember that William would sometimes come back to the house late, and to check whether Ivy was up, he'd throw his hat through the door – if it came flying back, she was!

Ultimately, Whitsbury and Sezincote must be regarded as perhaps William's most important personal achievement. 'I am a racehorse owner and breeder. I have never asked anybody to subsidise my pleasures,' he wrote in 1967. 'In fact, it has never been necessary, for over the years I have managed to show a profit on both these undertakings, simply by going in only for top quality and really trying to put something back into racing by breeding only the very best.' 'He's a breeder of horses,' confirmed Phil Bull, 'and this means more to him than anything else in life.'

He's only an owner insofar as he wishes to retain fillies that he has bred to go to the stud, and he wants to win races with them, as a breeder, to put them to stud. He has never really been an owner. All he has been concerned about is to breed good horses, sell them at the Sales, and those that he didn't sell at the Sales because they didn't make their very modest reserves, or those animals which he doesn't want to sell because he wishes to retain them for stud, high-class, well-bred fillies – these are the animals he put into training.

And as for the source of this love of Whitsbury and Sezincote, in the heart of the Hampshire and Gloucestershire countrysides, his friend Peter Campling put his finger on where it all started:

Talking to William Hill and retracing his steps, you begin to realise that the early days on the farm were the real turning point of his life. It is this dream of being a farmer which has been the driving force that has led him on and made him the organising genius and dynamic business personality he is today. His eventual memorial will be found ... in the annals of the Stud Book.

CHAPTER 10
PLAYING AWAY

There was a secondary benefit to William's purchase of Sezincote. When Peter Parsons retired and moved out of the house, William had it completely renovated – installing amongst other things carved oak doors – so that he could spend weekends there. But not, it seems, alone.

Sheila Baker was considerably (some say 30 years) younger than William, and was his mistress for 20 years. William's nephew Chris Harper tells the story of how they met:

> William took me to the 21 Club in London once, and introduced me to Harry Meadows, the owner – he'd come out of the air force penniless and needed £500 to set up the club. William wanted to help him and loaned him the £500, asking him to pay it back whenever he could afford it, although he never really expected to see the money again. Harry rented what was initially little more than a bomb site, and built up the club using tarpaulins which he painted to look like pillars, and other cheap materials. William visited the club, became a regular and was generously paid back. Sheila was one of the girls working at the 21 – William couldn't resist a pretty face and they became very close.

Sheila was no country girl, much preferring to spend her time in London, but she'd come down when William did, generally at weekends, says Douglas Ventress, who worked as a groom at Sezincote. It appears the liaison was no secret to Ivy, who referred to Sheila as 'the doxy', an interestingly archaic term, while William is reported to have named one of his horses Willshe. But if she knew, Ivy had no intention of confronting her husband and his girlfriend together: Douglas Ventress says that in 17 years at Sezincote he only saw Mrs Hill there once – 'and that was after Mr Hill had died'. William and Ivy lived in the house at Whitsbury for 25 years – 'Well,' says Chris Harper, 'they both occupied it, but living one at each end. She was potty about him, but she was very jealous. If he was away she'd spend the week preparing for when he might come back. She was still madly in love with William, but he had girlfriend after girlfriend.'

'Ivy contracted a bug whilst on holiday in Las Palmas with William in 1954' wrote Joe Ward Hill. This resulted in a chronic disease of the hip. 'She was unable to walk without the aid of a stick and suffered great pain.'

'She had one of the first modern style hip operations but wouldn't, or couldn't, do the necessary rehabilitation afterwards', says Harper. Her weight increased as her mobility did the opposite.

'In some ways Bill was a most unsatisfactory person,' says Phil Bull, his closest friend for 30 years – 'especially in his personal relationships and in his attitude to women, which was deplorable in the extreme.' Bull remembers William behaving badly towards Sheila, and then being 'knocked out [when] she'd left him and was about to shack up with another guy'. Phil had had to drop everything, give William 'a salutary dressing-down and sort it out for them'. 'Bill was a womaniser,' was Ron Pollard's simple verdict, and for William his propensity for female company was 'the sort of behaviour that Bill considered merely a minor part of his life's pattern'.

> Bill could never resist and few women resisted him. After racing we would sometimes go off to the Embassy Club [in Old Bond Street in London]. Bill would say to me, 'There's a pretty girl over there. Go and say that William Hill is here and would very much like her to join him.' I would go over and if, as mostly happened, the girl decided to join Bill, I would simply disappear.

In 1961 William's relationship with Sheila Baker produced a daughter, Miranda, and 'whereas Bubbles looked like her mother,' says William's niece, Peggy Evans, 'Miranda grew up to look incredibly like William.' However, possibly seeking to portray him in a better light, William's younger sibling Joe Ward Hill claimed that 'promiscuity had no attraction for him, and his extra-marital relationships were on a long-term basis.' What evidence there is suggests that this is an inaccurate assessment and Ward Hill himself also noted of an employee of William's called Jack Green, that his duties included 'entertaining William's current girlfriends when the guvnor was otherwise engaged, possibly touting jockeys'.

There were rumours within the company that one of William's girlfriends was Florence Desmond, a very successful actress, impersonator of female stars and radio performer who appeared in many shows and films. Angus Dalrymple, working at Park Lane in the mid-1940s, remembers her as 'stunning', and that she went on to star with the comedian Arthur Askey in *The William Hill Show* on Radio Luxembourg. As for whether she and William were having an affair, 'She certainly paid enough visits to Hill's private office on non-racing days.' In his book about his brother, Joe Ward Hill mused that a possible reason for William's backing of three West End theatre shows 'is that he was interested in a member of the cast'.

William would often take a girlfriend with him when he visited France for big races. Major Peter Blackwell would then be co-opted too as he could speak a little French, and one night in France, Blackwell recalled, William tired of his latest female friend and told her, 'I can't think why I brought you along.' Blackwell, as treasurer for the trip, had been informed by his boss that she had been given £700 to cover her hotel bill and still leave change. But when he saw her later and asked whether the bill had been paid, she claimed the money had been 'to buy myself some presents', leaving Blackwell to find more money at a time when there was a limit to the amount of currency that could be taken abroad. William was not amused, and refused to speak to the brunette on the flight home. At the airport the brunette was challenged over duty on the 'presents' she'd bought herself – and then on the mink coat she was wearing. This was genuinely one she had had for some time, and as she explained to this customs official he asked William for confirmation, whereupon, wrote Joe Ward Hill, 'He announced that he had never seen the coat until that morning, stalked out and into his waiting Rolls Royce and was driven back to Hill House.'

Another 'mistress' was with William one day at the races where Ron Pollard was clerking for him – only for him to realise that Ivy had also arrived at the course. 'Bill did not turn a hair. "Your job this afternoon," he said to me quietly, "is to keep Mrs Landa in the bar. No matter what she says or what else happens, she is not to come down here."' Pollard duly fulfilled his task: 'I fear Mrs Landa and I got rather tipsy.'

This liaison seems to have resulted in another child. When William Landa, a bank official born in 1953, got married in 1975, the marriage certificate listed the father as 'William Hill (deceased): Bookmaker.' 'I remember one conversation about Landa with various cousins/aunts in Birmingham,' says Christopher Foott, the family's archivist:

> The gist of it seemed to be that there wasn't much of a family resemblance and thus there was some doubt as to whether Billy was actually William's. But obviously William must have 'known' Miss/Mrs Landa, and apparently he took it in good faith that she was telling the truth and so accepted Billy as his son. I do think William was involved in Billy's life [as he was] growing up.

Billy Landa does seem to have been accepted as William's son by most, if not all, of the family; it is said that William paid for his namesake's schooling.

Marilyn Gowler, meanwhile, was born in the same year as Billy Landa, but her parentage is still a matter of dispute. In the early 1950s her mother worked in a central London club – she thinks she remembers her mentioning the Embassy Club, but cannot be sure. Perhaps it was one of William's other haunts – his nephew Sandy Brown remembers 'being entertained (and paid for!) by the Old Man, who would take us to his favourite haunt, Churchill's in Bond Street,' owned at the time by Bert and Harry Meadows – who also owned the 21 Club where William had met Sheila Baker.

Marilyn's mother always told her that her father was 'a man called Sidney Lewis, who doesn't seem to have really existed,' but after she died, she says an aunt told her who her father really was, and she has since spent years trying to prove that she is definitely William's daughter as there is no record of his ever being aware at the time that she was.

And then there were William's regular visits to Jamaica. Nigel Pemberton met him out there around 1959 and got to know him well. Would it be fair to say that when Ivy was not in residence, William treated Bogue Hill, the retreat he and Ivy had purchased soon after the war, as something of a bachelor pad? 'YES!!' was Pemberton's answer, in capital letters.

Bogue Hill overlooked Montego Bay, and William had purchased it from the Duke of Sutherland, whose family had had it constructed in 1840. William and Ivy had gone to Jamaica soon after the war for a winter holiday and fallen in love with the place, and on their third visit William decided to buy a house there. It offered such a relaxing and attractive way of life that eventually he was spending three months a year there, returning in time for the Cheltenham Festival, though he did remain in touch with the office. 'The other day I was talking to the builder who built most of William Hill's house,' says Nigel Pemberton, who in 2014 was still working in the real estate market there, 'and he was telling me that it was pretty much of a shack when William bought it. But it was a wonderful piece of land of about seven acres with the most magnificent view over Montego Bay and the Caribbean.'

William modernised the house, equipped it with a gymnasium and swimming pool, and, revealed Richard Baerlein, 'became a keep-fit and diet fanatic,' adding that William, improbably, 'would appear naked every morning at 6am for his first dip of the day'. The diet appeared somewhat half-hearted, though. 'While boasting he never ate bread rolls and was sticking to his diet, his neighbours at meals used to notice how quickly their rolls disappeared!'

'Of course you have to remember that Jamaica was at the peak of its popularity with the "rich and famous",' Nigel Pemberton points out.

Montego Bay was still a pretty small place, so up to a point any foreigner who had a winter house here probably knew the owners of the other houses. When famous actors from theatre and cinema came to stay in a place like Round Hill they always knew someone with a house here and were quickly drawn in. I remember having dinner with William Hill when Stanley Holloway was here and was playing in *My Fair Lady*, and after dinner he got up on our table and sang us 'Get Me to the Church on Time'. The great thing about Jamaica has always been that nobody puts on any airs and graces, however grand they are, because they know it has no effect. In William Hill's day here the rich in Palm Beach were still fawning over the Duke and Duchess of Windsor, but in Jamaica nobody took much notice of the Duke of Marlborough, who bought the house next door to William. I remember asking him as a good socialist how happy he was about that – William had a love/hate relationship with dukes, and particularly 'Bert' Marlborough. But he said to me, 'Nigel, I have no worries, because I am in control. The Duke's water supply runs through my garden. With one turn of the tap I can turn his house from an oasis into a desert!'

A 1968 article by Betty Beale in Washington's *Spokesman-Review* newspaper referred to the two neighbours, adding 'it amuses residents that the only other house belongs to the famous English bookmaker – at least he's conveniently available.' Was she suggesting he was taking bets there, one wonders?

Pemberton continued: 'My first introduction to William was being invited to one of his lunches at Bogue Hill, where he welcomed us like long-lost friends, which was pretty impressive to me, as I was still in my twenties and struggling on Wall Street. My memories of William and his house are seen through a haze of wonderful food, good wine and the best Havana cigars, which, somewhat surprisingly to me, William kept in large canisters of tea leaves. Most importantly, you always had the best food in Jamaica, which was in the hands of his trusted aide Harry Metcalfe. Harry had been the manager of the Bay Roc Hotel in Montego Bay – he had been a pentathlon or decathlon Olympic contender – and was highly qualified in what today would be called food and beverage. William was a great host, and he loved to entertain his friends. He was a very generous man, and whenever we were invited for lunch or dinner there seemed to be a cast of thousands. Of course, being William there was a heavy racing influence – Lester Piggott was a visitor. I have very fond memories of Phil Bull, I seem to remember we always called him Electric Whiskers.

William loved to tell stories and was a very good raconteur, and I do remember some of them quite clearly to this day. Our favourite was about the days when the homosexual act was criminal, and a man was brought up in court on a charge, and the magistrate noticed that the police officer seemed quite old. The magistrate said to the police officer,

'I really feel terrible that you have been given this job of monitoring the Men's toilet at Green Park underground station, a particularly unattractive job for someone who has served the Metropolitan police force, obviously for quite a few years.' Whereupon the police officer said: 'I wish to thank you, Your Honour, for your remarks. It has been the most unpleasant task I have had to perform in the force. In fact, Your Honour, when someone came in for an honest-to-goodness shit it was like a breath of fresh air.'

A strange deviation from the socialising came in 1959, when William announced plans to set up a laundry in Jamaica. The idea may have been prompted by the acquisition a year earlier of Debretta, the blouses and children's dresses business, in an attempt by Holders Investment Trust (see page 127) to diversify a portfolio then almost totally reliant on William Hill. The plan was to take in laundry from hotels and local residents, and William's business partner was to be a former Olympic skier, Peter Waddell, who had opened London's first 'launderette' and personal hand laundry in 1950. As the pair flew off to Montego Bay to finalise the details William revealed to the *Daily Express* that they already had 14 hotels signed up: 'I don't know much about laundries, but I know to my cost the laundry facilities in Jamaica are just not adequate.' Waddell chimed in with the less than tactful observation that 'At least we'll offer something better than having your clothes thumped on a stone in the river by an old washer-woman.' What became of the venture is unclear.

But otherwise William was determined that Bogue Hill be not work but pleasure. Tony Vincent was out in Jamaica on a cricket tour, and invited with his tour party by William – 'he was a great cricket fan' – to be wined and dined at the house. Vincent found William sitting in a corner in his morning coat with nobody paying him the slightest attention, and felt it his duty to converse with the man. He went and chatted away to him about fixed-odds betting and football, which was just coming into vogue at the time. Hill let Tony speak for about five minutes. Then, 'Listen, son,' he interrupted: 'I have come out here to get away from all that.'

Reg Griffin of the Timeform organisation first went to William's house in the early 1960s with Phil Bull: 'This was paradise, and I thought, "My God, what a pity we aren't staying here longer."' But William then invited Griffin to come and stay again, and:

It became a habit, perhaps every other year that I went out, and it was always done on the pretext that, 'Bring your form book and we'll do the pricing for the Classics.' But I used to go out there and, first day, I'd say, 'Do you want to do this?'

'Oh, no, you've only just come – sit still.'

This would go on every day until I told him, 'Bill, I'm leaving the day after tomorrow. If we're going to get anything done we ought to do it tomorrow.'

'Right,' and all the other house guests were told, 'You go to the beach today – Reg and I are going to be busy.'

Finally, we'd be sat at the table by the pool, and he'd have his little bag with cigars in, and his handkerchief and everything else, and then he'd get his cigar, and he'd sniff the cigar, then he'd get his lighter and he would light it, and blow his nose; finally, he'd get his pencil ready and so, there, poised to do this incredible job with the world's greatest bookmaker, was me, to do the pricing for the Guineas.

So, he'd start: 'What's the first horse?'

'So and so.'

'How do you spell that?'

Well, the fact of the matter is, we got nowhere, because we didn't want to do it in any case, and he'd been on holiday for about three months and you sort of get into a frame of mind where you just don't want to do anything.

William's jockey, Eddie Hide, visited Jamaica on honeymoon in 1961 and the couple were invited to Bogue Hill – 'His white coated manservant greeted us. We ate outdoors from a large glass table with fresh flowers arranged underneath – it seemed as though we were eating off a tablecloth of flowers.' Hide noted that William would befriend and feed local dogs.

Much later, William's granddaughters would spend idyllic holidays there, as Caroline St George recalls: 'The house was really pretty, perched on a hill overlooking sugar cane fields and Montego Bay in the distance, and it was a hugely happy place, filled with music and laughter and cigar smoke – which I love to this day as it reminds me of my Grandpa.'

Both Caroline and Sarah recall another visit when, with a variety of excuses and pleadings, they managed to extend their stay so long there was barely a fortnight of the school term remaining when they were finally sent home.

CHAPTER 11

KING OF THE RING

'To say that he revolutionised betting is an understatement,' said Willie Alsford, who joined William in 1948 to bet on the rails along with the great man himself. 'He hit racing like a tornado.' Alsford moved into the company's Trade Room in 1957 and eventually became its top racing odds compiler, known as the Wizard of Odds, but even after his retirement in 1983 he remained in awe of William. 'I used to stand behind him, mesmerised by the volume of betting. I saw him take as much as £50,000 on a race, and he knew every client by account number. £10,000 bets were frequent in those days, but he treated the 5/- punter with exactly the same civility.'

Despite the flamboyant acceptance of huge bets, William never forgot one of the bookmaking's eternal truths. Peter O'Sullevan put it this way: 'As Bill Hill used to say, "If you can sell a horse at 6/4, you're a fool to lay 13/8."'

This remains an unimpeachable bookmaking maxim.

'As a rails bookie you could see owners and trainers sidle up to William and enquire the price,' said Peter Campling.

'You can have four monkeys,' he would quietly say. He laid the odds strictly on his own reckoning of form and breeding and, of course, supply and demand. Few other bookmakers would chalk up their prices until they heard how 'H' was betting. His pitch was always surrounded by other bookies' runners, and the sharp punters hoping to hear owners strike a big bet.

By the end of the 1940s William had become 'King of the Ring', as many now called him, and this hadn't happened by accident.

'This was due to his shrewdness, his judgement, his boldness and his ability to work to percentages in a fraction of a second', wrote Richard Baerlein who would pay Hill a huge tribute when he later added: 'Sir Gordon Richards (multiple Champion Jockey); Henry Cotton (triple Open Championship winner) and William Hill have one thing in common. All three elevated their professions to an extent never known before.'

'He was a great one for meticulous detail in everything he did,' recalled John Brown, who would go on to become Hill's managing director.

I will always remember one occasion in particular, which proved it. He always liked to go through the form of every single Derby entry and he was always given a list of maybe 450 horses, complete with breeding and form, which he would study. One year he came on the phone in a raging temper – the breeding of one horse, about three generations back, had been given to him slightly wrong – and to make matters worse, the mistake involved a horse he bred himself. We didn't hear the last of it for weeks!

'I had not been with William long before I began to realise I knew very little about the game,' recalled another future MD Sam Burns, who joined the company with the acquisition of the Hurst Park Syndicate's betting shop chain.

In the next five years William was to teach me what it was all about. I owed my knowledge entirely to him. For instance, I always assumed that when a hot favourite won a big race the bookmaker automatically lost. I was amazed that when Meld, at 10/11, won the 1955 St Leger, the William Hill book showed a profit on the race. He had been careful to lay all the others to cover more than his losses on Meld.

A letter William wrote at the end of the 1940s to Dick Whitford of Timeform, one of Phil Bull's right-hand men, is fascinating evidence of how hard William thought about his trade, and how he was always working on ways to become better and stay ahead of the game. William had been advertising for someone to run what he called a 'Form Room', but despite 200 applications it was Whitford he really wanted:

> I wonder whether you would be interested in taking over complete control of an entirely new department that we are forming … It is to be known as the Form Room, and we have had form cards made for all last season's two- and three-year-olds. The idea is that between 3.30 and 4 o'clock in the afternoon, when we get a list of the probable runners for the next day, the form should be got out in detail with an analysis of the race given in brief, together with a forecast of the betting. Our object, in short, is to analyse the next day's racing, similar to *The Sporting Life* and *Sporting Chronicle*, only much better, as a guide to the office, but especially so for the Course Representatives. When I intend going racing it takes me three or four hours at night, studying intensively the next day's programme, and even then it is only in my own head and is very difficult to interpret to anyone else.

Whitford was tempted by the prospect of working for this 'big, impressive man with a stately way of talking – the very opposite of the image most people have of bookmakers. It was obvious he was a man with a big future.' But ultimately he declined the offer, took his ratings to *The Sporting Life*, and it's unclear whether the department was ever actually created.

When the journalist Robert Jackson accompanied William to the races one day in 1952 – William told him he was still making a book on the course because it was worth £150,000 a year to the firm – he soon appreciated the scale of the man. He tells a tale which indicates William's hold over the ring:

> He saw a titled millionaire owner with a mean streak scurrying from one bookmaker to another, trying to get a better price for his 10/1 horse. Hill decided to pull his leg.
>
> 'What price my horse?' queried the millionaire.
>
> 'Yours, sir? Hmm, it's difficult, but I'll lay 5/2.'
>
> The millionaire blenched and rushed to a bookie further down, but before he reached him, the tic-tac men had signalled Hill's jocular price and the horse became 5/2 favourite.
>
> Of course, it finished down the field.

The professional gambler and commissioner Nat McNabb, who would cross the Irish Sea to put hefty bets on for his clients, watched William in action at a Grand National meeting after the war, when a punter came up to him and asked for £9,000 to £3,000 as Hill was shouting '3/1 the field'. 'William Hill never batted an eyelid but continued to shout "3/1 the field." Another chap came in and took "£9,000 to £3,000". And a third. It was only then that Hill dropped the price to 11/4.' In the opinion of another financially fearless professional punter, Alex Bird, William was simply 'one of the most courageous bookmakers I have ever known.'

Bird knew first-hand what he was talking about, because not everyone was prepared to let William dominate the betting ring. At Newmarket on 13 July 1950, the third race on the card was the 25-runner Reach Selling Plate, and William, like his rivals, had chalked up Mavourneen Rhu as the 3/1 favourite. But the horse was trained, like one of its less-fancied rivals Royal Alligator, by Willie Satinoff, and he and Royal Alligator's owner Harold Wallington had been trialling the two horses against each other and Royal Alligator had been beating his stable companion by at least ten lengths. It was still a bold plot they hatched, given that there were 25 runners and the race was a mere five furlongs, but the two men deliberately stayed away from the track to give the impression they didn't particularly fancy their runners, and Satinoff brought Alex Bird in to get the money down for him.

Bird had recruited several helpers to get the cash on, with one of them ready to get the bulk of the money on with William Hill. With eight minutes to go before the 'off', Bird sent his men into action:

Herbert Howarth parked himself alongside burly, 17-stone William Hill. The bespectacled, trilby-hatted six-footer was betting for the firm. The first price he offered on Royal Alligator was 7/1, and Herbert asked him for £1,000 to £140. Hill then went 6/1, 5/1, 4/1, 3/1, 2/1 – and each time he offered the horse, Herbert stepped in and backed it to win £1,000.

Elsewhere, others in on the plot were also piling on as much as they could. Royal Alligator shortened to 13/8 favourite at the off – and won by two lengths, 'in a canter, pulling up'. The coup was landed, Satinoff cleaned up to the tune of some £23,000 and William, for once, was left licking his wounds.

By 1950 Ron Pollard had moved out of the office to become a Course Clerk, in which capacity he was able to see William working at close quarters.

There was no-one to touch him. He was always the leader of the market. His true ability was in actually making a book, in thinking faster than anyone else, to see the way the market was moving fractionally before anyone else. He would appreciate precisely how much money was being laid, perhaps 30 or 40 seconds before anyone else.

Hill was a giant of a man in every way. Burly and be-spectacled, he stood the width of a betting slip under six feet, was always smartly dressed, generally sporting a brown trilby. But had he been only 5 feet 2 inches tall he would still have had this immense presence. The moment he stepped on to those little wooden stools bookmakers still use on racecourses William Hill commanded attention as his voice boomed out.

On-course betting was in decline in the era of rationing after the war, which lasted until 1954 during which the company was putting greater emphasis on fixed-odds football business. William found himself having to spend more time on corporate develop-ment and started to cut down his course betting, and by the early 1950s as a general rule he was only betting on Saturdays. The race-course bookie Simon Nott heard a story from around that time from a betting acquaintance known as Rocky, who bets as Kelross on the rails, and comes from a long family line of bookmakers. Rocky's father used to get the train to and from the races, and on this particular day, Rocky was told,

William Hill had left the racecourse before the last and was already sat in the buffet car when my father and others got there. He asked what had won the last, they told him and it didn't seem to bother Hill too much. They ordered: all the others had a big meal, steak and the like, but William Hill just sat there with a small piece of cheese and a spring onion, looking longingly at his companions' food. The oth-ers commented that the result couldn't have been so bad for him that it had left him so 'ribby' he couldn't afford a decent meal! He explained quite forlornly that wasn't the case, but due to health reasons his doctor had put him on a strict diet.

Then, one morning in 1955, William turned up at his office with no intention of going to the races. Changing his mind on a whim, he suddenly announced that he was off to bet at Brighton. Later that afternoon Norman Pegg, who wrote as 'Gimcrack' for the *Daily Sketch*, met him at a cafe on the way back to London where they had both stopped for a pot of tea.

> There was a sick and sorry-looking William Hill seated in his car, and sipping tea. 'I don't know what made me want to come to Brighton, but I do know I've lost a fortune on the rails this afternoon,' he confided. If he does not know why, I'll tell him. He's too restless to stay in his office. He must be up and doing. Maybe that restlessness accounts for his occasional tummy trouble.

Maybe losing that 'fortune' played on William's mind. Could he even have felt he might be losing his touch? Soon he had also managed to fall out with his old friend Peter O'Sullevan, who opened a registered envelope from Hill's at breakfast one morning notifying him of the closure of his account. O'Sullevan knew the reason: a 'sequel to my criticism in the *Express*, following the telegraphed complaints from readers, of Hill's advertising ante-post odds which were either unavailable or remarkably short-lived.' (This is of course the type of comment levelled at bookmakers to this day, often by clients who feel they should be offered unlimited amounts at special-offer odds or who missed out because they were tardy in asking for them!) A 'less than entirely friendly discussion' with William ensued, and 'we did not speak for many months.' They eventually reconciled when both arrived early at a race meeting at Maisons-Laffitte in France and 'circled each other warily' before deciding 'more or less in unison, we'd best have a drink'.

Royal Ascot was one of William's favourite meetings, as well as one of the biggest betting weeks of the year, and Ron Pollard found it 'an education just to watch him, let alone work alongside him'.

He would always arrive early and then, around 1 o'clock, perhaps an hour and a half before the first race, he would stand and start to make a book on the big race of the day. If it was the Royal Hunt Cup day, for example, with 23 runners, Bill would go through the whole field, one runner after another, quoting a price on each and, quite incredibly, taking bets at the same time. I never saw another man do that with such precision. As he finished he would say to me, 'I think you will find that Horse A is in for £2,000, Horse B is in for £12,000, Horse C is in for ... until he had covered his whole book.

The 1955 Royal Ascot meeting, however, was a memorable one in several ways. It took place almost a month later than scheduled, in July, as a result of the national rail strike, and the banning of divorcees from the Royal Enclosure was finally lifted. (Undischarged bankrupts, those who had served a prison term, along with betting debt defaulters, were still excluded.) Sipping champagne in his private box at Ascot with the *Sun*'s Claude Duval and Peter Campling some 15 years later, William relived the drama of the Royal Hunt Cup, always one of the great betting races of the year. Pointing out from the balcony the part of the racecourse where he had stood – 'That's where I used to bet, there – in the middle' – William told Claude, 'I laid a horse to lose fifty thousand in the Royal Hunt Cup – it was beat a short head. Lucky, wasn't I?' No bookmaker would have been more relieved than William when the 50/1 outsider Nicholas Nickleby prevailed by a short head over the hotly fancied 11/2 favourite Coronation Year. The following day of the meeting also stuck in William's memory, he told Duval, because he had seen a flash of lightning strike the course near to him – which killed someone 'stone dead'. (In fact, two spectators were killed, and the remaining racing was abandoned.)

But the 1955 Royal Ascot meeting was historic for one more reason. On what presumably was the last day of the meeting William tried to put £1,000 (other sources suggest £4,000) on a runner in a certain race, recalled Richard Baerlein – perhaps it was to try and lay off another bet.

> None of the rails bookmakers would take the bet, and Hill got nothing on. He got up, and said he would never appear on the rails again. They all laughed and none of them took him seriously, saying, 'Good day William, see you here tomorrow.' [The following day, Saturday, would have been the Ascot Heath meeting at the same track, not then officially part of the Royal Ascot fixture.] But none of them ever did, and he never again bet himself on the rails.

Sure enough, as *The Sporting Life* of those days, which would list Hill's big meeting course 'reps' shows, this was his last working day at any racetrack. His narrow escape with the Hunt Cup had been on the Wednesday. Next day the lightning had struck, with fatal consequences. On Friday came the knock-back in the ring. An unholy trinity of traumatic omens. Finally, perhaps, enough was enough. Geoffrey Hamlyn, who considered William 'a mathematical genius', ascribes his friend's dramatic, unexpected reaction to a sudden conviction 'that the money had dried up'. Perhaps it was also that William realised he was no longer running the company for himself. His decisions now impacted on a large, Stock Exchange-quoted company and work force. He could no longer bet specific horses up to potentially damaging liabilities and afterwards face no critic other than his own reflection in the bathroom mirror. He could now be held accountable for his actions by other, lesser employees of his business. It was said that at this point William was owed some £750,000 by late – or non-paying credit clients – how much was ever recovered is not clear.

Whatever the reason, it was the last meeting at which he would ever stand, and his action certainly marked the end of an era in racing. *The Sporting Life* paid tribute to his 'fantastic memory for faces. When he was betting on the rails he knew the names of all his clients, however small, every tic-tac, however humble.'

With his time on the racecourses now over, William was asked to speak on 'What makes a successful bookmaker?'

> Without doubt, integrity is the most important quality you need. Let your client see that he can trust you and show him that you trust him. Whatever you promise, live up to your word – and always give the client the benefit of the doubt. Nothing is so hard to live down as a bad name, so don't do anything to get one! It is an old and trite saying that honesty is the best policy, but in bookmaking those are the truest words ever spoken.

But what if a client did not display the same 'honesty'? When a highprofile punter defaulted consistently in the mid-1950s, William showed restraint by giving him time to pay his four-figure debt, refusing to accept family jewels in payment. But when he then struck lucky and won £9,000 William decided to sit on the winnings in the hope he would bet again and lose them. There was a stand-off when the client, Prince Aly Khan (1911–60), demanded the money. William eventually paid but complained to the Prince's father, who history, and his brother records, told him: 'Do you mean to tell me, Mr Hill, you are foolish enough to accept bets from my son? You should know better.'

Hill was already seeing his business in the same way as City dealers regarded their stock-in-trade:

The Sporting Life looks forward to fireworks as William wins the right to make a traditionally controversial speech after his Be Careful wins the 1958 Gimcrack Stakes. He didn't disappoint.

Modern bookmaking is a highly organised business in which you are dealing in horses and dogs or football matches just as the merchant buys and sells commodities. If you misjudge the value of what you're offering you'll soon be in the red. A bookmaker is no use to man or beast if he hasn't the ability to assess value mathematically.

[But] it's no good having the judgement if you haven't the courage to back it. Nor is it any good having dreams without the courage to go after them – they'll stay dreams. The bookmaker owes it to himself and his clients not to go bust, but he has to be more than a bookmaker if he wants to rise above the crowd. He has to think fast, decide what risks he is justified in taking, and then really give the customers something to go after. And I've found the same thing true of life as a whole – make sure you know what your aim is, then gamble on it with all you've got.

William soon made another significant mark on the turf when his two-year-old filly, Be Careful, won the prestigious Gimcrack Stakes at York in August 1958 – entitling the owner to make the traditionally outspoken Gimcrack Club Dinner speech. William, the first of his profession to be so honoured, duly called for the 'cleaning out of undesirables' amongst bookies, described the fact that some racecourses still debarred bookmakers from becoming Members as 'out of date and undemocratic', and suggested turf accountancy should be given 'statutory recognition by a Royal Charter or Act of Parliament'. He advocated 'overnight declarations' for races as well as 'action against the overcrowded calendar – five meetings a day are far too many'.

William's inability to give others their head showed up again in 1959 when Dan Abbott, from Hill's advertising agency S.H. Benson, devised a new cartoon-style ad as a successful alternative to the company's usual 'mundane' daily ads. It worked so well that applications for accounts poured in. William must be delighted, thought Abbott, when 'summoned to his huge office'. Not a bit of it – he was 'given a serious bollocking and we returned to the old style'.

In 1967 William hit out again in *The Paddock Book* ranting against a Tote monopoly which, he wrote, 'is aimed at lining the pockets of rich individuals who own and breed racehorses. The British public has shown it prefers to bet with the bookmaker.'

William feared a Tote monopoly would, like the Levy, divert punter cash to increased prize money and away from 'reducing admission charges and improving catering facilities'.

'I am a racehorse owner and breeder', he admitted, 'but I have never asked anybody to subsidise my pleasures.'

In an interview he gave to *Reveille* in 1969 William was outspoken about the state of horse racing, and had some forthright and radical recommendations:

> I think the people who have been responsible for the government of racing have been archaic. The retired admirals and generals – if some of them had the sole monopoly of a winkle-stall on Southend Pier they couldn't make it pay, let alone promote racing. You've got derelict courses, derelict stands, corrugated toilets, cardboard cups – and courses of 150–200 acres used for 10 or 12 meetings a year, and for nothing else.

William's solution?

> The country has 60 or 70 racecourses – 20 would be ample. They should centralise it in regions. Concentrate on three or four tracks round London, one in the south, a couple in the west, one in the Midlands, a couple each in the North Riding and Lancashire, perhaps one or two in Scotland, and give those courses more fixtures so that you could always have, say, two race meetings a day, a good way apart. Four or five meetings on a Saturday are too many.
>
> I wouldn't subsidise the smaller tracks, or inefficiency, which is what the Levy Board's doing. A lot of meetings are mediocre, and they complain about prize money being too low at them – people should think themselves damned lucky that they can race tuppeny-ha'penny horses for prizes of £500 and £600 – because the whole bloody field's not worth £600 at some of the races.

A company publication of the time boasted of the construction of 'a great new Hill's headquarters which will cost a million

pounds. As it rises to take its place amongst the City's famous institutions, the new building will symbolise much more than one
man's achievement – it will be a monument to British sportsman-
ship founded on the solid support and goodwill of millions of ordinary people'. The man and his company were acknowledged as
the undisputed leaders of horserace betting; the fixed-odds business was flourishing. But the day William quit the racecourse was
perhaps the day his 30-year upward trajectory peaked. Even as the
company's great figurehead withdrew himself from the frontline
perhaps the seeds of setback were being sown. Hill's great rivals
Ladbrokes would shortly be sold and enter a new era under a dynamic younger leader, and just down the road would be definitive
proof that William was now capable of flawed business judgement,
which would see his company falling behind even up-and-coming
competitors.

CHAPTER 12

BARBER AT BLACKFRIARS

In 1951 a crucial part of Team Hill was slotted into place when William finally managed to bring Lionel Barber into the company as co-director. Barber, 'a taxation expert of almost worldwide repute', according to *The Sporting Life*, already had a brilliant career of financial guidance behind him as a senior partner in a respected and substantial City firm of chartered accountants. He'd been auditing William Hill's books since 1939. But now, attracted by Hill's personal drive and the vast potential of the organisation he was building up, he freed himself from all other commitments, including a number of high-profile directorships, to be able to accept the co-director role William was offering. By December 1952 Barber was on the board of William Hill (Football) Ltd. 'His City background,' William would acknowledge a few years later after more relentless expansion, 'has been of immense value as a stabilising force.' So pleased was he to have brought Barber on board that the souvenir programme for the annual William Hill Festive Party featured a prominent drawing of Hill House with a large barber's pole jutting from a second-floor window!

As the company's accountant, Barber set about transforming the organisation. He was deeply involved in the introduction of an accounting system called Hollerith, a mechanical accountancy machine that could produce and print clients' accounts while making out winners' cheques ready for signature, which was way ahead of anything the opposition had. Then he turned his attention to the firm's corporate structure, which by 1953 comprised three main and four subsidiary companies: William Hill (Park Lane) Ltd; William Hill (Glasgow) Ltd; William Hill (Football) Ltd; William Hill (North Eastern) Ltd; Whitsbury Farm & Stud Ltd; Sezincote

Stud Ltd; and Racing Review Publications Ltd, based in New Bridge Street, London EC4, and the proprietor of *Racing Review* magazine.

Barber's search for a suitable financial vehicle in which to incorporate the vital main parts of the William Hill businesses eventually bore fruit in 1954 when he identified Holders Investment Trust, a relatively small but well-established investment trust company with some £55,000 of capital, whose shares were worth at the time 2/9d (13.5p) each, and acquired three-quarters of the shares for 2/10d each. Then, on 31 March 1955, in a reverse take-over, William Hill became a subsidiary of Holders Investment Trust, as the latter acquired the whole of the issued capital of William Hill (Football) Ltd. This was one of the first times, if not the first, that a 'shell' company had been used in such a manner; not everyone had been convinced that the Stock Exchange would permit it. 'I think William Hill used HIT in order to get some outside investment into the business [25% of the Trust was owned by third parties], and also to realise some profit from his businesses,' explained David Farmer, William Hill's Head of Tax in 2014: 'The Trust was able to borrow to buy the three William Hill companies, and hence enable William to turn his investments into cash whilst still retaining control. Capital gains tax would not have been an issue as it was not introduced until 1965.'

After the acquisition of William Hill (Football) Ltd at a cost of £1.05 million, the share capital of HIT was increased again in April 1956 in order to purchase William Hill (Glasgow) Ltd for a reported £1.875 million, at which point *The Sporting Life* woke up to the fact that this signified 'the first bookmaking concern to receive a Stock Exchange quotation'. By 1960 Frederick Ellis of the *Express*'s City desk had been looking at HIT's share register, and noted that William, or 'Britain's Mr Betting, probably the biggest bookmaker of them all', had a shareholding worth £2.35 million (over £45m today), while Holders' chairman, Lionel Barber, held two blocks of shares worth an estimated £3.11 million. 'Holders made a profit of £1.9 million last year,' noted Ellis – 'a sign of the efficiency with which Mr Hill runs his business.'

The final stage of the absorption of all three William Hill companies did not happen until 1961, when William Hill (Park Lane) Ltd was bought by HIT for £2 million – half in cash, the remainder in instalments of £200,000; William himself, chairman of the company, was listed as owning 80% of the shares, and Barber 20%. The accounts of William Hill (Park Lane) Ltd for 31 July 1961 saw a net profit before taxation of £613,779, which meant directors got a remuneration of £17,500, and £306,437 was paid in dividends. This represented vast riches for William Hill and the other directors in a year which saw Johnny Haynes become the first £100-a-week footballer, and when the average yearly wage was around £799, the average house price £2,670, a pint of the milk that William was never far from the equivalent of 4p, and a pint of beer 8p. The company also had a healthy £1.342 million cash in the bank. 'Thus, Hill was one of the first bookmakers to adopt a corporate structure in the changing market of the post-war era,' said Roger Munting in *An Economic and Social History of Gambling in Britain and the USA*, 'and in many respects was ahead of the game.' William now bought out from William Hill (Park Lane) Ltd the two stud farms, Whitsbury and Sezincote, which he had always wanted to own personally.

'Barber's finesse with numbers was helping to turn the rails layer into a man of substance,' writes the racing journalist Jamie Reid. Barber's finesse with members of staff seems to have been less apparent, though. In early 1962 almost 20 years after joining the company, Ron Pollard parted company with William Hill – indeed, even defected to the 'enemy', Ladbrokes – deciding he was unable to endure Barber, whom he described as 'a very difficult man to work with. Indeed, I would have to say that he was impossible to work with.' Matters had come to a head when Barber put him on a special project which he worked on for weeks, finally, and proudly, to show him the results. 'With no more than a cursory glance, he threw it on to a table and said dismissively just one word: "Bollocks."' Pollard wouldn't be the only one to find Barber a man of few words. Future managing director John Brown dealt with him in the mid-1960s over an application for a mortgage loan which the company used to offer staff: 'He made me write out all the details and go through it with him, and then just said: "No."'

With the absorption of the 'Park Lane' company came the next step: the construction of a new headquarters at the top end of Blackfriars Road. The contract for the new Hill House was awarded to the builder Bernard Sunley's company. Sunley, it is well documented, enjoyed a bet: in 1964 he staked £20,000 on one of his own horses, Out And About, in a big race at Cheltenham. The horse started at 5/1, and Sunley stood next to the bookie's representative who had accepted his wager and gave a running commentary as the race unfolded and his horse was well beaten. There were rumours that at the time of gaining the contract for the Blackfriars building Sunley owed William a considerable sum from ill-advised wagers and, according to one source, 'built the place almost for nothing'.

The new Hill House, on the south side of the Thames for the first time, opened in March 1962 at a total cost of £2 million. Staff mucked in to help with the move – a number recalled William ('no one put in more physical effort', said Roy Sutterlin) inviting them for a drink to thank them for their efforts, only for William, as so often, to find he had no money on him to pay and had to 'borrow' from them! 'No one can tell me why William never carried any money on him,' wondered Joe Ward Hill. 'Maybe it was a throwback to the days when, as a one man band, it was potentially dangerous to carry too much cash.'

To Angus Dalrymple the new headquarters was a 'breathtaking' place: nine storeys high, 153,000 square feet, air-conditioned

The proud boast on the side of Hill House, Blackfriars, was justifiable when the building opened in the early 1960s.

and double-glazed, housing 1,500 employees dealing with '100,000 credit accounts and a quarter of a million weekly letters, serving 'more than two million racing and football clients'. A year later, William Hill would embrace the new computer age with the installation of a state of the art ICT 1500 computer (which would sell for up to £150,000 at the time, it used a 6 bit byte and had core stores of 10, 20 or 40,000 bytes). On the lower ground floor a 'fabulous staff restaurant' could accommodate 450 at one sitting for a 'first class' three-course meal 'prepared under the supervision of a former West End restaurant manager' that would set them back a mere 2/6d (12.5p), which even the newest of recruits like Tony York, a 17-year-old grammar school leaver who had joined the very day it opened, could comfortably afford. On the top floor there was a penthouse flat for William himself, as well as 'magnificent' executive suites and a conference room with 30 chairs and a long table. Hill's own private office, however, was described as 'a little austere' – somewhat like the modest home from which he emerged to conquer the bookmaking world: 'nothing ostentatious, furnished on simple, utilitarian lines'.

Such a comfortable place of work confirmed how well William treated his staff these days, giving them 'security, peace of mind and dignity' in a manner very much out of the ordinary for the times. The industry's traditional 'winter lay-off' was a thing of the past for his employees: 'He gave the five-day, 40-hour week,' wrote Dalrymple, 'optional overtime, all-round wage increases and security. His non-contributory pension scheme [which was already rewarding over 30 former staff members who had now retired] means that a man or woman earning, say, £21 a week, will retire on two-thirds pension of £14 a week' – and that, remarkably, 'without having paid a single penny in premiums! And, all the while, his or her life is heavily insured.' Ron Pollard adds that 'William Hill was … one of the first firms to have a profit-sharing scheme for its employees.'

Hill's Sporting Annual for 1962–3 described the new Hill House in action:

Bets by telephone are taken in a room 170 feet long where 300 telephonists work. The bets, after being taken down and called back, are timed and placed on conveyor belts which carry them to the field tables to be entered in the field books. Here the bets are collated and the departmental manager, watching with one eye over the shoulder of his clerks as they enter the bets, sees how betting is going – while with his other eye he watches the fluctuations of the prices as they are phoned back from the course and written up on huge blackboards.

All letter bets – racing and fixed odds – having been collected from the central Post Office in armoured vans under strict security, are then pierced with a special coding device indicating time of arrival. The cash enclosed is checked against the client's bet and the form or coupon photographed on micro-film before checking. It provides a permanent record of the bet. Before any bet is checked the postmark is examined against the time of the race. Any bearing a late postmark is declared void and money staked refunded to the client. All winnings are sent off by post that day. As fast as bets are checked they are placed on conveyor belts and carried direct to the Cash Office.

The opening of this new and expensive headquarters coincided, however, with a significant downturn in trading, overwhelmingly due to the fixed-odds football betting, which had lost the company £600,000 during the previous season, not least thanks to the big winter freeze when 'little or no business was obtained' for 11 weeks, a good chunk of the whole season. For the year to July 1963 the group moved from a profit of £227,000 the previous year to a loss of £295,000, and the half-year dividend was cut. Profits recovered the following year to £1.23 million, though Barber complained bitterly at the AGM about the new 25% duty on fixed-odds turnover. Pronouncing himself 'shocked and amazed', he explained why this made the business effectively uneconomic:

No business, however well managed and efficiently operated, can expect overhead expenses to be less than 20% of gross turnover. In fact, the reduction in turnover [caused by the duty] has caused overhead expenses – after every possible saving – to increase to 33% of gross turnover. How can a fixed odds business exist if it is necessary to retain 58% of the amounts invested to pay duty and expenses, with no profit?

The obvious and undeniable answer was that it couldn't and didn't.

An intriguing story in the *Daily Express*'s City pages, meanwhile, claimed that the recent sale of the Debretta ladies' and children's clothing firm was 'in order that a bookie could pay what is owing', and additionally that the tougher trading in the fixed-odds business had meant HIT had 'fallen behind in its payments to Hill and Barber for the purchase of the William Hill business'.

In November 1965, HIT reported a loss for the year of £2.67 million (£2.6 million had gone out in tax) – against a profit of £1.23 million the year before – and, for the first time since it bought Hill's business, scrapped its dividend. Two weeks earlier, Joe Coral had reported their first loss, also blaming fixed-odds tax. HIT's share price, which had been at 26/6d (£1.32) in 1961 when the takeover of Hill's business had been completed, crashed on the day the figures were announced to the City to just 5/6d (27.5p), nudging back to a closing price of 6/9d. To finance what the *Express* called this 'monumental' loss, Hill House was mortgaged for £1 million.

It was a pivotal moment for the company. According to Joe Ward Hill, William believed Barber was attempting to put the blame for the huge annual loss 'entirely on his shoulders', and hit back by delivering 'a tirade' against Barber to a pre-Christmas board meeting, souring forever the previously excellent business relationship and tolerable, if not warm, personal relations between the pair.

William had suspected Barber was looking for a way to quit the company, and not long after, in January 1966, while William was away in Jamaica, he did bail out. 'The rift was so deep,' said Joe Ward Hill, 'that they seldom spoke to one another again.'

Though the company's fortunes did soon improve, the overall trend was gloomy.

The new 6d (2.5p) in the pound betting tax in the autumn of 1966 pushed the shares to a new low of 4/9d, turnover fell in 1967 to £21.15 million and staff numbers were reduced from 853 to 785. The outbreak of foot-and-mouth disease in 1967, causing the suspension of horse racing for weeks, added to the misery, and now the jewel in the crown, the magnificent, custom-built Hill House, had to be sold, for £2.92 million, and leased back.

CHAPTER 13

OUTCAST AND BEREFT

In December 1953, William's daughter Kathleen, now a mother of two, married again, having been divorced two years earlier. At 25 her new husband, Edward St George, a barrister, was four years younger than her.

By the time he married Bubbles at Westminster Register Office, Edward St George had already led an extraordinary life, to be revealed in full in his daughter Sarah's obituary of her father. Growing up in Malta the son of Count and Countess Zimmermann Barbaro of St George, he had as one of his early memories being strafed by a German Messerschmitt as he bicycled home. Another was of being patted on the head by Mussolini as he paddled in the sea in Italy. At the height of the siege of Malta in the Second World War, at the age of 12, 'Teddy' had left Malta alone, his ship in a convoy torpedoed nightly by German U-boats, to attend a Dickensian prep school run by cane-wielding monks. At Oxford he got a First in Law and met Burt Kerr Todd, an eccentric American globetrotter who became a life-long friend. In Kathmandu on a post-university world tour, and despite no experience of mountaineering, they secured permission to climb Everest from a never-attempted face, but, having hiked 500 miles across the Himalayas, unfit, unprepared and unaccustomed to dysentery, they gave up. Called to the Bar in 1951, Edward continued to build on the ties he'd made with the small Himalayan kingdom of Bhutan through his friendship at Oxford with two members of its royal family, and became adviser to the King, proposing a constitution along Westminster lines and setting up a judicial system. The King then sent the crown prince, daughters and a nephew to England with Edward – where they would visit Whitsbury – to be educated. The assassination of one of his

William and Ivy's daughter Kathleen with her second husband, Edward St George, and their daughters Caroline and Sarah.

university friends, Jigme Dorji, who had become Prime Minister, occasioned the kingdom's first formal trial by jury.

It seems, however, that his father-in-law was not Edward's greatest fan – although, given William and Ivy's extravagant pandering to their daughter's every whim, it is difficult to think that any male suitor would have found favour. But there is maybe a clue in the last interview Edward St George gave before his death. 'The secret of life,' he advised, 'is to find something you really enjoy doing, then find someone else to pay you for doing it.' One thing Edward seems to have enjoyed was spending days at the racecourse with his brother Charles trying to earn extra 'loot' by punting. Edward often had trouble making ends meet, and when really broke he would find a two-horse race and back both horses with two different bookmakers. He would then collect his winnings in cash from one, and delay paying his losing bet – frequently to his father-in-law – as long as possible.

In 1956, still aged only 28, Edward accepted what was considered in the colonial service a playboy's post, that of Chief Magistrate in Nassau in the Bahamas. Once again Kathleen found herself following her husband abroad to set up home in a strange country. She, Edward and their new daughter Sarah, who'd been born the year before, sailed out in the November, and the following year a second daughter, Caroline, arrived. Edward fell in love with the Bahamas and dispensed island justice there leniently and with humour, as well as being a popular fourth at the bridge tables of Lyford Cay society. Once he provoked the ire of the Solicitor-General there by proposing a 60mph speed limit for the long road home to his house in Lyford Cay, pushing for and eventually persuading him to split the difference from the existing 30mph at 45.

The year after William's daughter and her new family settled in the Bahamas, he was continuing to innovate and lead his industry, this time by becoming the first bookmaker ever to sponsor significant horse races. The clerk of the course at both York and Redcar, Major Leslie Petch, was a man William had 'a very great regard' for, so when he learned that York's major betting race, the Ebor Handicap, needed financial bolstering for the prestige of being the most valuable of its type in Europe, he stepped in to top up the prize money. It was quite a philanthropic act as, apart from the credit for '5000 sovereigns given by the William Hill Organisation' noted in *The Sporting Life*'s race details, and for such munificence attracting a record field of 31 runners, he wasn't even granted the right to append his company's name to the 1957 event.

Evidently undeterred, William supported another high-profile betting contest in 1958, the Redcar Five Thousand, with William Hill and the Race Committee each contributing £2,500 to the prize

William Hill became racing's first bookmaker sponsors in 1957 when the company funded the Ebor.

money, which also included a Gold Cup to the value of £200, and 11 days later the Ebor Handicap, now the richest handicap of the year in Britain, was run, again featuring £5,000 contributions from both Hills and the Race Committee at York. An enormous gamble on Lester Piggott-ridden, Vincent O'Brien-trained Gladness, from 10/1 to 5/1, was duly landed. The use of some rather coy language in the *Bloodstock Breeders' Review* of the time suggests that this new kind of arrangement didn't meet with universal approval (except presumably from the owners who benefited from the bumper prize money). To the toffs and titles of the racing world, bookies were to be tolerated and taken advantage of but never to be regarded as equals. One somewhat snide comment noted how the Clerk of the Course at Newcastle was able to increase the value of the Northumberland Plate 'without the aid of any form of sponsoring'.

Within eight years William had invested a six-figure sum in sponsorship and since this first involvement there has never been a year when William Hill have not been major sponsors of horse racing, and the company has poured millions into maintaining and boosting the financial rewards and prize money on offer for hundreds, if not thousands, of different races. As a result of William Hill's example, other companies eventually realised the benefits of sponsorship and followed, only enhancing the status and value of many, many contests.

The absence of universal acclaim for William's innovation sprang almost certainly, as so often over the years, from the racing hierarchy's snobbish, hypocritical attitude to bookmaking, which had prohibited bookies from displaying their odds in Members' Enclosures at racecourses, from even being allowed in certain areas of the courses as racegoers, and from becoming members of the Jockey Club. William's great friend Phil Bull understood very well how hurt William's feelings were:

> No person in racing that I know has put back into racing as much of what he has made out of it as Billy Hill has done. And the humiliations that he has had to suffer from places like Ascot and Epsom, when he has wanted to go into the Members' Enclosure there, are a disgrace to British racing. I have known him be so angry and upset by being refused admission to the Members' Enclosure at Epsom – a man who had two large studs, is sponsoring numerous races, and has a dozen horses in training. The sole reason for this is that he is a bookmaker.
>
> Now, any visitor who comes along from America or France, or somewhere else, they walk into the Clerk of the Course's office and get a complimentary ticket which takes them into the Members' Enclosure – whether they happen to be people of consequence in the racing world and contribute

Cantelo is led in after winning the 1959 St Leger for William.

something to it or not is irrelevant, provided they have a name. Yet Mr William Hill has to go and argue the point to try to get a ticket and in the end can't get one. Can you imagine what an insult this is, what humiliation?

William's greatest racecourse moment, aside from Nimbus' Derby triumph, came in 1959 when, two days after being controversially beaten when favourite for Doncaster's Park Hill Stakes, the filly Cantelo, bred and owned by William and running in his claret and blue colours, started at 100/7 for the St Leger, and won by a length and a half under Eddie Hide.

Some of the gloss was taken off this Classic victory as the horse and jockey were greeted by a chorus of boos as they returned to the winner's enclosure. Ill informed punters and racegoers felt the horse must have been 'pulled' deliberately in the previous race. The

Daily Mirror's Dick Ratcliff rushed to William's defence, calling this 'quite the most unsportsmanlike demonstration I have ever witnessed.' Tom Nickalls in *The Life* lambasted the 'ignorant minority' but the *Daily Sketch* declared it 'the Turf's most embarrassing big race result for years'. The Stewards were happy, though – there was no enquiry into the race.

Bubbles returned from the Bahamas in 1960 when Edward became legal adviser to the United Nations Organisation, and went to live with her young daughters in a flat in Belgravia. The following year, on 28 November 1961, a maid found Kathleen's bedroom door locked and could not get an answer when she knocked. She telephoned William, who broke down the door and found his daughter dead on the bed. Beside her was an empty bottle which had contained sleeping tablets. There was no note. She had apparently been dead for some time. She was 37.

Her own daughter Caroline was only four and a half at the time, but says her mother had had dinner with her parents only a night or two earlier. Just three weeks earlier Kathleen and Edward's home had been burgled, and £2,500-worth of jewellery stolen ('There was no sign of forcible entry,' reported *The Times*), which cannot have helped Bubbles' mood. But the *Daily Mirror* reported that the day before her death Bubbles had been 'busy decorating her new "dream house" in South Audley Street, Mayfair'. Sarah, who had celebrated her sixth birthday just ten days earlier, recalls that her mother had gone to bed that night leaving a note on her door asking not to be disturbed as she was tired and had not been sleeping well recently. There is a suggestion that William and Bubbles had recently had a terrible row and not been on speaking terms, according to William's niece, Peggy Evans – but she also says her mother Ida, William's sister, had recently been to visit Bubbles and Edward and found them 'busy renovating properties and selling them on – they seemed very happy'. 'William could never believe she meant to do that, and always claimed that it had been a cry for help,' says Chris Harper. 'He believed it was brought about by her husband, Edward, having an affair.' Sarah remembers that her father, who had been away working on a trial in the north of England, was haunted by the thought that he might have prevented his wife's act: 'He told me, "I knew your Mum was a bit down – I meant to send her flowers to cheer her up. If only I'd sent them. But the train was late and I didn't send them."' Sarah retains the belief that her mother's death was accidental.

The inquest into the death of William and Ivy's daughter opened on 30 November and returned a verdict of suicide, with the Coroner concluding, in a phrase open to varying interpretations according to the *Mirror* (no official record is available) that she had been 'under stress over family arrangements'. The death certificate gives the cause of death as 'Barbiturate poisoning (Seconal) self-administered while suffering from mental stress.'

Kathleen is buried along with her parents at the tiny St Leonard's Church in Whitsbury. A local resident living there at the time says that William Hill had the road dug out to the church, which stands elevated above the village, so their daughter's coffin could be driven to the church instead of having to be carried up the steep, narrow track. A small brass plaque inside the church reads:

> To the Glory of God and in Loving Memory of their daughter Kathleen Lavinia; Born 10th Feb 1924; Died 27 Nov 1961. This church was restored and refurnished in 1963 by William and Ivy Hill.

'We visited Mummy's grave every time he came home on weekends,' says William's grand-daughter Caroline. 'He loved her unconditionally – she was the light of his life, and he never got over the pain of when she died.'

Joe Ward Hill described his brother as an 'agnostic' but William's friend Phil Bull believed that he turned to religion after Kathleen's

A family's final resting place – at Whitsbury's St Leonard's church.

suicide: 'He's not really a religious person at all, never was. I think this began with the unfortunate suicide.' he told an interviewer.

William had met Father John Byrne when in Ireland with the RIC and they became very friendly.

Byrne became William's 'private parson', said Bull, and the pair regularly shared fishing trips to Ireland. Byrne visited Whitsbury, and Chris Harper suggested that he 'came to rely on William for funds in the latter part of his life'.

During this one year, William had to deal with the deaths of his daughter, his mother (in May) and his very good friend Jack Bloomfield as well as the birth of an illegitimate daughter and the traumatic impact of betting shops on his business.

CHAPTER 14

BETTING SHOPS

On Monday, 1 May 1961, perhaps the most significant date in the history of the bookmaking industry, it became legal to open a betting shop. But William Hill did not open any. That may not be what a reader of a book about a business bearing his name which at time of writing operated almost 2,400 betting shops – more than any other company – would expect to hear. It may even cause the firm a little embarrassment. But in the same way that Scrooge was absolutely sure Marley was dead, before being confronted by his shade in *A Christmas Carol*, so William Hill was absolutely positive that betting shops would play no part in his business.

In 1850 there were some 400 betting shops operating quite legally in London. They had emerged during the first half of the 19th century, when popular interest in horse racing was beginning to flourish. On-course and credit bookmakers were already well-established, but with the latter in particular too concerned with 'gentlemen' clients to worry about lesser fry, others were quite happy to provide a home for the pennies, tanners and two-bobs the smaller punters wished to stake. These pioneer betting shop operators began by setting up business in tobacconists and barber shops – people would already gather in such establishments to gossip and peruse the sporting papers, so gradually the proprietors began to encourage their customers to indulge in the occasional wager. Soon hordes of punters were flocking in purely to place bets; the interiors were upgraded with carpets and comfortable furniture to encourage them to stay; the walls were hung with lists of runners and prices, and the shops became known as 'list shops' or 'listers'. As they became more profitable, shady characters from the criminal world muscled in on the booming business to push the original small owners out

– at which point the reputation of such shops began to slump. One estimate at the start of the 1850s put the proportion of betting businesses that were properly run and fully solvent at a mere 4%. Such dodgy establishments were all too willing to decamp and welsh on their liabilities. One of the best known betting shops, Dwyer's in St Martin's Lane, London, vanished overnight after the 1851 Chester Cup, owing punters an estimated £25,000 (worth at least 100 times that today). When they turned up to collect their winnings they found every moveable item had been spirited away and all that was left was the deserted shell of an old cigar shop.

The authorities now turned a closer eye on the phenomenon. It was said at the time that to own up to working in a betting shop 'was about as unfavourable a description as a man could give himself, short of admitting he was an outright criminal'. Towards the end of August 1853 legislation was introduced to close them down. But betting shops continued to operate illegally, and there is little doubt William would have been aware of them as he was growing up. By 1924 'our industrial areas are permeated with these secret and illegal betting houses,' declared a Select Committee on the Betting Duty, in a report which also drew attention to shopkeepers who would 'double up' as bookies, such as greengrocers in Birmingham and Coventry, butchers in Warrington and Nottingham, as well as pie shops, fishmongers, tobacconists, chip shops, coal merchants and even a second-hand furniture shop, while pubs were frequently happy to dispense punts along with pints.

How To Make A Book (1945) explained the current bizarre situation whereby it was illegal to use any place 'for the purpose of betting with persons resorting thereto, or for receiving money on deposit, or ready made bets'.

An occasional occupational hazard was the police raid, but by 1958 a *Daily Mirror* article revealed how easy it was to find an illegal shop, its reporter stopping a policeman in Redcar to ask him, 'Can you direct me to the nearest place I can put a bet on?'

'Certainly, sir, straight along the road – you'll see a little door-way, go right in.'

Many of the illicit establishments boasted telephones, relayed commentaries, board displays, comfortable furniture, television, radio, refreshments and carpeted floors.

They were illegal, but tolerated. They would occasionally be raided, but usually with the manager being tipped off, and the outcome a token fine, usually levied on a volunteer without a police record of any sort, who would then be recompensed for their minor inconvenience by the owner of the establishment.

In 1951 the Royal Commission on Betting, Lotteries and Gaming had recommended the legalisation of off-course betting, but an alternative proposal was for a levy on bookmakers, 'to be applied for the benefit of racing'. In 1959 the snappily named National Bookmakers' and Associated Bodies Joint Protection Association, of which William Hill was a member, passed a resolution that it was not in favour of the legalisation of betting shops. William Hill called Conservative Home Secretary R. A. Butler's proposed legislation 'a charter for small bookmakers'. The bookmakers' opposition had been hardening towards the end of the decade: they feared it would lead to a tax on betting – which of course it did. They objected to the petty restrictions they felt sure would be imposed on betting shops, as indeed they were. And if betting shops turned out not to be a success, they feared this could be used as grounds to give a monopoly on betting to a government-run Tote. Once it became obvious that both shops and levy were inevitable, though, most bookies began to focus on getting the best deal possible. So why was William Hill himself so vehemently opposed?

In 1961 William Hill was Britain's, if not the world's, biggest bookmaker. His company was leading the way on the racecourses. It was the biggest credit betting operation in the world. Asked in 1955, 'What makes a successful bookmaker?' he had shown himself to be a true visionary in how he assessed the changing marketplace:

'Last but not least,' he had pondered,

> I would say the initiative to know what the public wants and
> to give it to them in full value ... There's been a revolution
> in our national betting habits since I lost my first bob or
> two as a lad. It's the big turnover of small sums that counts
> nowadays, and the successful bookmaker must have the vi-
> sion to cater for this new demand, plus the organising power
> to cope with it.

There was William almost foreseeing the new dawn, and the
imminent demand for betting shops, yet he would fail to react until
it was nearly too late. In *A Licence to Print Money* the knowledgeable racing and betting observer Jamie Reid describes his stubborn
opposition as 'Hill's biggest mistake' as a businessman.

But is it possible that William was more than a little concerned
that the arrival of betting shops and a new level playing field for
the industry might put his pre-eminence at risk? Letter bets poured
in to his offices from all over the country. Would so many letters
be posted if betting shops appeared in every high street? On the
other hand, were he to enter the field the sheer size of his organisation posed a problem: Charles Sidney, a respected chronicler of the
bookmaking scene, remembered 'William Hill remarking that the
number of betting shops needed by the Hill organisation (should it
enter that business) would be prohibitive, as they would need one
in almost every town of the United Kingdom to provide a service to
their clientele, so vast had it become.'

He wasn't the only major player of the day to be a little wary
about the arrival of the new kid on the block. Ladbrokes didn't
come in from day one either: 'There were early doubts about their
profitability,' wrote Ron Pollard, who worked for both companies –
'worries that drugs and crime might become associated with them.'

William's friend and rival Joe Coral was another who was uncertain: 'I agreed with many bookmakers at the time that it would be like reopening street pitches in shops.'

Pollard thinks part of William's 'suspicion stemmed from the fact that his only experience of betting shops was in Ireland, where they were poor and rather run-down establishments'. They had, though, been legal there since 1926. Ultimately the big bookmakers, suggest Wray Vamplew and Joyce Kay in their *Encyclopedia of Horse Racing*, saw the new shops as 'merely a continuation of the old, unrespectable street bookmaking in a new legal guise'.

But William's objection went much deeper, and came from a different source. An interview he gave to the BBC in 1956 offers a fascinating insight into his point of view. He began by conceding the current muddled position: 'You cannot have a ready money bet with a bookmaker through the post. You cannot legally have a bet with a street bookmaker, but you can send money with a pools coupon, but not with a racing coupon. It is ridiculous.' But, asked why betting shops wouldn't offer a solution, Hill responded: 'Why is it necessary to have betting shops? It will be quite sufficient if the law is changed to permit sending stakes through the post to a bookmaker and have a legal bet on the street.'

'Don't you think,' probed the interviewer, 'there would be more social evils created, more street betting and, therefore, more loitering?'

'Certainly not,' came back Hill.

If betting shops were allowed I can visualise crowds of people inside and out during racing hours, and I don't think it would be very nice to see at every street corner a betting shop with all these people hanging about … I have seen many betting shops, and I have seen these unpleasant types hanging about. I believe there is some law against crowding inside, but there is no law about crowding outside … You cannot have 'hole in the corner' dens.

And now another bombshell: 'Most important of all, they will have to have proper hours allocated, like public houses, and all betting shops must close during racing hours.' They would, concluded the rant, 'be responsible for a vast amount of misery, and in some cases broken homes'. Joe Ward Hill wrote that the interview 'evoked considerable merriment' the next time William went to the races, with few of his fellow bookies agreeing with him.

William was not alone in his opinions – they were echoed even at parliamentary level: also in 1956, in the House of Lords, Viscount Astor raised the question of whether bookmaking as a whole should be handed over to a (state-run) Tote monopoly, as 'The Tote has no temptation to corrupt jockeys and employees do not engage in gang warfare.' The threat is still raised occasionally today. William dismissed that idea: 'The British public has shown over years of opportunity to patronise the Tote that it prefers to bet with the bookmaker … The Tote, with all the facilities at its disposal has made little or no impact on betting.' But at heart William's objection to betting shops was a combination of moral misgivings and financial self-preservation – this is the only explanation that can justify him declaring betting shops 'a cancer in society'. He may have been an agnostic but Chris Harper, who became warden at the church in Whitsbury to which his uncle contributed so generously, emphasises William's great belief in 'Christian values'. It was no secret that William held strong left-wing views: Robin Hood was apparently a boyhood hero; Keir Hardie, the first independent Labour MP, had been an influence during his formative years; Harry Pollitt, the General Secretary of the Communist Party of Great Britain for more than 20 years, was a long-term friend; Joe Ward Hill goes so far as to say that Marx's *Das Kapital* was 'William's Bible'. 'He is perfectly able to distinguish between a Harold Macmillan and a Harold Wilson,' reflected his close friend Phil Bull. 'He was a great admirer of Aneurin Bevan.'

He is a left-wing man. His position both politically and so-
cially is – better say he takes his position in the fight from the
belly and not the head. Not from the belly now because he's
no longer hungry, but because his upbringing from early days
pre-conditioned him to be so. This is the case with most of us
... and this is why, as a millionaire, he finds himself on the left.

The real reason, therefore, Ron Pollard believes, 'was that
... while he thought it right and proper to take money from the
wealthy, he had no ambition to take it from the poor.' Howard
Hodgson, a distinguished secretary of the National Association of
Bookmakers, also puts it down to William's 'social and political
views – certainly not because he may have had any doubts that
such a move would have proved highly successful commercially.'
William maintained this line shortly after the legislation was
introduced in an interview with American writers Henry D. Paley
and John A. Glendinning, who were studying 'off track' betting in
England as a possible 'pattern for New York', that betting shops
could encourage working people to bet too much:

> People have gone into a betting shop for the first time. They've
> seen a blackboard. They've seen the runners. They've seen
> the fluctuations in the betting. Then up comes the winner
> and the price. Then they can play the next race. They have
> never seen that before in their life, and this is a new toy to
> them, and this will probably last. Previously they might have
> been encouraged by fancy to bet just spasmodically, but then
> they wouldn't bother again for months. So they might have
> been betting just on big races. But now they go and see the
> actual fluctuations on the board. They must like it and they
> hear it and they get the atmosphere of excitement and the
> payoff quick. Of course, it's like if you're a very small eater;
> all of a sudden you went into a community where they had

eight- or nine-course meals. You'd soon get attuned to it, wouldn't you?

'Integrity,' had been William's answer in 1955 to the question posed to him, 'What makes a successful bookmaker?' 'That is the most important quality you need.' 'I am not suggesting that William's concern was not genuine,' wrote Joe Ward Hill, however, 'but why in the world did he not allude to this ... instead of confining himself to a dissertation on the undesirable types which would frequent these shops? A betting shop at the corner of the street would be a convenience,' William's brother reasonably pointed out, 'but it would not necessarily increase the size of a man's bet.' The younger sibling detected self interest: 'William foresaw that betting shops would completely transform betting in this country. The volume of starting price and racecourse betting would inevitably dwindle, and he would have to reorganise his business from scratch,' so, thought his younger sibling, 'he pretended that his opposition to the new form of betting was based on moral grounds.' Many bookies agreed, feeling 'that he was against betting shops not because of his high principles,' writes Carl Chinn, 'but because he was scared that they would draw trade away from credit businesses such as his own.'

However, with the alternative a return to street betting and illegal bookies, customers were voting with their feet and the new betting shops flourished immediately – within a month of the legalisation there were reported to be 7,000 betting shops up and running. After two months a Manchester bookmaker was boasting a turnover of 'fabulous' proportions – between £500 and £600 per day, against his 'expected £50. On Derby Day we took £1,000.' *The Sporting Life* was already campaigning for evening opening – with a survey coming out clearly in favour. 'It's trebled or quadrupled the number of people who are interested in betting,' William complained to his American interviewers. Ominously, less than a month after legalisation, *The Times* reported 'Holders Trust Warning of Profit Slump': William Hill's holding company's profits for the year were not expected to exceed £1 million – almost half the previous year's. Questions about whether the company could afford to stay out of the betting shop market were already being raised behind the closed doors of the boardroom. It was, observed the American economist Richard Sasuly, 'as if a thoroughbred swung wide on the turn for home, allowing fresher horses to slip through on the inside and grab the lead.'

Angus Dalrymple, who'd formerly been a settler for William Hill, was working for Jack Swift on the day betting shops opened, 'running London's biggest betting shop … Jack Swift's gambling emporium at Dover Street and Piccadilly.' He has a different take on William's intransigence. 'From the outset, William didn't have the slightest interest in owning even one shop,' he says. 'All he saw was the chance to get small betting shop owners to open hedging accounts with him.' Many of Hill's trade accounts belonged to betting shop owners, hedging their bigger wagers to his company, which was better placed to deal with liabilities that might be ruinous for the smaller bookies. 'As if to prove he posed no threat to the little people, he actually used these reassuring words in his trade advertisements: "We are not in competition with you."' John Brown, who began working for William Hill in 1959 and went on to become managing director and chairman, agrees: 'When the shops were opening up, William said he didn't need them. He thought that people with shops would need someone to hedge with, and that he could get 10% of all the shop business without opening any of his own.'

'For a while he was right,' concedes Brown, 'and the trade room business boomed.' His 'Wizard of Odds', Billy Alsford, had another take, reckoning 'William couldn't trust anyone – so if he set up a string of shops he wouldn't trust the people running them for him.'

In 1963 William compared his Trade Department figures for 1960–1, pre-shops, with 1962–3: its share of business coming from credit bookmakers had remained fairly constant since the legalisation of betting shops. Moreover, whereas in 1960–1 his lowest weekly turnover had been £75,000, in 1962–3 it was £250,000; the highest for 1960–1 was £90,000, for 1962–3 £300,000 – and the 1962–3 figures included a period of 12 weeks when there was no racing due to bad weather. Such figures seemed to back William's conviction that the new betting shop operators would need to use his hedging facilities.

However, confirmation that William was missing out came from close to home. John T. Chenery had previously worked as a solicitor for William Hill and now, recognised as an authority on the economics of bookmaking, was a director of the Hurst Park Syndicate, which owned a chain of betting shops. Chenery pointed out that the growth in betting shop business was in excess of what William's figures indicated, as the amount hedged ('multiplied fourfold', said William) was 'directly related to the individual bookmaker's own capital reserves'. While the majority of shop businesses were indeed hedging, he explained, a lesser proportion of total turnover was being laid off, as the proprietors were becoming able 'to accumulate sufficient capital to themselves carry risks which had previously required laying off to a larger business'. His own company, he showed, was a prime example of such growth: in 1961 Hurst Park's profit was £5,687; the following year £28,524. For 1963 it was expected to be not less than £90,000. With the likes of Jack Swift, Mark Lane, Joe Coral, City Tote and Eric Barber reporting similarly buoyant growth it is no great surprise that within his company, which until now had always led the industry, William's lieutenants were becoming uneasily aware of how his attitude was adversely affecting future prospects.

The new shops were heavily regulated, however, to encourage people not to loiter, and with their blacked-out, closed windows

Tastefully Yours...

These are the sort of high-class shops throughout Great Britain in which every Holders Investment Trust shareholder has an interest.

Top right Inside of a James McLean Shop.
Bottom right Inside of a Jack Swift Shop.

Late 1966 and Hills finally buy into betting shops, soon taking over a string of established companies to create their own chain.

and murky, smoky atmosphere did gain something of a reputation for being dens of iniquity. 'Their saddest feature is their discomfort,' wrote John Morgan in the *New Statesman* in 1964 in an interview with William in perceptive words that are likely to have been music to his ears. 'With a delicate hypocrisy the government has encouraged gambling by making the shops easily available, but salved its conscience by insisting that they are graceless, utilitarian places without coffee or soft drinks and even without television to watch the horses.' In fact, they were less welcoming to customers than the illegal shops had been.

Three years after legalisation, in his interview with the *New Statesman* at Blackfriars Road – 'the biggest gambling factory in history', where 1,500 men and women sat 'at telephones or chalking odds on blackboards until, from some distant racecourse, the last sweating horses flash past the post' – William was not about to soften his views. 'Licences have been given to undesirables, gangsters and thugs,' he thundered, 'and to people who don't know the first thing about racing. We had spent a very long time making bookmaking respectable, by clearing out the thugs and welshers, and now this Tory government comes along and undoes all our good work.'

But by 1966 a town like Merthyr Tydfil, with a population of just 58,000, had 64 betting shops. The top English betting-shop town was Gateshead, with 73 shops for just over 100,000 people. Coral alone had a chain of 149 shops, and there were 15,000 in all across the country. Future MD, Len Cowburn, believes fellow bookmaker John Hudson, whose business William would buy, had already been persuading him to acquire some himself. That year William had a 'stormy' showdown with director Bill Balshaw, who would subsequently become chairman, in which Balshaw and other senior staff such as John Ullman, the company secretary, spelled out the situation to him in stark terms: 'It's either betting shops or we go bust.' This may have been a slight overstatement of the company's quandary, but the point was well made, and ultimately William's principles had to give second best to the financial welfare of his company and its employees.

At long last William Hill took the plunge, and on 30 December 1966, two months after the introduction of a contentious 6d (2.5p) in £1 tax on all bets – on course, credit and shops, in a deal worth £825,000 the company purchased the Jack Swift betting shop chain, with Swift himself coming on board 'to expand its betting shop interests'. Swift had 18 betting shops (some sources say 23), mainly based in London's West End, which were expected to produce an annual profit before tax of £300,000 for the current year. His Dover Street premises, where Angus Dalrymple worked, had quickly become the largest ready-money establishment in London. William soon confirmed he meant business with the acquisition three months later in March 1967 of Manny King's five London shops. 'He also let it be known that this was only the beginning,' reported *The Times*: 'The William Hill betting shops venture has the aim of 100 prestige shops' – a landmark it would take three years to achieve.

'When Hill bought Jack Swift's business, we started to buy up shops like mad,' says John Brown. Next was the John Hudson Group, a well-established credit business with a 35-strong chain of betting shops based in and around Hull – and with it the services of one Leonard Ponsonby Cowburn, who already had experience of most aspects of the bookmaking business having joined Hudson after his National Service in 1954. Cowburn took responsibility for the development of Hill's betting office business in the Midlands and north of England. Both he and John Brown were to enjoy stellar bookmaking careers within the Hill empire. Bill Balshaw, meanwhile, was opening some new shops for the company in Scotland, and Len Cowburn was soon impressed by what he saw: 'Bill Balshaw opened for William Hill the best of the betting offices, which I saw with my own eyes. Jamaica Street, Buchanan Street. They were superb. They were five-star hotels compared with some of the other betting offices throughout the country, which were one-star.'

Having run the Glasgow office, Balshaw was appointed Hill's deputy chairman in 1967, the year in which William's celebrity status was marked by his inclusion in a photograph for *Queen* magazine by Patrick Lichfield which also featured F1 ace Graham Hill; comic Ronnie Corbett; authors John *'Rumpole'* Mortimer and Anthony *'Clockwork Orange'* Burgess; the Bishop of London and politician Reginald Maudling. At the turn of the New Year, racing was called off because of a foot-and-mouth epidemic – costing Hills £1m per week in turnover for several weeks. In 1968 betting tax on horse racing was doubled to 5%.

By 1969 the company was on the way to recovery: back into profit, finally pulling out of fixed-odds coupons for good and investing some of the proceeds from the sale of Hill House in buying more betting shops. Ladbrokes had taken their total to 330, but Hills were catching up with 128. In 1970 the aggregate of average turnover per betting shop was expected to reach £28 million, according to an article in *The Times* that year, against £20.6 million in 1969, and there had even been 'preliminary talks with Joe Coral' about a possible takeover. The extent of the improvement was signified by William's projection for the year of profits 'something in excess of £800,000', with turnover likely to top £50 million for the first time.

In a 1969 interview – by which time William Hill were in their third year of owning betting shops – with what was then one of the country's best-selling weekly magazines, *Reveille*, William offered more robust wisdom:

As far as betting shops are concerned, if a man knows enough about the service he's selling, yes, he will get on; but he doesn't have to be an expert. He still won't be a bookmaker – that's one who can compile prices sufficiently to attract custom, and knows figures, and knows the form, and knows psychology. The people they call bookmakers today are just shopkeepers.

Racing was called off due to the country's worst foot-and-mouth epidemic in 1967. For several weeks turnover slumped and a spokesperson said: 'Our total loss could run into millions.' The Hill House Race-room was deserted.

But it was when the interviewer asked him whether he approved of 'gambling' that William's considered reply again presumed a moral dimension to the issue:

Not of gambling as such, no ... Betting I do approve of. Betting is intelligent study, and backing your opinion. But I call a gambler a person who bets what he can't afford. Getting out of your depth – that's gambling. We go to a lot of trouble to prevent people betting recklessly and getting out of their depth. I never was a gambler and I don't approve of gambling. I don't believe in gambling, but I will back an opinion. That's the art of making a book. It's only buying and selling money.

That may have been an attitude ahead of its time; his answer to the question, 'Are women punters more or less successful than men?' was emphatically not so. 'Oh, less. The average woman just sticks a pin in, or picks a fancy name. I wouldn't know one professional woman punter. They do it for fun.'

But while his company fully embraced betting shops, William himself never did. In an interview two years before he died, he was asked if he still disapproved of them. The Betting and Gaming Act of 1960, he maintained, was 'very bad legislation. Betting shops are costing the country millions of working man-hours lost.' At last, though, he was realistic about the situation: 'They are part of British life now. People have got used to them and they'll always want them.'

CHAPTER 15

BATTLE LINES DRAWN UP

The genesis of the rivalry between William Hill and Ladbrokes may well have been a dismissive remark by Ladbrokes' director Harry Green. Asked his opinion of William Hill, who was making a significant impact on the bookmaking world during the war, Green responded: 'I have seen plenty of those sort of people come and go.' In 1942 Ladbrokes' head man of the time, Arthur Bendir, had cast aspersions on William's liquidity. The rivalry lives on today, and shows few signs of abating: as recently as 2013 Hill's CEO Ralph Topping told *The Times* that 'there's a £2 billion gap in the capital value of the two organisations. So you're thinking to yourself, should we really be thinking about Ladbrokes as a competitor?' Respected gambling scene website, CalvinAyre.com's Steven Stradbrooke noted in August 2014, 'Hills enjoyed a World Cup wagering total nearly twice that of Ladbrokes.' This is the story of William Hill, not Ladbrokes, but we need briefly to consider the history of its rival to explain the challenge it posed to Hills in the mid- and late 1960s.

Unlike William Hill, the founders of Ladbrokes came from the English upper class, and in the years leading up to the First World War it unashamedly serviced aristocratic clients. Founded via a partnership between Harry Schwind, who trained horses at Ladbroke Hall in Worcestershire – hence the name – and a gambler, Mr Pennington, the firm was largely the creation of Arthur Bendir, a bookmaker, racehorse owner and punter who had joined the company in 1902 and driven it forward, making much of the fact that his clients were members of the top St James's clubs such as the Reform, White's, the Carlton and the Athenaeum. Ladbrokes saw itself as bookmaker to the gentry, and the word was put about that to open an account the person had to have an entry in *Debrett's*. As the company's history puts it, bets 'were settled in the splendour of a four-storey Queen Anne house amid feather pens, ledgers, brandy and cigars'. Ron Pollard moved from Hills to Ladbrokes in 1962, and 'when I first walked through the Ladbrokes front door I remember still being greeted by Richard Kaye [one of the directors] in the most gentlemanly way: "Morning, Pollard. Care for a sherry?" And this before 11 o'clock.' 'It was straight out of a Dickens novel,' reflected its chairman Cyril Stein, looking back to when he joined the firm. 'There were only 15 phones.' Lunch was still served to the staff by dinner-jacketed waiters, and 'the directors were mostly knocking 70 and wouldn't open an account for a man with humble beginnings.'

Cyril Stein, a grammar school boy who went to business college, was a smart operator who, still to reach the age of 30, was appointed as boss in 1956, shortly after his uncle Max (known as Parker, rather than Stein) had bought the company. According to Joe Ward Hill, William could have bought Ladbrokes for £225,000 had he wanted to – the actual figure Parker paid is disputed, but may have been as much as £250,000. Instead, 'he let it slip through his fingers – it was one of the biggest mistakes of his life.' Stein was the son of Parker's brother Jack, who worked for an agency transmitting information between bookies and the racecourse. Another of Cyril's uncles, Harry, aka 'Snouty' Parker, was a leading racecourse bookmaker of the 1930s. The family name was Stein, reflecting its Jewish origins, the Steins having emigrated from Russia, and it is a measure of how much Cyril felt that anti-semitism was no longer something to be worried about that, unlike his father or uncle, he seemed to have no hesitation in using it. 'Quiet, slim, pale, elegantly dressed, smokes an occasional cigar, drinks little,' was how the journalist Noel Whitcomb described Stein in 1967, when he was 38. Stein was physically very different, therefore, to the well-built, imposing William, but both loved racing and betting, both shared

By 1974 William's objections to political betting had been consigned to history.

a left-wing political inclination, both were generous with charities. Both, in their own minds, were never wrong, and both appear to have been happy to bend rules to promote their businesses when it suited them. Stein, married at a young age with two sons and a daughter, was by all accounts devoted and faithful to his wife.

Stein quickly realised that, whatever his uncle Max felt, he had to take Ladbrokes into the modern age, and he used his razor-sharp business skills to take on William Hill. At first he was in awe of his competitors and the clients they had – Ron Pollard recalled that the first question Stein asked him when he joined was, 'Have you brought any names and addresses with you?' – clearly an attempt to use Pollard's 19-year knowledge to poach William Hill's wealthier clients – and when Pollard bristled and said this was not how he did business Stein quietened down.

The two companies soon went toe-to-toe, cranking up the odds they were prepared to offer in an effort to attract floating punters. The problem was the fixed-odds football business, where Stein, as we have seen, was so keen to challenge Hills. Eventually the companies would become embroiled in lengthy legal proceedings over the alleged copyright infringement of Hill's coupon by their competitors, with Hill's pyrrhic victory costing them far more than the £1 damages they were awarded. The weekly competition proved financially suicidal for both companies as results frequently went against them. Neither was prepared to blink, even when in September 1963 there were 21 draws in 59 matches, costing them each estimated seven-figure payouts. On the last Saturday of 1963 Ladbrokes lost another £500,000, the following week £1.5 million. 'It was the fast lane to ruin and we paid the penalty,' wrote Ron Pollard:

£2 million in two weeks. Hills must have suffered similarly, but they were in a much stronger position than us. I remember one of our accountants, a Mr Holmes, bursting into my offices shouting, 'You're insolvent, you're insolvent!' and rushing out never to be seen again. But few knew how close we were to putting up the shutters.

Stein returned from his traditional Christmas holiday in Israel to warn Pollard and the racing manager, 'The firm is in a bad state. You must not lose. If you do, it is the end.'

Ladbrokes was saved because the National Bank of Ireland provided a loan of £250,000, but the following year in the 1964 General Election the firm came within a few results of going bust. The company took £640,000 on the election, on which it had called a Labour victory, and with £191,000 in advance bets, this was money in the bank. But election night was fraught, as Labour's lead dwindled.

Pollard was aware that the firm had offered odds it shouldn't have, and were the Conservatives now to win they might struggle to pay all of their winning clients. He only relaxed when Labour won Meriden by 363 votes and eventually ended up with a five-seat majority, making them a 5% profit on turnover. Only three years later a company that had survived bankruptcy twice would become a public company and, with a turnover of £39 million and a profit of £426,000, be able to claim to have overtaken William Hill. And though neither firm had taken the initial plunge when betting shops had been legalised, it would be Ladbrokes now taking the lead and acquiring outlets, starting with shops on the Isle of Wight in 1962, and approaching 500 by the middle of 1969.

For the next General Election in 1966, Stein began to eyeball William Hill in the full glare of the media. Until now William had only reluctantly tolerated his company betting on the outcome of General Elections; Ladbrokes had no such qualms, and Ron Pollard had been promoting their political odds to the media with little competition. Now, as the Labour Prime Minister Harold Wilson sought to hold on to power by defeating his Conservative rival Edward Heath, William finally weakened and allowed a range of prices to be offered and more widely publicised. BBC Radio then decided to run a debate on whether politics was 'a suitable subject for large-scale betting', and invited William and Cyril Stein to discuss the matter. It made for intriguing listening.

'Your firm has been a pioneer,' Stein was asked. 'Do you think this is a perfectly proper subject for betting?'

'Absolutely. If the public want to bet on Elections, they should be allowed to do so … They have shown for the last three years that they want to bet when the odds are right, and we give them the opportunity to do so.'

'Now, Mr Hill,' said the interviewer. 'Why, in your view, isn't a General Election a proper subject for betting?'

'Frankly, I think it is undesirable, because if this became a fever and millions of people went for it, I think it could affect the ballot box. And electing a government is a very serious business.'

Cyril was not convinced: 'I cannot believe that the Conservative member in a particular constituency would vote Labour because he has backed Labour. To me it is idiotic that this could be so.'

The interviewer asked William, who was revealing a serious lack of public relations nous by his clumsy answers, if he was actually saying that 'because people see Labour as the favourites, more people will be induced to vote for the Labour Party?'

'Exactly,' said William. 'There is always a certain majority [*sic*] of people who don't go to the polls. I believe 15–20% … If people had a financial interest, and it was a mass interest going into millions, I think people would go and support their own money.'

Stein: 'They would be just as much influenced by the various polls.'

'Mr Hill was suggesting that maybe a General Election is too serious a thing to bet on: now,' Stein was asked, 'would your firm be prepared to bet on anything?'

'Anything living, yes.'

'If the public wanted to bet, Mr Stein, on the number of people killed in the Vietnam War during a certain period, or dying during a cholera epidemic, would you accept that?'

'No, I said that we bet on anything living. We do not want to bet on anything that is going to affect human life.'

William: 'I remember during the war we were pressed by Fleet Street to give a price when the war would finish. And I refused to do it. Recently, we were asked if we would lay a price about the rail strike. And I refused to do it. I think election betting could lead to a certain amount of evil and I think it most undesirable in the long run.'

'I am completely mystified by Mr Hill's attitude,' declared Stein. 'It is a one-man campaign on Mr Hill's part. The views are held by him, and so far as I can see, by no one else. MPs of all parties have not taken this line. MPs have come to me in the last few weeks, phoned up and asked what the odds are on their being returned to their individual constituencies.'

'What do you say to that, Mr Hill?'

William seemed a touch rattled, and rounded on Stein: 'For your information, long before you started betting on Elections we were pressed by Fleet Street, asking us to offer odds on Elections and I resisted it. You started it. We did not interfere, we let you have it. And it's only in the last Election, I think, that we ever bet on the Election.'

'Yes,' said Stein, 'I think Mr Hill has really put his finger on it. He said he had to come into the business. But why? Because the public demand it. And although Mr Hill takes the line certainly that he is running this only for his clients, well, he knows as well as I do that the public wants to bet on this.'

The interviewer then asked William about 'a lot of businessmen putting a lot of money on Labour as a sort of re-insurance against a Labour victory'.

'It's a form of hedging, or insurance,' replied William, 'and from that point of view I do not think that is wrong.'

Stein spotted an opening: 'He is saying it is all right for the businessman, but not all right for the public. This really doesn't go. I can see no reason why one person who is not a large businessman should not be allowed to bet, if he wants to bet.'

William's response was a harmless lob served up for Stein to volley back over the net: 'Do you think a little small man can afford to lay 10/1 on?'

'He doesn't want to!' declared a triumphant Stein. 'He doesn't want to, but he's betting on the majority, and he's enjoying it, and getting 10/1 and 16/1 against.'

That seemed to be game, set and match to Stein, leaving William appearing as out of touch with public opinion as he still was at that point on betting shops.

'William was never at a loss for words,' reflected Joe Ward Hill, but he was fairly inarticulate and incapable of making a convincing case on any subject off the cuff. William, of course, would never admit he was wrong, so it was pointless to question the accuracy of his statements. He had an obstinate streak, which more than once came near to bringing about his downfall.

William, naturally enough, had an explanation for such obstinacy, describing himself as by nature a 'dissenter'.

The somewhat prickly relationship that now existed between William and Ladbrokes is further illustrated by an anecdote told by the commission agent-cum-bookie Benno Miller, recalling an occasion when one of his high-rolling French clients wanted several hefty wagers on Arc de Triomphe contenders:

They were a little too rich for me – ten grand a time – and would have put me in 'schtuck' had any one of them won, so I decided to pass the bets on to Billy Hill, but I had to do so by getting someone who had an account with him to place them for me.

Billy was very good friends with an American music publisher called Lou Leeds Levy [and] he agreed to put the bets on with Billy for me. Somehow Billy found out that the bets had been placed on my behalf and he rang my office in a foul mood after the race, which one of the backed horses won: 'Don't you ask me to take bets for that fucking firm round the fucking corner again,' he shouted at me. I soon realised he thought I'd put the bets on behalf of Cyril Stein at Ladbrokes – and he wasn't happy at all!

As the *Daily Mirror*'s Noel Whitcomb observed in an article in the late 1960s of the heads of the two bookmaking firms, 'I found both men likeable in different ways, but they do not like each other.'

Now the rivalry shifted to the question of who could claim the title of 'World's Biggest Bookie'. It seems to have first made headlines in late 1966, when the Daily Mirror demanded: IN BOOKIE'S LANGUAGE: PUT UP OR SHUT UP.

The story explained that in a *Sporting Life* advertisement Ladbrokes had included the phrase, 'Undoubtedly the biggest turnover of any bookmaker'. Hills had responded by offering to stake £50,000 'that no bookmaker could prove a bigger racing turnover for the week ending 29 October', the losers to donate the £50,000 to charity. Ladbrokes declined to pick up the gauntlet unless 'Hill's would accept the appointment of an independent chartered accountant to examine the horse-racing figures of the two companies for the last six months, or the next six,' and there the matter rested, unresolved.

The argument would continue to simmer for the remainder of the 1960s as the two companies traded claims over turnover. In 1968 Ladbrokes' was a record £39.5 million – 'possibly the highest in the country', it suggested; in 1970 Hills predicted theirs to top £50 million. Then events intervened to call a temporary halt to hostilities – but the battle would soon resume …

CHAPTER 16

WILLIAM'S RETIREMENT

Although William had begun to retreat from the front line of the war between punters and bookies, Derby Day 1968 proved to be a reminder of why he had acquired his unparalleled reputation.

The Vincent O'Brien–trained Sir Ivor was the hotly fancied, 4/5 Derby winner. His victory landed one of the great gambles of this, or any other, era.

How this bet came about is somewhat unclear, but that it ended up costing William Hill a substantial £62,500 (worth, according to one website which calculates such values, £946,000 today) is not in doubt.

Joe Ward Hill wrote that it happened face to face between William and the great Irish trainer O'Brien at a racing-themed social gathering; Vincent's wife, Jacqueline, wrote that it came about when owner Raymond Guest, the United States ambassador to Ireland, contacted William by phone when the latter was enjoying a jaunt on a boat in one of his favourite destinations, the French seaside resort of Deauville.

A third version by Vincent's biographer, Raymond Smith, has it happening in a phone call from one of Guest's friends, to William.

For sure, it happened in the autumn of 1966.

William was asked by Vincent, Raymond, or Raymond's friend, whether he had yet opened a market for the 1968 Derby. He was told the breeding of two colts, from the O'Brien yard, quoted them each at 100/1 and accepted bets of £100 for each.

Then, in what may have been a well orchestrated 'ambush', William was asked the same question about an American-bred colt, by Sir Gaylord out of Attica, for which he again quoted 100/1.

By now, whether at the event, or around the phone conversation, others had begun eavesdropping, and there were gasps when O'Brien (possibly Guest or his friend) asked for a 'monkey' (£500) each-way – the equivalent today of some £7,500 each-way – at the three-figure price.

William must have experienced a small pang at the potential liability he was about to take on for his company. His ego and reputation would have made it impossible for him to refuse.

So, displaying not the slightest outward reaction he reached towards Vincent and accepted the bets with a firm handshake (or agreed over the telephone by giving his word).

William was well aware of the potential publicity dividend involved in laying, and even paying out on such a wager.

Sir Ivor won two of his races as a two year old and became winter favourite for the Derby. He won the 2,000 Guineas and went odds-on for the Derby.

Guest's absence from Epsom, as he had to plant a tree in President John F Kennedy's honour elsewhere, was ' the greatest disappointment' of his racing life. But he watched the race on a portable television, surrounded by government ministers, diplomats and bishops. He ended up 'knelt on the ground, visibly trembling in front of the set'.

William may also have felt that in betting terms he, too, had been brought to his knees, as Lester Piggott steered the favourite to victory.

Despite the hefty payout, the bet repaid William many times over in terms of enhancing his reputation amongst betting men, and went down in history as perhaps the most famous ante-post gamble of all time.

William never won the money back from Raymond Guest, though. In June 1968 he announced that he did not intend ever to place another bet.

Seven years earlier, William had risked a loss which would have dwarfed the Sir Ivor payout. The impossibly exotic, wealthy and attractive Maharani of Baroda backed her 20/1 chance Victoria to win the 1961 Stewards Cup at Goodwood, staking £500 each way for a potential profit of £120,000 – equivalent to a staggering £2,300,000 today.

The horse was unplaced but won the race at 10/1 in 1962.

In 1948 William for once was hoping for a £33,000 (£1,125,000) profit from his own £500 at 66/1 on his Vertencia to win the Cesarewitch – only to see her touched off by a neck as Edgar Britt won on Woodburn, and then revealed William had promised Vertencia's jockey, Doug Smith, a £500 'present' had he won.

Whether the Sir Ivor setback had influenced his decision is not known, but on 13 May 1970 William Hill announced his retirement. 'William Hill closes his book at 65,' shouted the *Express*, getting his age wrong by a year. He would henceforth concentrate on his bloodstock and breeding interests, he explained. The new chairman of the company – in those days this was not a non-executive position as it is today, but really running the business – would be his current deputy, Bill Balshaw, formerly managing director of William Hill (Glasgow). William became life president.

'The pattern of the betting industry has changed considerably since I began my career,' he mused to the *Express*.'The emphasis has changed from credit and course business to betting shops. The specialist technique of understanding horse racing and form is not necessary to anything like the same extent with betting shops as it was formerly. Positive and able administrative ability are now the main essentials,' he reflected, with apparent regret. He also revealed that this was not the first time he had decided to quit the game – several years earlier he had resolved to retire at the age of 60 – but had changed his mind two days later! In *The Sun* William told his old chum Peter Campling, 'Curly [his nickname of 30 years], I've had my chips.' Despite having bred Nimbus to win the Derby in 1949, he admitted he still regretted missing out on the purchase of 1945 Derby winner, Sir Eric Ohlson's Dante, who he believed he could (and should, as Phil Bull had urged him) have bought for a five-figure sum and for whom a later offer of £200,000 was turned down. To his friend, Bill – as he always was to Campling – was prepared to make a rare, if somewhat unconvincing, admission that in recent years he had 'changed his mind' about betting shops, but only because 'I was forced to – it's the only place where there's any growth now.' William's rival Joe Coral paid tribute to the man he had known for 30 years – 'we both used to make a book at the dogs. He's the man who brought respectability into the profession. Bill got to the top by sheer hard work – years ago, when bookies finished work and were living it up in pubs or clubs, William Hill would go home and study the form of every horse running next day – that's why he always led the market.'

Probably by now used to such flattery, William nonetheless believed he deserved it: 'He was just as certain he was the greatest bookmaker as Muhammad Ali was that he was the greatest boxer,' explained brother Joe.

It seemed certain he would not be taking on rival bookies in the betting ring in his retirement. 'I gave gambling up years ago. Most people bet because they want to make money. I didn't need any more money. I no longer got a kick out of a bet if I won. And if I lost – I was damned annoyed! You can't make a book and gamble,' he noted, however: 'that's fatal.' Yet William still believed that if a backer remained disciplined it was possible to beat the bookie. Fellow racecourse bookie John Banks, who is credited with coining the oft-repeated phrase that 'betting shops are a licence to print money', recalled William telling him:

When I was betting I made it more than pay by careful study of the form book. Any man, provided he is intelligent and industrious enough, can make betting pay. The backer who makes a regular, intelligent study of form will come out on top 99 times out of 100. It is not necessary to go racing

– sometimes it is fatal to go to the course. One error punters make is to change their mind, because a horse may be quoted at 10/1. If you fancy a horse, back him, don't let the price put you off.

That year the 11/8 favourite Nijinsky proved William's theory right by romping to victory in the Derby, and condemning William Hill to a loss of £500,000.

On 15 June 1970, on the eve of Royal Ascot, leading names from the racing and betting world gathered at Claridge's for a glittering black-tie dinner to pay tribute to William following his retirement. He had been voted 1970 Bookmaker of the Year, but according to Chris Harper didn't quite rise to the occasion in the ceremonials, when 'he just got up with no notes and mumbled and fumbled his way through a terrible speech in which he droned on about racing not being what it used to be, and complained about a whole range of things. William – although he thought he was – was definitely not a good public speaker.' Amongst those on the William Hill table was Len Cowburn, still in his early thirties, who had come to the company with one of its first betting-shop acquisitions, the John Hudson chain in Hull, and was now the director with responsibility for developing the betting shop business in the Midlands and north of England.

William beckoned me over to talk to him. 'Mr Cowburn' (he never called me Len, and I never called him William), 'I'd like a word with you and your wife.' He sat us down and said to Tanya, 'One day your husband will no doubt take the chair at William Hill – and he'll need your total support . . .'

So why did William pick out Cowburn, then so much younger than the others round the boardroom table, to be a future head of his company? 'I have no idea. I can only assume that William wouldn't want an accountant, he'd want somebody with a bookmaking background, and I had that.'

Bill Balshaw, the new chairman of the company that was taking 75 million bets a year, was nowhere near as well-known as the man he had succeeded. The press hurried to make his acquaintance. 'I am not a bookmaker at all!' he protested to Claude Duval of the *Sun* in October 1971: 'William Hill and I are two worlds apart. He was the greatest bookmaker of them all – I just rank as a very efficient businessman.' Indeed, when it came to horses this 'blunt-talking Scotsman' didn't mind acknowledging, extraordinarily, that 'they are wonderful animals. But I have only been on three English racecourses in my life – Ascot, Newbury and Newmarket. I could not tell you where Epsom is.' He couldn't resist what may have been a sly dig at the founder: 'I was just lucky to see the good sense of betting shops. This year our turnover will be £85 million; last year it was £55 million. Last year we had 240 shops; now we have 528.' Duval would paint a picture of the man in one of his favourite watering-holes, the Albion, just round the corner from Fleet Street and an easy 63 bus ride over Blackfriars Bridge from Hill House – 'not that Balshaw would have dreamed of catching the bus.'

> Bill Balshaw would stand in the corner with his Glaswegian mates, chomping on a huge cigar. After a few glasses his accent could be difficult to understand, but I remember him telling me that 'the Tote is so out of date that they think a Yankee is an American tourist.' All very amusing – but ironic as he later went on to work for the Tote!

In September 1970, the company had made a sensible change of name, the holding company Holders Investment Trust becoming the William Hill Organization, a move widely approved by the bookmaking and investing community. By now the company's commercial performance was improving significantly, the results for the previous year released in February 1971 showing profits up from £467,000 to £1,420,000, with turnover increasing by £10 million to £55 million, harking back to 'the golden days of 1961'. It was due above all to the contribution from the expanding chain of betting shops.

The company lost out to Ladbrokes on the Solomons & Flanagan chain of 31 betting shops built up by the boxing promoter Jack Solomons, despite William's friend Bud Flanagan being a co-owner, and merger talks with the Mark Lane chain, which boasted some 250 shops – and would have brought a combined total of in excess of 460 – went nowhere (they subsequently merged with Coral). However, two months later, in February 1971, the company agreed a £1.76 million deal with the Hurst Park Syndicate to add 65 more shops to the William Hill chain and take the total to 277. The deal was good news for Hurst Park's major shareholders, the former world champion boxer Terry Downes and the boxing promoter Sam Burns – who later ran William Hill – both of whom were said to have benefited by up to £500,000 each from the bid. William Hill now found itself for the first time diversified into other sporting fields, as along with the shops it also became the owner of the wrestling company Dale Martin Promotions – the grappling superstars of the day such as Mick McManus and Jackie Pallo would frequently be seen wandering the corridors of Hill House – as well as golf ranges, billiard halls and a closed-circuit TV company, Viewsport, with plans already afoot for a further company called Hearsport, which would provide a sports service to the 60 commercial radio stations due to be given the go-ahead by the government.

The managing director of the Hurst Park Syndicate, Jarvis Astaire, would later become an extremely influential figure at William Hill, and play a major part in its reshaping in the 1970s, but, as he recalls, his involvement came about 'in a very strange way, soon after the start of the 1960s, after they liberalised betting.'

[William] had a great personal friend called Jack Bloomfield who was a famous ex-boxer (and almost certainly also a 'minder' for William, who would pay for him to stay in a Swiss sanitorium shortly before his death in 1961), and at that time Bloomfield was running the Regal, Marble Arch, which was a ballroom and a tearoom. I used to just go there to have a cup of tea every afternoon with Bloomfield, and nine times out of ten William Hill would be there. He had known him when Bloomfield had a pub in the West End. We used to talk and got on well. He was a big man, and the sort of fellow to dominate a proceeding. Whenever I went to a racecourse, he was always there and you knew about it straight away, he had that presence.

Astaire was 20 years younger than Hill, and had a background more similar to Cyril Stein's. His grandmother had migrated to England from Chotin in Ukraine; his maternal grandfather was a cantor who led synagogue services. His mother was born in the East End; his father had arrived with his family in London from Pinsk, a town which had alternated between Russian and Polish ownership over the centuries. The war had scuppered Astaire's plans to become a lawyer, but by the time he started having tea with Hill he had married well, become a successful businessman, had an interest in racehorses, enjoyed betting and was involved in boxing and other sports. He and Hill also had their politics in common, both being Labour men – indeed, Astaire got involved in the party following its surprising defeat in the 1970 election and was made a member of its Finance and Industry Committee of businessmen who backed Labour. But there was one thing that kept Astaire and Hill apart: their very different opinions on betting shops. 'I was in Deauville having dinner with William and another bookmaker,' Astaire recalls:

The subject of betting shops came up and William said they would be a disaster. I dared to disagree with him and, being

the dominant sort of man he was, he didn't like it. He became very hostile and unpleasant. We didn't meet again so-
cially for seven years, but when we did, he was ready to
admit he had been mistaken.

An added reason for William's rage, believes Astaire, was that
across from him at the dinner was Sam Burns, whom Astaire had
lured away from running Hill's trade betting department to start
some betting shops. Astaire had been the right-hand man of Jack
Solomons, widely accepted as the greatest British boxing promoter
in history, and together with Burns he had also co-managed Terry
Downes. The three of them together built up a betting shop chain
of 38 shops, and Astaire then engineered a deal with the Hurst
Park Syndicate, which owned the famous Hurst Park racecourse
beside the Thames in Surrey, whereby the racecourse land would
be sold for house-building, and the money raised used to acquire
and expand the Burns and Downes betting business. It was then
that William Hill made their approach, and when they announced
their acquisition of Hurst Park at a lunch at the Café Royal in early
1971, Astaire was struck that Hill came out of retirement to make
one of his rare public appearances. 'We had not spoken since his
tirade in Deauville and now he said to me, "I'm glad you've joined
the company because I am looking to you to turn it into a real
business. These fellows don't know what they're doing."' It was a
remark that revealed how Hill felt about the management he had
bequeathed.

Though it had been Jack Swift who had brokered the deal, a
last-minute falling-out between him and Bill Balshaw had seen him
depart the company, leaving another space on the board which
provided the chance for Astaire to bring in Sam Burns, and on 13
April 1971 they both became directors, making Astaire a director
of 31 companies in all, ranging from Alexandra Park Racecourse
to finance and properties companies; Burns was the director of 16.

William Hill had asked Astaire to provide 'good management', and this he proceeded to do, buying up businesses all over the country. 'When I was a director,' Astaire says with great satisfaction, 'more and more betting shops opened, there were more purchases of shops, generally smaller businesses. There were rules on how to operate them. They weren't restrictive at all. We made some excellent acquisitions in Manchester and picked up several businesses in London.'

A major acquisition was the 146-strong Fred Parkinson chain, which dominated the north-west, was expected to boost Hill's annual turnover by £10 million and increased its total number of shops to 428. Pleased as Astaire was, he felt this was still not enough. 'We made great strides in catching up with Ladbrokes, but even so we were still striving for some sort of public respectability.' The way that would be achieved would mark one of the most significant changes in the William Hill story.

The company went into the second half of 1971 with profits up 166% at more than £1 million for just the previous six months, and from a hefty rise in betting shop turnover from £8 million to £20 million set against a simultaneous drop of 20% in on-course, ante-post and credit betting, Bill Balshaw adduced the long-term trends:

The men who bet £1 million a year each on horses and dog tracks are a dying breed. They are being replaced by the ordinary man who puts a quid or two on the nose in the betting shop. That is good for us, because it means that we do not stand to lose large amounts in one go.

William would not, you would imagine, be wholeheartedly in agreement with that sentiment!

CHAPTER 17

THE GREATEST BOOKMAKER OF ALL TIME

By the beginning of the 1970s William's health was far from robust. In 1969, after suffering from severe chest pains, he had been diagnosed with angina, prescribed pills and warned to avoid stress. He tried to make light of the condition, complaining that a trainer friend with similar problems had 'bigger pills than I've got'. After several 'bad turns' he'd been told to cut out cigars and drink, but he didn't change his ways for long. He may have had other, long-standing health problems: Ron Pollard recalled that he 'lived on milk puddings and was never without a bottle of milk close to hand'. He was sporadically affected by arthritis. In early October 1971, three months after his American granddaughter Linda made him a great grandfather when her daughter, Melissa, was born, his youngest granddaughter Caroline, who was at boarding school in Lausanne in Switzerland, was surprised when out of the blue her grandfather came to see her, having recently returned from the Keeneland Sales in America, selling a $200,000 filly in a deal which did not play well with some of those close to him, amongst them Chris Harper:

He took me out, and we went to see my mother's old school in Montreux, Chatelard. He had never done this before. We had to take a small train to Les Avants, where the school is, and I noticed that he became very out of breath as we were hurrying to the train, and he took his heart pills. He stood quietly looking at Chatelard, lost in thought. I held his hand tightly until he dropped me off at my school.

A week later, William was at Newmarket for the Houghton Yearling Sales, a highlight of the year for him. 'There was a little room for the press, facing the auctioneer's rostrum, where William always liked to sit,' says Douglas Ventress.

There was a note, PRESS ONLY, which he clearly did not believe applied to him, and he would invariably be sat in there. Only this time he wasn't there, so I went off to look in the bar behind the restaurant and arrived there at the same time as Mr Hill's chauffeur Smithy, who was also looking for him. Mr Hill's voice boomed out, 'Smith!' He was sitting there with [stud manager] Norman Lonsdale.

'Sorry, sir, I didn't see you, I was looking for Mr Lonsdale,' said Smithy.

'Well, while you're here, what would you like to drink?'

'I'll have a small light ale, sir.'

'What would you like, Douglas?'

I wasn't a big drinker, so I said I'd have the same.

'You bloody well won't, lad. It's whisky or nothing!'

Douglas had his whisky. Later, he had to drive back to Sezincote with some of the other staff. On the way back they were talking about the dramatic story they'd heard of how William had 'saved someone's life' by whipping out the heart pills he carried with him at all times in a small snuff box and telling the wife of a man who had been showing the early signs of a heart attack, 'Give him one of these – he'll be fine.' William, meanwhile, was able to celebrate that night: 13 lots from Sezincote and Whitsbury had been sold for a record aggregate for one breeder of 93,150 guineas. He dined well with his guests, his trainer Bill Marshall and his wife Pam – Phil Bull should have been there, but 'something cropped up to stop me'. William had a drink, smoked his favourite cigars – all against doctor's orders. What he had to say shocked and delighted them. 'He told us he would have £10 million to spend on yearlings,' remembers Bill, 'and he wanted me to spend the money buying Classic prospects. I couldn't believe my luck . . .'

William was sharing his suite, Room 14 of Newmarket's Rutland Hotel, with his former stud manager Captain Peter Parsons, and the next morning Parsons went down for breakfast leaving William to follow on. But on his way to or from the bathroom William had a heart attack. 'He obviously realised, and tried to reach his pills in the bathroom,' says Chris Harper, 'but couldn't quite make it.' The bathroom was where Smithy found him, slumped on the floor. He was 68. On his death certificate, showing he died on 15 October, his occupation was listed as 'Farmer and bloodstock breeder,' which he certainly would have appreciated. The cause of death was recorded as 'Coronary Occlusion, due to long-standing ischaemic heart disease.'

Hearing the news on his car radio, Bill Marshall 'nearly swerved off the road. I thought "poor old bugger." Then I thought, "Just my bloody luck!"'

The next day *The Sporting Life* saluted 'the man who made his name a household word.' Bill Balshaw, the William Hill chairman, paid tribute to 'probably the most courageous bookmaker of all time. He transformed bookmaking from standing on racecourses, to giving the public in general the opportunity to win a lot of money for a small stake. He would back his judgement for hundreds of thousands of pounds against other people's judgements.' In the *Daily Mirror* George Fallows wrote of a bookmaker who 'was reputed to have members of the Royal Family amongst his punters, but who thought gambling was a mug's game. He loathed people who, on sheer chance, risked money they couldn't afford.' To Phil Bull, who had tried in vain to persuade William to stop smoking and drinking, his death 'wasn't exactly a shock', but he wrote that 'I have lost my staunchest friend of longest standing.' His granddaughter Caroline, who had seen him just a few days earlier, mourned 'Sweet, sweet Grandpa – the greatest man and the best grandfather.' Interviewed for this book, she said sadly: 'I am still heartbroken to have lost him.'

Inevitably, following William's death, it was 'business as usual' behind the scenes at the company, and Bill Balshaw emphasised that 'the death of Mr William Hill, president and founder of the William Hill bookmaking company, will in no way affect the position of the family trust with regard to the running of the company' – indeed, somewhat inappropriately, he also announced that it would be going ahead with plans for expanding its betting shop chain, with the purchase of four in Liverpool soon followed by 15 in and around Blackpool.

In his will William left the majority of his possessions to Ivy, and also specified £5,000 each to his brothers and sisters, and £10,000 for Sheila Baker. This last detail was immediately followed by the sentence: 'I wish to place on record my sincere appreciation of the love, loyalty and devotion of my wife throughout our married life.' He left £2,000 each to his stud manager Norman Lonsdale, to his chauffeur George 'Smithy' Smith, and to his butler Wolfrano Raimondi and his wife Ida, who worked as Ivy's maid. The last of these bequests demonstrates William's innate sense of fair play, for in 1968 he had 'summarily' dismissed Wolfrano for gross misconduct, 'culminating in your seeking to fight with me', which had in turn required the couple to vacate their flat at Whitsbury, although he permitted Raimondi's wife Ida to continue working for Ivy. The income from four secretive, probably multi-million-pound, family Trusts he had set up for the benefit of his grandchildren and their families, as well as nephews and nieces, seems to have been generous in its effect: one relative confided that 'it changed my life and brought me back to England. It also helped a number of young cousins to establish themselves.' Others, though, such as William's American granddaughter, Linda, seem not to have been convinced they received their just due.

The net value of his estate was £1,006,866.47 (by some esti-mates, £12,428,854.59 today).

William was buried according to his wishes at Whitsbury in the local churchyard, where Bubbles had already been laid to rest. At his memorial service at St James's Church, Piccadilly on 12 November, attended by some 200 people, Phil Bull broke down as he gave the address. He had known William for over 30 years and was almost certainly his closest friend – and certainly not one who was blind to his pal's faults. Despite their permanently combative relationship, his true feelings emerged in this moving tribute:

It is my privilege to put my feelings and my tribute into words; for William Hill was my firm friend for over 30 years. Of his career as a bookmaker, I shall say little. William be-gan at the bottom of his profession, rapidly rose to the top and lifted the whole profession with him as he went.

He took from bookmaking the check suit and gold-watch-chain image and gave it a new respectability and in-tegrity. He became the greatest bookmaker of all time, both on the racecourse and off, with a centralised SP organisation on a national scale, such as has not been seen before. It will not happen again. William's death was the end of an era. There will be none like him again.

William also made his mark upon the Turf itself. Cantelo, Nimbus and Grey Sovereign were products of his studs. These, and the stallions he imported, Chanteur II, Ballymoss, Sica Boy, Celtic Ash, Taj Dewan and Gyr, will have a big influ-ence upon the British thoroughbred for many years to come.

I wish to speak to you, however, not of William Hill the breeder or the bookmaker, but of William Hill the man. I will not pretend he was a paragon. To those who worked with him he was a perfectionist who could be a demanding taskmaster, sometimes too quick to criticise and blame, and

Above: William's father (circled)at a meeting of the local pigeon club, of which William Hill Jr became a member in 1912.

Right: The earliest known photograph of 'Willie' with five siblings outside their home in Malmesbury Road.

Mollie. Ethel. Fred. Willie. Cissy & Dick

Above: 'Bubbles', William and Ivy's beloved daughter.

Above right: William and his granddaughters, Caroline and Sarah, at his house in Jamaica.

Below: Joseph Appleyard painted the finish of the 1959 St Leger, won by William Hill-owned and bred Cantelo. The painting was hung in the Doncaster Art Gallery.

Nimbus (bred by Wm. Hill) winning the 1949 Derby from Amour Drake and Swallow Tail.

Left: The moment William Hill claimed he literally jumped for joy! His finest racing moment as the colt he bred, Nimbus (centre), won the 1949 Derby from Amour Drake and Swallow Tail. William said: 'I vaulted the rails of the Members' enclosure and rushed to the unsaddling enclosure.'

Middle: He backed, bred, owned – and also rode racehorses! William, in tie, formal attire but no helmet, rides out at either Sezincote or Whitsbury.

Bottom: William proudly stands between two of his favourite stallions, St Leger and Arc winner, Ballymoss, and Belmont Stakes winner Celtic Ash.

Above: Sezincote Stud.

Below: William's home from 1943, Whitsbury Manor
Stud and Farm. It is still in the family today, run by
nephew Chris Harper, wife Nicky and son Edward.

Top: Brighton racecourse in the early Fifties – is that William relaxing against the fence?

Middle left: William greets boxing promoter Jack Solomons, whose chain of betting shops he bid for, but failed to buy.

Middle right: William in business mode.

Left: William's chauffeur, Smithy, opens the door of the 'Roller' for his boss outside the Blackfriars Road HQ.

Above: Business as usual in the Hill House, Blackfriars Road race-room – the nerve centre of the company in the 1960s and 1970s.

Left: A somewhat idealised image of William Hill's Piccadilly headquarters.

In an appropriate setting for the world's foremost bookmaking organization, Hill House stands in Piccadilly Circus at the hub of the Empire — typifying the pre-eminent position which The Hill Organization holds in the estimation of sporting men and women everywhere.

THE Hill ORGANIZATION

The World's Biggest Bookmakers

Left: By royal command! William hands a trophy to the Queen Mother.

Below: Len Cowburn pulled off a unique PR coup when Princess Anne donned a William Hill branded sweatshirt during a charity showjumping event held at Ascot Racecourse in 1992 which the company sponsored.

Ace accountant Lionel Barber.

Military bandsman turned William Hill top man, Bill Balshaw.

It was 'betting before six, boxing after six' for MD, Sam Burns.

Sir Charles Clore helped bestow 'respectability' on the bookmaking industry when his Sears Holdings acquired William Hill and he became chairman.

Jarvis Astaire, director and often power behind the throne.

Len Cowburn was a prominent figure in industry politics.

Bob Green took control of the 'new' William Hill when it was merged with Mecca under the Grand Metropolitan umbrella.

Turbulent times were almost the norm during the George Walker era.

John Brown introduced a plain speaking, no-nonsense style of management.

David Harding made it his business to overtake Ladbrokes.

Ralph Topping ensured that William Hill stayed ahead of the field.

James Henderson took over the hot-seat on 1 August 2014, after 29 years with the company.

Above: Wolverhampton couple, Mr and Mrs Atto, collect a cheque for £13,500, signed by Hill's director Harry Hodgson, in August 1954, for a successful fixed odds flutter.

Left: Morecombe builder Darren Yates and wife Annaley (previously no fan of the Italian jockey) with Frankie Dettori, who won them over £550,000 when he went through the card at Ascot for a 'Magnificent Seven' in 1996.

Above: A talented team – Tommy Graham (back, left) who was Hill's golf, tennis, football and athletics odds compiler, stands next to the 'Wizard of Odds' Willie Alsford, the racing form expert, while shirt-sleeved William is blissfully unaware that the be-quiffed youngster sitting immediately below him, John Brown, would rise to run the company.

Below: One of the annual company highlights, the 2014 HOME awards ceremony was staged at Brighton's Grand Hotel just before the 2014 World Cup, gathering staff stars from around the domestic and international offices to receive well deserved plaudits and prizes.

Left: The Angel of the North promotes odds for England in the 2012 Euros in a stunt devised by PR man Tony Kenny.

Middle: Joe Hart shows off the safest pair of hands in English football as he endorses William Hill's role as an official sponsor of the England team, since 2012.

Bottom: Maradona is about to 'score' past a startled Peter Shilton during the England v Argentina clash in the 1986 World Cup. Hills 'disallowed' the goal and paid out to those betting on a 1-1 draw, thus creating the first ever high profile punter concession, to the dismay of its competitors.

Above: The William Hill branch in London's Fenchurch Street.

Middle: Exterior of Slough – a flagship shop.

Bottom: An inaugural broadcast from the company's Leeds £1m broadcasting studio in 2014 as Hill's Stephen Powell introduces PR director Kate Miller, John Francome and Jim McGrath.

International Headquarters in Gibraltar (*left*), Tel Aviv (*middle*) and Nevada (*bottom*).

Left: Tony McCoy took time out of his 2015 'retirement' season to meet William Hill's oldest betting shop customer, 104 year old George Atkinson from Norfolk, who had chosen AP's intended mount Shutthefrontdoor in an effort to back the winner of the great race for the first time in his lengthy life! William Hill course representative, Simon King, prepares to confirm the bet.

Bottom: Ralph Topping with pupils, staff and volunteers at the Project Africa school.

Left: Billy 'Big Yin' Connolly was one of the most popular celebrities called upon to make the draw for one of the rounds of the William Hill Scottish Cup, which the company have sponsored since the 2011-12 season.

Middle: Eastenders actor Jake Wood started a massive (losing) gamble from 12/1 to 4/1 on his character, Max Branning, to be revealed as the killer of Lucy Beale in the soap's 'whodunnit?' story-line when he held up this sign during a visit to the 2015 William Hill World Darts Championship, won by Gary 'The Flying Scotsman' Anderson. And, no, we didn't ask him to do it!

Bottom: John Inverdale announces Jamie Reid as the winner of the 25th William Hill Sports Book of the Year for his book *Doped* as he is congratulated by Graham Sharpe.

all too slow to praise and compliment. He was flawed in other ways, too. Which of us is not? But William was a man whose qualities of character far outweighed his failings and disabilities. Best of all, he had a real concern for justice and the welfare of people. Not theoretically, but practically.

During the war, his cashier at Hill House embezzled over £20,000 and was sent to prison for 12 months. Bill immediately provided the man's wife with a job, and I was instructed to find a school for her two young sons ... Bill then arranged for the education of the boys and also made a substantial donation to the school funds.

That experience gave me a regard for William Hill that nothing could ever destroy. For a rich man to accept a financial responsibility is easy; for a man voluntarily to accept a moral responsibility that is not his, is another matter. But for a man to disregard the demands of his own pressing affairs and go to such trouble to help the dependents of someone who has just done him an injury, is an education in ethics.

This was but one of many such actions in the life of William Hill. He was a man scornful of snobbery, impatient of incompetence, rough and uncompromising in his judgements, and forthright in the expression of his views. He was a man who could be a very charming and considerate host. There will be few of us here who have not frequently enjoyed his hospitality. Few who have not received some kindness at his hand or been helped by him in one way or another.

The most important thing in life is not success in one's affairs, but personal relationships. Friendship. We are lucky indeed if in a lifetime we make two or three real, lasting friendships that are proof against all adversity and all vicissitudes. That was how it was between William and me.

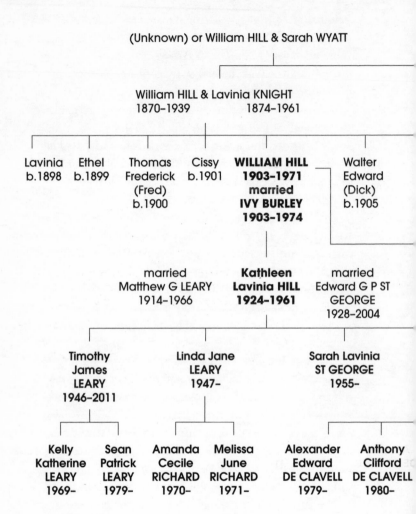

(Unknown) or William HILL & Sarah WYATT

William HILL & Lavinia KNIGHT
1870–1939   1874–1961

| Lavinia b.1898 | Ethel b.1899 | Thomas Frederick (Fred) b.1900 | Cissy b.1901 | **WILLIAM HILL 1903–1971 married IVY BURLEY 1903–1974** | Walter Edward (Dick) b.1905 |

married
Matthew G LEARY
1914–1966

Kathleen Lavinia HILL 1924–1961

married
Edward G P ST GEORGE
1928–2004

| Timothy James LEARY 1946–2011 | Linda Jane LEARY 1947– | Sarah Lavinia ST GEORGE 1955– |

| Kelly Katherine LEARY 1969– | Sean Patrick LEARY 1979– | Amanda Cecile RICHARD 1970– | Melissa June RICHARD 1971– | Alexander Edward DE CLAVELL 1979– | Anthony Clifford DE CLAVELL 1980– |

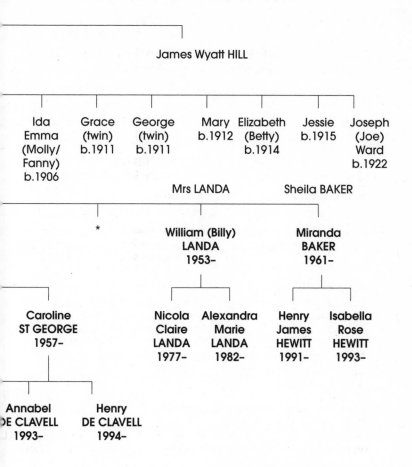

James Wyatt HILL

Ida Emma (Molly/Fanny) b.1906 — Grace (twin) b.1911 — George (twin) b.1911 — Mary b.1912 — Elizabeth (Betty) b.1914 — Jessie b.1915 — Joseph (Joe) Ward b.1922

Mrs LANDA — Sheila BAKER

* — William (Billy) LANDA 1953– — Miranda BAKER 1961–

Caroline ST GEORGE 1957–

Nicola Claire LANDA 1977– — Alexandra Marie LANDA 1982– — Henry James HEWITT 1991– — Isabella Rose HEWITT 1993–

Annabel DE CLAVELL 1993– — Henry DE CLAVELL 1994–

* Marilyn GOWLER (1953–) claims to be William's daughter

There were times when what he said or what he proposed to do, I could not countenance. No doubt he felt the same about me. But our respect for each other always bore the strain. And if my ship had run upon the rocks, he'd have been right there to throw the lifebelt to me.

To very many people, William's death will have brought a real sense of personal loss. That is its own tribute to him. My own personal loss is very real indeed. Most of the important events in the last 30 years of his life I shared. It seems that I stood beside him most of the way along the road – from the time I went with him to buy Whitsbury, until three weeks ago when they lowered his body into the grave in the churchyard there.

Watching there on that cold, sad day, I saw a little boy at the back of the classroom in a school in Birmingham, intent upon his painting, maybe dreaming that one day he'd be a famous painter. I saw a happy 12-year-old lad on a Warwickshire farm – the reluctant apprentice in a BSA tool room – the 18-year-old Royal Irish Constable, enlisted in his brother's name – and the newly-married 20-year-old, running a dance hall back in Birmingham. And then the young man in London, learning his trade on dog tracks, betting on the outside at Epsom, and making a name for himself at Northolt Park.

At last, I fancied I saw again the William Hill I lately knew, whose body they were lowering into its last resting place with all his other friends around.

PART TWO

Betting shop exterior designs have changed over the years. Here is a selection of Hill High Street shop frontages.

CHAPTER 18

THE SEARS TAKEOVER

For years Sir Charles Clore had been dead set against investing in bookmakers. A decade before William's death he had been asked whether his financial stocks-and-shares-related company, Investment Registry, would handle the flotation of Joe Coral. 'I don't want to be involved with bookmaking,' Clore had exploded. 'It's a terrible business. It's not respectable.' Clore would have grown up with illegal bookmakers, and it is clear that at this stage he shared the Establishment view that betting was to be distrusted and, like drinking, curbed. But now, says Jarvis Astaire, 'Clore wanted anything he thought would make money.'

Born in 1904 the son of a Russian Jew who had fled anti-Semitism in Latvia, Charles Clore had been brought up in the East End in a family that made a living from the textile trade and small property deals. He had not exactly shone at school, and had not been to university. He landed his first big business deal in 1924 by picking up the film rights for the Gene Tunney-Jack Dempsey fight, and selling them to South Africa on the boat going over to Cape Town. (This would immediately give him something in common with Jarvis Astaire, who would go on to promote Muhammad Ali.) Clore went on to buy a derelict ice rink in Cricklewood where he had once worked as a boy, then the Prince of Wales Theatre in the West End; he invested in a South African gold mine, and then acquired the Richards chain of dress shops, expanding the business from 30 to 45 shops and eventually selling it for £1 million. That such a successful businessman was denounced by the City says much about the British business world of the 1950s. By the 1970s the major components of his retailing empire were shoe shops – a whole host of high street chains including Freeman Hardy Willis, Dolcis, Saxone and Lilley & Skinner, all consolidated under the name British Shoe Corporation – and the department stores Lewis's and Selfridges. He was also a keen racing man, and even at the time of his death had some 60 horses in training in Europe and America, and at his studs, over 20 high-class mares with nominations to some of the best stallions in the world. His best horse was probably the 1966 Oaks and Irish 1,000 Guineas winner, Valoris.

The acquaintance between Clore and Jarvis Astaire had begun inauspiciously in the 1950s, during a holiday weekend at Deauville. 'He did not leave that much of a mark,' says Astaire of that meeting in the French resort and horseracing centre.

He was already well known as one of the country's leading entrepreneurs, but that weekend he did not seem anything special. If great men carry a certain aura about them, then it was completely absent with Clore. Far from being at the centre of the social group, he was at the edge, more a listener than a talker, an observer rather than a doer. As I was to discover, he liked the company of friends but never dominated proceedings.

But when it came to business, Astaire encountered another man: 'In the boardroom it was very different. There he moved with the swiftness of thought and purpose that was truly breathtaking.' Over the years Astaire came to be so impressed by the Clore of the boardroom that he called him Britain's version of Nelson Rockefeller: 'In America, if someone made an eyebrow-raising financial demand you would say, "Hey, do you think I'm Rockefeller?" In Britain we substituted Charles Clore for Rockefeller.'

However, in 1953, when Clore launched an audacious and successful takeover of Sears, a large and successful business which had 920 retail premises, mainly in the shoe trade, breathtaking was not the word being used to describe him. Now he was seen as behaving in an ungentlemanly and deplorable fashion, bringing disreputable American business practices – the contested takeover, rather than the customary approach to the board of directors – to a City which still retained its starchy pre-war traditions. Let Jarvis Astaire take up the story:

Clore's great ability was approaching problems from an angle that no one else had seen or thought about, and this was to lead to his huge success with Sears Holdings. Charles would look at companies with a stock exchange price well below the value of their assets and then approach the shareholders with an offer they could not refuse. He did this with Sears, offering 40 shillings a share against the quoted price of 14. Now, such a way of doing business is so commonplace that during takeover battles the bidder positively advertises the fact that shares being bid for are much below their asset value. When Clore did it with Sears, it was a totally unheard-of tactic and caused controversy. The City was outraged and dubbed him, with no affection whatsoever, the 'takeover king'. He was accused of asset-stripping, but his crime was simply to be ahead of his time. Indeed, far from stripping companies, he built them up. A typical example of this was Selfridges department store, which he acquired after a bitter battle. He certainly made great improvements there. When Clore moved into Sears they had 2,000 employees. By the time he died in 1979 there were 60,000. 'Find your opportunity and work hard', was his creed, and he was true to that.

Clore had helped Astaire get out of a hole by taking off his and his business partner's hands the jewellers Mappin & Webb, which they'd overstretched their resources to buy as the price for getting out of a messy business situation, and eventually William Hill provided Astaire with the ideal opportunity to return the favour. 'Soon after becoming a director of William Hill in 1971, I met Charles at a party where he told me he thought I had a good deal and that he wouldn't mind becoming involved himself.' By the beginning of the 1970s William Hill was making significant money. 'Not more than the shoe business,' says Astaire, 'because the shoe business was very, very big. We're talking about the largest shoe business in the country, probably the largest in Europe at that time. But William Hill was very, very profitable.' Hills had 550 shops and a positive cash flow which could finance other group activities and acquisitions, and Clore had noticed how both Ladbrokes and Coral were using their profits to diversify into businesses such as hotels and casinos. Clore always liked to have businesses that were the best in their industry, so the rising competition from Ladbrokes under Cyril Stein was also a challenge that excited him. 'So I told Charles I could probably have some shares placed with him,' says Astaire, 'because the firm needed cash for a number of acquisitions we wanted to make. Virtually the next day, Charles's lawyer Leonard Sainer came on the phone and told me that I'd got Charles very excited … He had got the bit between his teeth and was not going to let go.'

However, when Astaire put it to the William Hill board that Charles Clore wanted to invest – 'with his own money, rather than Sears' – he received 'a pretty sharp negative response. At that point,' admits Astaire, 'I was unaware that there was bad blood between Charles and William Hill.' It emerged that William had advised Clore in the building of his stud farm at Stype, and the two men had fallen out because William felt he had not received enough credit. Astaire decided not to relay this snub back to Charles, and arranged for him and William to meet at the races in Deauville, where they had talked very amicably, leaving Astaire hopeful that something could be salvaged.

Then William suddenly died. After the funeral Astaire gave a lift to Chris Harper, who, he says, told him that his uncle's will stipulated that the Whitsbury stud was not to be sold while Ivy was still alive. Astaire realised this was clearly going to put a lot of pressure on the business, because through another trustee of the will he'd heard that the death duties on the estate were going to be substantial. Four weeks later, Clore's lawyer called Astaire to say that Clore had had a change of heart and was now talking of making a Sears bid for the company. Astaire went round to the company's flat in Grosvenor House where Bill Balshaw was staying.

I arrived there at 4.30pm to see Alan Wyborn leaving. He was one of the William Hill trustees, a member of the board and an accountant. Still in the flat with Balshaw was one of his closest allies, Harry Hodgson, the company secretary. It transpired that Wyborn had just left after spelling out loud and clear that the shares had to be sold, and worse, he had brought news of an approach from Grand Metropolitan, owners of Mecca Bookmakers. So, when I turned up to say I'd been contacted by Sears on the same subject and with the first move in a bid, the William Hill men were delighted. I was the white knight in shining armour, because it meant their jobs could be saved. Grand Met, with Mecca Bookmakers, already had staff who were experts in the betting business and they would stick with their own management. Sears were making a first foray in to it and would have to rely on the existing team. That night I was the toast of the William Hill chairman.

However, there were to be more twists to this takeover saga, as Astaire to his great surprise soon discovered:

I was working on the price and putting together a draft for the deal when I had a hand-delivered letter brought to me from Balshaw, in which he said that he and the rest of the

William Hill board now wanted to remain independent. This stunned me, as well as Wyborn, who knew there was no alternative but to sell out, to raise the money for estate duty. But Balshaw, who had risen from employee to chairman and during Hill's lifetime had been not much more than a yes man, now saw his chance of glory.

Sears originally bid £20 million for William Hill, equating to £1.35 per share. *The Times* quoted Balshaw, interrupted in mid-celebration of annual profits having risen from £1.4 million to £2.5 million, dismissing the bid as 'inadequate', and the following day the *Express* was reporting that the William Hill board was split, with the suggestion that four of the ten directors had voted 'against rejection'. Hill's shares rose 8p nevertheless to £1.52, possibly in anticipation of a rival bid. However, the *Mirror*'s 'Your Money' column claimed that the Hill family trusts, which controlled nearly a third of the voting shares, had already said yes. William Hill's rivals, meanwhile, were enjoying the confused situation, Cyril Stein declaring that 'it will be a pleasure to work together with Sir Charles Clore.'

'[Bill Balshaw] flooded the board with his own people,' says Jarvis Astaire, and used Hambro's Bank, where he won over one of their directors, to act as his adviser in this mistaken bid for independence. The director, Cecil Berens, said that Sears' shares were nothing but Chinese paper, a ridiculous notion considering the standing of Sears and Clore at that time. Balshaw was fighting a losing battle and all he did was delay the eventual success of the Sears offer, as Charles Clore typically remained on top of every twist and turn.

On 13 December, Sears raised their bid to £1.40 per share, which seemed to satisfy the William Hill board (even though it meant that William Hill would not be paying a dividend for the year just ended), and from 29 December 1971 the William Hill Organization

Ltd became a subsidiary company within Sears Holdings Ltd. 'Part of the package meant that Balshaw stayed on,' says Astaire,

> but he continued to display his resentment and only lasted a few months after the deal was completed ... My William Hill shares were now transferred into Sears and I became, in effect, a Sears representative on the board remaining there for several years after Charles's death in 1979.

The deal had cost Sears some £21 million, and Clore was formally appointed as chairman of William Hill at the AGM on 13 June 1972. He didn't even move offices, though, and for a man then running a huge British conglomerate his, at 95 Park Street, could not have been smaller, with his personal assistant Leah Gelman, a distant relative whom he had hired when he discovered she had a typewriter, a ferocious gatekeeper. The office had a huge switchboard to keep Clore in touch with his various businesses, but he much preferred using a wind-up telephone. From Sears, Leonard Sainer and Geoffrey Maitland-Smith, once Paul McCartney's personal accountant, joined the Hill's board (more than a decade later they would become chairman and chief executive of Sears), as did Alan Wyborn and Len Cowburn. Cowburn, apart from being the only existing Hill's employee to be elevated at this time, was also the youngest of the new directors. A further consequence of William Hill now becoming part of a conglomerate was the appointment of a number of executive directors.

When Bill Balshaw resigned towards the end of 1972 – albeit not without a little encouragement from the Sears hierarchy – Sam Burns, now joined on the board by Hill's senior racecourse representative Leslie Spencer, was nominated as his successor.

Sam became managing director in 1973, with, at Jarvis Astaire's behest and with Sears' approval, Len Cowburn soon becoming his understudy.

The same year also saw the death of Cowburn's mentor John Hudson, the acquisition of whose betting shops had really set William Hill on the way to establishing a belated, but significant, presence on the high street. And Jarvis Astaire was both prophesying the future and echoing William's own wish when he declared that 'of the people in William Hill, the man that I would trust would have been Len Cowburn.'

CHAPTER 19

AFTER WILLIAM

Shortly after William's death, Ivy had called her housekeepers in to see her. Joan Sims, her son Graham remembers, was given several of William's white silk shirts for her husband, and then called back in the next day as Ivy apologised for forgetting the cuff-links to go with them – 'and handed her William's own gold Cartier cufflinks embossed with the image of a horse's head.' Another housekeeper, Ada Johnson, was handed a silver ashtray William had received from the British Friesian Society. Ivy didn't like the idea of having William's guns in the house, so she gave them to Chris Harper.

She remained living at Whitsbury with her Pekingese dogs, rarely venturing out, surrounded by a loyal team who looked after her, amongst them butler-cum-gardener Ken Ellicot, and house-keepers Ivy Miller, Ruth Partridge, Ada and Joan (who had to brush the dogs every day) – all local ladies. Kathleen Bassett was her trusted cook. 'It was very much "business as usual" following Mr Hill's death,' said Mrs Johnson, who joined the household in late 1970. 'She was obviously upset, but made it clear she wanted everything to carry on as normal. She would often tell us how it had been her money that got William started, that she'd given it to him in the early days, probably from her hairdressing salon.'

'Mrs Hill was virtually housebound,' explained Mrs Johnson, 'but she would spend the occasional week at the Carlton Hotel in Bournemouth for a break. Ivy's sisters would come to stay with her from time to time.' There was a lift in the house to enable Ivy to be manoeuvred about, and Mrs Johnson and her husband Alan, who worked for Chris Harper on the Whitsbury farm, would often go up to help with Ivy's preparations for bed on a Sunday evening, when she would love to listen to the Max Bygraves records Mr

Johnson would play her. 'Ada – get me another drink,' Ivy would request as she listened, and Ada would bring her another whisky, having given up on watering it down for her as requested by her doctor – 'she always knew and made me top it back up.' Alan would be invited to eat with Ivy, while Ada was left to get on with chores around the house. Ada would stay over on the Sunday night. 'Ivy was a kind and generous person to work for,' she says.

William's widow died on 30 June 1974 at a Bournemouth nursing home into which she had been moved days earlier. The cause of death was heart disease caused by high blood pressure. Ivy left instructions that she should be buried in the family grave at St Leonard's, Whitsbury where William and Bubbles were buried. The majority of the household staff were unable to attend the funeral, as when William died, having to prepare for guests at the house afterwards.

Following the conclusion of William's probate, the Whitsbury estate went on the market 'lock, stock and barrel', as Chris Harper puts it, and it was eventually bought by the Legal & General Pension Fund in October 1975. After prolonged negotiations Chris Harper became the tenant of L&G on an agricultural tenancy, but had to find substantial funds to meet the trustees' asking price, as L&G had only agreed to pay the leasehold value because they were taking on a tenant. The Majors Yard and its accompanying house were sold off separately. In 1977 the Manor Yard stables were rented out by Chris Harper, and James Bethell became the first trainer to take up residence. Chris planted a horse chestnut tree in the middle of the main stable yard on 12 December 1977 to commemorate the occasion. James's wife Emma Higgin retains her love of the place to this day:

On 14 July 1978 there was great excitement as the immortal Red Rum and his stable lad Billy Beardwood came to stay at Whitsbury. Red Rum was 'opening' Fordingbridge Show and spent a night at the yard. I have a photograph of him and Billy in the small paddock to the side of the main thatched stable yard. The stable yard itself was built to last and of outstanding quality – brass fittings on the indoor stables, and doors which I think were made of teak, so any horse trying to chew them found the task impossible and gave up! Our trainer's office was above the stables on the right hand side in the main yard and I believe that in William Hill's day this was where the stable lads slept. There were showers at the bottom of the stairs leading to this loft area, which had lovely beams that formed natural compartments for a dormitory of single beds. All our stable lads loved being at Whitsbury, and when we left to buy our own yard quite a few stayed on there to work for David Elsworth. Whitsbury has to my mind been in a time capsule of a bygone age, where proper values on how to treat and look after those who worked for and with you are still upheld.

James Bethell moved out in 1980, to be succeeded by David Elsworth, who occupied all three training yards from 1980–94 with considerable success, with horses such as the mighty Desert Orchid and the enormously popular Flat veteran Persian Punch being prepared from Whitsbury. He returned in 1995, adding Majors Yard in 2000, before moving to Newmarket in 2006. In 2010 Whitsbury's prize dairy herd – a pride and joy for William – was sold, and in 2012 jumps trainer Paul Henderson took the tenancy of the farm's Dairy Yard. The current tenant of Majors and Manor is Marcus Tregoning, who moved in 2013 from Kingwood House in Lambourn with 40 horses and celebrated 'a wonderful place to train, with the facilities and gallops being second to none'. Tregoning won the Derby in 2006 with Sir Percy, and told the *Racing Post*: 'It is great to be able to train on downland again. In fact, the gradients here are very similar [to Kingwood]. I'm confident you could train a

Derby winner here.' Now that really would meet with William's posthumous approval!

Stallions standing at Whitsbury in 2014

COMPTON PLACE: Foaled in 1994, an amazing servant to the stud and a rare example of a commercial stallion who never seems to go out of fashion.

SAKHEE'S SECRET: A champion sprinter. The leading second-season sire in Europe in terms of numbers of winners.

SHOWCASING: A Prince Khalid Abdullah-bred sprinter. As we went to press Showcasing was the leading British based first crop sire by European earnings, individual winners and number of wins.

FOXWEDGE: Australian-bred and -raced 'superstar' who covered his first season at Whitsbury in 2013, before returning to Australia for their covering season.

SWISS SPIRIT: Winner of £141,500 and three important sprint races at two and three, beating ten individual Group 1 winners, including Kingsgate Native, Sole Power, Reckless Abandon and Lethal Force. New for 2014, a son of Invincible Spirit – both were rated 121 by Timeform.

In 1983 Chris and Nicky Harper had a son, Edward, which gave long-term agricultural succession rights to the Harper family, and therefore in 1986 L&G sold the estate to Chris, though to fund the purchase he had to sell the majority of the stud's broodmares. Chris is currently churchwarden at the parish church where William, Ivy and Bubbles are buried; because access to the church necessitated a steep, tiring climb, William had built a road up to it. Chris maintains William, Ivy and Kathleen's beautiful family gravestone. There are still small mementos of William Hill in the house, says Chris's son Ed. 'Other than the furniture we still have his humidor (full of cigars), his engraved ivory hair brushes, his binoculars which he gave to Dad. We also used to have his pocket pen knife, but this is now in the Newmarket racing museum!'

Meanwhile, the early years under Sears saw the William Hill Organization continue to grow and to innovate. Within six months of the takeover a substantial betting-shop chain, Windsors (Sporting Investments), with nearly 200 offices in Leeds and the West Riding, was acquired. The purchase was a great illustration of how Clore made his deals. Both Coral and Ladbrokes were interested in the company and had made offers that the chairman Jim Windsor had refused. Clore trumped them by offering Windsor and his family trusts £2.9 million for 66 per cent of the equity, and when the news broke Hill's rivals were furious but could do nothing about it. But if this was Clore the deal-maker at his best, Cowburn was not impressed with the business: 'Windsors was a big purchase, a big company, but badly run from top to bottom. It was the worst company I came across.' He was asked to draw up a report for the Sears board. 'I'd never seen Charles Clore get angry. He banged the table. "We should never, Mr Sainer, Mr Maitland-Smith, we should never have made this purchase!"' Cowburn was sent to Leeds to sort things out, and retains some entertaining stories to tell of what he found, including 'leakages and 'fiddles':

> There was a particular problem with how Windsors handled cash. Windsors had the old-fashioned system of the leather wallet that you used to put money in and go and deposit it in a bank safe, outside a bank. It was commonplace for someone to produce themselves at head office and say, 'I've lost the float, I've done it in.'

[Cowburn was incredulous that little more than a light rap on the knuckles of the offender appeared to result.]

On one of my visits, I said, 'I want to see some of these shops,' and we visited a whist club. Our conversation went as follows:

'What is this? A whist club?'

'Oh, it's one of our betting offices.'

'Well, how did you get a betting office permit for these?'

'We didn't.'

We could not have that at William Hill. The betting office was closed the next day.

Whatever the original state of the chain, though, its Leeds base made strategic sense, as Cowburn explains: 'We had the finance department based in Leeds and the security department based in Leeds and all the acquisitions about the same time were in the north.'

In late 1974, a smart new logo made its debut on racecourse banners and on the company's new rules list. Conceived by Murdoch Design Associates, the replacement for the trusted, if inaccurate, 'globe' trademark of previous years was a slanted, script-style 'William' followed by a very upright, upper-case 'HILL'. It actually bore more than a passing resemblance to William's own signature. This was to be the first step towards a proper corporate identity, rolling out a uniform look for everything from shopfronts to headed notepaper, betting slips to press advertisements. The first new-look betting shop was unveiled in Watford High Street on 31 January 1975, with spotlights illuminating the William Hill sign above the window, prompting passers-by to wonder whether it was a 'boutique or a disco'. The effect was slightly spoiled, though, by the mis-spelling in the 'Licenced [*sic*] Betting Office' sign outside!

In 1975 William Hill opened a betting shop at the Wimbledon tennis fortnight –
so successful was it that the sport's authorities took fright, and this remarkable coup
was never repeated.

A couple of months later William Hill announced that the
company would be operating a betting marquee on-site at the
All-England Club in Wimbledon – an extraordinary coup – the
first, and at time of writing the only, time such a facility had been
permitted at the tennis tournament. It was not universally welcomed: 'I will attempt to get a rule passed that will forbid any of
our players betting on individual matches,' declared Arthur Ashe,
then president of the Association of Tennis Professionals. 'If betting comes in and spreads, the opportunity for a little hanky-panky
would be limitless.' Players were indeed banned from visiting the
betting marquee, but William Hill employed the British number
three Buster Mottram, just 20 years old, to advise the tennis odds
compiler Tommy Graham during the event – not that Tommy was
one to take advice from anyone! It was hardly a radical development: if they had wanted to, players had always been able to place
a bet at one of Hill's shops. 'At Wimbledon I would bet on myself
in each round,' Jimmy Connors confessed in his autobiography

The Outsider. 'Every year. The local bookmakers knew me well.' In fact, the year before the marquee's arrival, Connors' manager Bill Riordan collected £8,800 winnings after staking £800 on his man to win the 1974 men's singles title at 11/1 with Hills – but he also staked £2,500 on Connors' beaten opponent Ken Rosewall at even money on the day of the final to hedge his bet.

By 1975, four years into the Sears ownership, Charles Clore had reason to feel the business was going well. The William Hill Organization accounts were now consolidated, including nine subsidiaries consisting of various regional William Hill companies such as Southern, North Eastern, North West, Glasgow, William Hill (Football); Park Lane; James McLean, a Scottish company taken over by Hills in 1963, and Windsors (Sporting Investments) Ltd. The accounts for the year to 31 January 1975 showed turnover up from £146.2 million to £161.6 million, largely due to the growing income from licensed betting offices and other betting. Profit before tax was down, however, by nearly a million at £2.4 million and after tax by half a million at £1.3 million.

Keen as Clore was to expand the business, however, one area, says Astaire, was taboo: 'We never went into casinos. Never. He [Clore] didn't like it.' Len Cowburn also recalls the response when he suggested to Leonard Sainer that William Hill should become involved in casinos. 'His response was, and I particularly recall his words, "We don't like people running our businesses while we're asleep, and I'm sure that Sir Charles would agree with me."'

In December 1976 Charles Clore announced he would step down as chairman of Sears, remaining as life president. His health had not been good ever since an operation for bowel cancer, and having spent a lifetime making money he now wanted to enjoy it without the hassle of running his business. He had Inland Revenue approval to take his vast fortune away from the UK, and had decided to become a tax exile in Monte Carlo. Leonard Sainer would take over as chairman. Clore soon discovered, though, that exile, even in Monte

Carlo, was not the life for him and, miserable and missing the activity of business, would be on the phone every morning to London to keep up with what was happening. On his death in 1979 his worldwide assets were estimated at £123 million. Jarvis Astaire has no doubt that Clore's contribution to William Hill, indeed to the whole bookmaking industry, was 'almost too great to gauge':

> Grand Met might have been a big company, but they had casinos. When William Hill became part of Sears they moved into a different league. Sears was part of the business establishment, part of the fabric of British life, and got a gravitas for the bookmaking business that had not been there before.'

CHAPTER 20
THE EIGHTIES

The 1980s were a time of great change in Britain as a result of the economic policies followed by Margaret Thatcher's Conservative government. Much as William Hill the socialist might have deplored the Thatcherite revolution, overall the business he founded could be said to have benefited from it. But the turmoil in the outside world during the decade was mirrored by extensive changes within the company.

The biggest was the move of the company's administrative base in 1981 from London to Leeds. By the start of the decade William Hill occupied only a relatively minor portion of its purpose-built Hill House in Blackfriars Road, the majority of the space having been sub-let to British Telecom (now BT). 'Hill House was built to accommodate the sizeable postal betting, horseracing and fixed-odds football coupon business and the telephone credit betting service,' explains Bryan Robinson, the group's property executive at the time, and at its opening the company had occupied the entire building, somewhere in excess of 100,000 square feet, but two factors, the legalisation and rapid growth of betting shops, and the imposition of a tax on fixed-odds betting, had had a dramatic impact on staff numbers. 'It was not a good building,' adds Robinson, 'in terms of the quality of its construction, nor was it well located in terms of investment value,' and it had already been sold and leased back after William's death. Its fate was sealed when Len Cowburn, who by then was managing director, arrived for work early one morning to discover that some cladding had fallen from the exterior of the building. A surveyor's report subsequently discovered problems, including asbestos in the basement, and defective curtain walling which meant the windows no longer shut properly; the overall cost of repairs was estimated at millions.

It was decided that William Hill would take redundant space, in the order of 30,000 square feet, in the Lewis's department store owned by Sears Holdings in Leeds, on two upper floors its customers could not be enticed up to. Leeds was centrally located for the company's nationwide betting office network, and well served by rail and motorway links; Lewis's would pay the conversion and refurbishment costs, and Hills would make a considerable saving on office costs – Len Cowburn remembers the rent being £1 a square foot. Initially the telephone credit business remained in London, but in due course that moved up too, taking 24,200 square feet in the new £18 million St John's Centre adjacent to Lewis's, despite risible internal objections that clients would not stand for having their bets taken by staff with northern accents. Recently founded British Telecom became sole occupants of Hill House, and not long after were persuaded to take an assignment of Hill's head lease for the substantial sum of £750,000. Hills still maintained an office in London for selected senior executives, and the PR department in nearby Valentine's Place, the argument being that as far as the media was concerned, without a presence in the capital, it would no longer be perceived as a national company.

Many years on the Leeds move remains controversial. For all the good business sense it made, many employees did not like it. 'I don't think anyone really, given the choice, would like to go somewhere away from where they've been born and bred,' acknowledges Len Cowburn now. 'The fact is the majority of the employees didn't move. Very few people moved. The majority of people who worked at Leeds would have been recruited there.' Even Cowburn's deputy, John Brown, didn't make the move but stayed in London. Cowburn's sensitivity on the issue is easy to understand, as he had never moved from his home in Hull. 'People at the time said it was because of me,' he says now. 'I did not move the business to Leeds.

Believe me, it's the greatest load of nonsense. At the time, I was still looking for a relocation in London, and Sears, or Leonard Sainer, was directing me towards the best places to look.' But he feels it was logical to move north, as many of the acquisitions Hill's were making were in that part of the world – indeed, one of Sears' first acquisitions for Hills had been the Leeds-based betting shop chain Windsors, following on from Bill Balshaw's purchase of Parkinsons in Macclesfield. 'The move to Leeds,' says Cowburn, 'was, ultimately, principally because of the Windsors purchase.'

Having understudied him for some six years, Len Cowburn officially succeeded Sam Burns, by now in his late sixties, as managing director, as 1980 gave way to the New Year. Interviewed by Graham Sharpe shortly after standing down, Burns was very aware of how the world of bookmaking as he knew and loved it was changing. 'The modern bookmaker only wants to cater for the small punter who is guaranteed to lose,' he reflected. 'Even if William Hill were alive today, circumstances would have forced him to change his tune. He could not have betted as he did in the past by laying tremendous bets against a few horses. Today, the big punter is only after live bets, and that is why the ante-post market is inclined to dry up so quickly.' In a 1985 interview the company's senior course representative, Leslie Spencer, echoed Burns' diagnosis from the point of view of the rails bookmaking where William himself had excelled. 'There is no longer so much big money about generally, and it has got to the stage where you have to take whatever money you can.' The largest bet Spencer had ever taken on course was for £40,000, he revealed: these days 'you still get one or two having ten or twenty thousand on, but there is a well-known saying in racing that this game tames lions, and the big punters usually fall by the wayside, for one reason or another.' The 'real racecourse characters', he felt, 'showmen like Prince Ras Monolulu' (a forerunner of John McCririck with his eccentric, colourful attire and gesticulating manner) 'and the tipster Gully Gully' (who wore a teacher's gown and mortarboard while 'educating' punters), men who 'commanded audiences and were showmen' – had died off and not been replaced.

At least in 1987 the Chancellor of the Exchequer, Nigel Lawson, offered an unexpected boost to the traditional side of Hill's business by abolishing on-course betting tax.

Sam Burns had always had outside interests, already part of the foundations of British boxing before entering the worlds of bookmaking and racing, and at William Hill he summed up his approach as 'betting up to six o'clock, and boxing after six.' An East Ender whose trademark was a genuine friendliness, he differed from the founder, who could rarely bring himself to praise his staff, by following up intense rollockings with a consoling arm around the shoulder a few minutes later. He gained his love of boxing from his father, Sid Burns, who twice challenged for the British and Commonwealth welterweight titles, got involved with Jack Solomons, the leading promoter of the day, and promoted top fighters such as Freddie Mills, heavyweight Brian London and his eventual betting shop business partner, Terry Downes. Despite his frantically busy business life Burns continued to manage boxers, most notably the world-class brothers Chris and Kevin Finnegan – the latter of whom seemed to train on Guinness, said Sam, but was still 'the best pound-for-pound fighter I ever had' – and towards the end the exciting Commonwealth and European middleweight champion and light-heavyweight world title challenger Tony Sibson.

Sam once confided to a meeting of his Advertising and PR department that although he was delighted one of his fighters had just won a title, 'now I've got to teach the ****** to box!'

Within a year of taking the top job Sam was able to act on one of his most strongly held principles – that it was the duty of bookmakers to plough some of their profits back into racing, a principle acted on to this day. That year, thanks to him, William

Hill assumed sponsorship of the three big Newmarket autumn two-year-old 'Classics', the Cheveley Park, Middle Park and Dewhurst – important pointers for ante-post punters to the following year's real Classics – and soon the company had become the largest sponsor of horseracing in this country with such prestigious and, importantly, competitive events as the Cambridgeshire, the Stewards' Cup, the July Cup, the Scottish Grand National, the Lincoln and the November Handicap carrying the William Hill name. In 1976 he introduced an American flavour to sponsorship in the UK by importing for the first time the word 'Futurity' to a British race, when the William Hill Futurity became the new title of what began life in 1961 as the Timeform Gold Cup. The company won the inaugural running with its own horse, Sporting Yankee. In 1981 it sponsored a race in America for the first time, also a first for any British bookmaking company, with the William Hill Trophy at New York's Belmont Park, in May, apparently in an attempt to attract leading American horses over to the UK to run in the William Hill July Cup and the William Hill Sprint Championship in August. By 1988, to celebrate its 30th year of racing sponsorship, the company contributed a total of £367,500 over 12 races. It also supported greyhound racing for a five-figure sum.

Burns also introduced the innovative scheme for the company to own horses, whose success could emphasise the Hill connection with racing. It resulted in Hills Yankee becoming the first, and probably only, bookie-owned horse to run in the Derby, running creditably behind 1978 winner Shirley Heights.

Jarvis Astaire, Burns' erstwhile Hurst Park partner, left the company in 1982, his relationship with Leonard Sainer having deteriorated irretrievably. At the end of the same year Hill's managing director of credit, Roy Sutterlin, famed for his immaculate, dapper appearance, also retired after 35 years with the company. Len Cowburn had been 'given' Bill Abbey, who had run Sears' golf driving ranges and Dale Martin's wrestling stable, as assistant managing director, showing that while Sainer and Geoffrey Maitland-Smith, Sears' deputy chairman, wanted a Hill's man in charge, they also wanted someone from Sears to shadow him. As managing director, Cowburn set about assuming a high-profile role in the bookmaking industry's politics, sitting on a wide range of organisations and committees, including the Council of the Betting Office Licensees' Association (BOLA), that generally represented the big bookmakers, and a much-praised two-year stint as chairman of the Bookmakers' Committee of the Levy Board. 'It was William's idea,' says Cowburn. 'William influenced me more than anybody else as regards my role in representing the industry.' There were criticisms that it must inevitably distract his focus from William Hill, but Cowburn's response is that 'if I hadn't done it, someone else would, and they may have raised the profile of their own company at our expense. By having the industry's best interests at heart I also had Hill's best interests at heart.'

Not everyone was convinced, with John Brown observing of Cowburn: 'He rarely seemed to be in the office, but was consistently involved in industry matters.'

Both Sainer and Maitland-Smith would see Sears through most of the 1980s, Sainer vacating the chairmanship in favour of Maitland-Smith in 1986 but remaining life president, and only leaving the company for good in 1988. Jarvis Astaire is not complimentary about either man, though, judging that Sainer was 'difficult in the boardroom. His involvement stopped the business growing. I think he was an inhibitor. And once Clore died, Sainer proved an unsuccessful businessman and he had Maitland-Smith as an accountant with him and he was just as unsuccessful.' The results seemed to suggest otherwise: 1984 saw the best ever profit for William Hill of over £11 million, with Sears Holdings also announcing record profits of £159.1 million.

Betting shop acquisitions, meanwhile, had continued apace. The Royal Commission on Gambling's report in 1978 showed the speed of the transformation of William Hill's business. In 1968 William Hill had just 90 shops, putting the company third behind Ladbrokes with 218 and Coral with 234. By 1977 it owned 969, 13 more than Ladbrokes, the first time the company had drawn ahead of its great rivals. The 1977 acquisition of the Ken Munden and Sherman groups, adding another 238 branches, was followed in 1982 with a reported £6.18 million deal for the Trident Group's credit business and 81 shops, trading as Playboy, mainly in the Greater London area. This was the only major purchase of a chain of shops John Brown ever became involved in – 'I could only ever see the risk in buying at high prices, not the opportunities, and could never bring myself to pay the price.' The report's statistics illustrated the financial impact of this massive change, with money staked with bookmakers in the year to March 1976 breaking down as £85 million (4.5%) on-course betting; £114 million (6%) off-course credit; £1,691 million (89.5%) off-course cash. John Brown was put in charge of the company's Southern Region, running some 200 shops, and set about creating a structured corporate approach to shop development for the first time.

A less successful betting-shop venture was a move into Belgium in the company's drive to expand abroad. 1984 had seen the company successfully introduce what it dubbed its 'International Credit Betting Service', a unique telephone betting facility aimed at top businessmen and frequent travellers who would often be abroad, that allowed bets to be placed from anywhere in the world simply by calling a special London number. But in 1986 Hills had heard that Mecca's negotiations to purchase a number of betting outlets in Belgium had stalled, and decided to hijack the deal. 'I don't know why the board wanted to buy the shops – about 250 of them,' wrote John Brown, then joint assistant managing director for Hill's betting shops, who was despatched to Liège. 'It was not a good move. They weren't betting shops as we understand betting shops. They were kiosks which opened at 11am. and closed at 1pm. All the bets were on French races, and no races were televised.'

Nonetheless, Brown did the necessary. The company had hoped the deal would establish a foothold in the untapped European market but, said Brown, 'when we investigated the legal and commercial situation, it was hopeless.' He ran the operation for two and a half 'difficult' years. The business was making about £2 million a year when Hills bought it: 'In the first year, it made £1.2 million, and the next year £700,000.' It was eventually sold off to Coral in 1989 for £10 million – 'God knows how!' said a relieved Brown, to whom it taught the lesson that 'William Hill should never set up abroad, because you cannot beat the home team, particularly in a business so heavily dependent on legislation.' Len Cowburn would later admit it had been a mistake sending Brown to Belgium, and though Sears had supported the deal they then stopped any moves towards expansion into Germany or the USA. Cowburn himself headed up a little known 1984 bid to take over the running of the New York Racing Association's off-track 'betting parlors [sic]'. The company submitted a detailed, compelling and viable plan, but despite serious discussions in New York, it was ultimately unsuccessful. In 1985 Cowburn – despite acknowledging that the two 'never got on' – appointed John Brown and Norman Vickers, who had moved through the ranks alongside him, as joint assistant managing directors with seats on the board, Brown looking after the company's three southern regions, Vickers the three northern ones.

With the 1980s confirming Hill's supremacy in the betting-shop sector in Britain, the major challenge of the decade was technological. 'New technology has impacted upon our business in a big way,' wrote John Boyd in the *Action Line* magazine the company distributed to clients. 'The technical support staffs and communications systems now required to operate a major bookmaking organisation are extensive and complex.' The end of the 1970s had seen the launch of the Post Office's Racing Information Service, 'Raceline', with only the Speaking Clock, Dial-a-Disc and Cricket Information boasting more callers than the 168 line that attracted 6.7 million calls a year. Much of the information provided on Raceline came from William Hill, with Graham Sharpe fielding late-night and early-morning phone calls from clerks of the course to report and update the latest going, even to the point where one old-school toff rang at 5.30am on Christmas morning to declare 'Firm going, old chap, off to church now, Happy Christmas.'

Then the service was taken over on a commercial basis by William Hill, with a staff of a dozen supplying race commentaries, betting updates and information. 'Within two years, Raceline was making about £2 million a year, when the whole of William Hill was only making about £20 million,' noted John Brown.

Up in Leeds, the new communications headquarters in the St John's Centre incorporated all the latest technology that enabled the company to introduce its own Hillsport service, an audio and text data communications system linked via two complete national cable networks to every shop, where it was broadcast through an eight-screen videotext system offering up-to-the-minute odds and information on a wide range of betting events.

In 1986 betting-shop proprietors were permitted for the first time to provide televised racing in their premises for punters, and also offer them light refreshments.

This prepared the way for the next major innovation the following year, on 5 May 1987, with one of Hill's Bristol branches chosen for the launch, when SIS (Satellite Information Services) began broadcasting daily televised live racing action into the shops. The service was a joint investment by the four major bookmakers, William Hill, Ladbrokes, Mecca and Coral, and owed its development to the initiative of Mecca's MD Bob Green. Len Cowburn, the managing director of William Hill when it was set up, recalls its origins:

'It was modern technology. Bob Green had a right-hand man called Professor Barry Stapley. He was a professor in technology, I believe, and Bob explained to us at a meeting at which I was the William Hill representative that there were satellites up there. We'd barely heard of satellites. We thought they were something that looked like flying saucers. The early days of satellite involved having a dish, and the main problem that the industry had was with landlords saying, "I'm not having that dish".'

Hills owned around 19% of the venture initially, and the proportion has fluctuated slightly over the years from 15% in 1990 to currently 19.5%. Outside broadcast crews transmitted pictures of the races to SIS's London studios, where they were fed on to the Telecom Tower (now the BT Tower), and from there to British Telecom's Teleport Satellite Earth Station. The transmission was beamed to a satellite orbiting 22,000 miles above the earth, which amplified the signal and bounced it back to betting shops equipped with receiver dishes – the whole process taking less than a second. 'William the Robot' – a distant ancestor of the 2014 'Confused.com' promotional speaking robot – was on hand to introduce the new service to punters in Hill's shops.

CHAPTER 21

THE BRENT WALKER YEARS

'I often thought,' John Brown would say later, 'that after Clore's death Sears didn't really want to be bookmakers at all.' Towards the end of the 1980s the conglomerate had hit problems with its British Shoe Corporation business, and now it was offered the opportunity of an exit. 'William Hill was a gleam in my eye throughout 1988,' says Bob Green, who at the time was the chairman and CEO of Mecca Bookmakers, one of Hill's three main rivals.

> We were number three in the pecking order, but I knew that if we could acquire William Hill, we would leapfrog Ladbrokes into the number one position and become the clear market leader. I believed it to be a perfect fit with Mecca's dominance in London (based on the original Ron Nagle and City Tote Shops, plus the James Lane and William Massey chains that I had acquired in the previous couple of years). These, together with Hill's significant representation in provincial towns and cities, would give us a formidable national presence. There was also the established name and reputation of William Hill, plus Mecca's known advances in technical innovation.

Mecca, which included the traditional bingo halls as well as just under 800 betting shops in Britain and 54 more in Ireland, was part of Grand Metropolitan, a conglomerate vested principally in catering, hotels and the drinks industry, where it had acquired Distillers, the brewers Truman Watney Mann and the licence to make Smirnoff Vodka. By December 1988, a deal (given the code name 'Operation Mountain' by Green) had been agreed for Grand

Metropolitan to acquire William Hill from Sears for some £331 million in cash, with Grand Met's Mike Smith (who declined an invitation to contribute to this book) the chief executive of the new merged company, its 1,700 UK branches now making it the equal largest betting shop operator in the country, and Bob Green chairman. Green told a meeting of senior executives in Hill's Leeds boardroom that Mecca had the best management team, the best technology, the best marketing and the best shopfitting style, but that William Hill (Green rejected colleagues' idea of simplifying it to 'Hills') was the stronger brand name, and that's what the new company would be called. 'Bob Green didn't explain how,' John Brown noted wryly, 'if Mecca was best at everything, William Hill had the best brand name.'

In 1961 Green had worked and lived above a Hornsey Road, North London betting shop. 'Now, here I was at the helm of the largest wagering operation, not only in the UK but worldwide.'

With the Monopolies and Merger Commission wondering whether to show an interest, in January 1989 Grand Met swiftly divested themselves of 119 betting shops to Brent Walker. Brent Walker had been founded by the ex-boxer George Walker (brother of fellow pugilist, Billy 'Blond Bomber' Walker), said to have once been a minder for the gangster Billy Hill (a case involving whom, a judge interrupted to make it clear that there was no connection between the villain and William), who had made his money in the 1970s by redeveloping Hendon greyhound stadium as the Brent Cross shopping centre, as well as financing films such as *The Bitch* and *Quadrophenia*. Brent Cross had since been sold, and now Brent Walker's business interests ranged from a large estate of pubs and the Tolly Cobbold brewery to the London Trocadero and Elstree Studios. According to his *Daily Telegraph* obituary Walker's 'infectious confidence suited the mood of the Eighties boom years. Investors and bankers backed him again and again … By the mid-Eighties he was courted from every corner of the City.' In 1989 his daughter even married a cousin of the Queen, the Marquess of Milford Haven.

John Brown had already been warned by Mike Smith that he would be leaving the newly merged company; now he took a call from Walker, whom he'd never previously met, asking him to come and run these 119 shops for him. It is a matter of dispute whether John Brown had been Walker's first choice. 'He was very persuasive ... You could not help but like and admire George. He was charismatic,' Brown recorded in his autobiography. Brown took with him a number of trusted William Hill colleagues who had been victims of the amalgamation, and would somehow wring a £1.5 million profit from what was by no means the strongest collection of shops.

That summer saw the retirement of Leslie Spencer, Hill's senior course representative, after 40 years' service with the company. Like William Hill, Leslie had seen big punters come and go – amongst them Terry (T.P.) Ramsden, a dealer in foreign financial markets, who, say some, was the biggest of them all. During his mid-1980s heyday he is said to have lost over £50 million. 'They say I was the biggest punter – maybe I was.'

John Smurthwaite started on course for Hills in 1966 working with former Air Commodore Walter 'Brookie' Brooks – the archetypal cartoon 'Honest Joe' bookie in a loud yellow and brown checked suit with a bowler hat.

He says of Ramsden: 'We referred to him as "Indian", a nickname derived from his initials. He once staked £100,000 on his own Chapel Cottage, which won at 9/2. I remember him arriving at Thirsk in his helicopter and announcing: "I'm going to skin you bookies."'

For a while he did, but he lost £57 million in the three years up to 1987.

Leslie Spencer's departure was followed in July by the shock departure of Bob Green from Grand Met for the USA, where he set up Greenwood Racing and bought a racecourse in Philadelphia. Green explains what happened:

> I knew that to further grow the William Hill business, the heady days of acquisition in the UK were over and that we had to develop organically and be expanding our business into the international market. I had already begun working at opportunities in the Far East and the US, and had made several trips and meetings in pursuit of deals that I thought brought added value to the company. The largest and, in my mind the most important, involved the acquisition of Philadelphia Park Racetrack on the outskirts of Philadelphia. Pennsylvania had recently passed a law that allowed the existing racetracks to open off-track wagering (OTW) outlets within their market area. Although the Act had yet to be implemented, it gave Philadelphia Park the exclusive OTW rights to the greater Philadelphia area of five million people. Clearly, we had the expertise to develop an off-track business and I saw it as a major thrust into a new and undeveloped market. Grand Metropolitan gave me the authority to negotiate a deal, and by the spring of 1989 I had reached agreement to buy the racetrack from the owners.
>
> However, Grand Metropolitan through its Foods Division had been looking at the potential acquisition of Pillsbury, a publicly-traded US company that owned such major brands and businesses as Green Giant, Doughboy and Burger King. It was bound to be a 'hostile takeover', and as the time of the bid became closer, the board of GM determined that it would send out the wrong signal if, at the same time as they were seeking to take over the homely 'Mom and Pop' brands of Pillsbury, they were getting involved in a betting business in Philadelphia. Accordingly, I was advised by Allen Sheppard, the chairman of Grand Met, to suspend the

potential Philadelphia Park acquisition and 'relax for a year or so and then go back into the US market once controversy over the Pillsbury deal has died down.'

My belief was that if the perception was wrong then, it would never be right, and that Grand Met, with its global food and drink aspirations, should decide whether or not it should be in the gaming and wagering business. In any event, I determined that it was probably the right time for me to move on, and it was amicably agreed that I would leave William Hill and pursue the acquisition of Philadelphia Park in my own right.

Green offers a postscript to his time in charge of William Hill: 'I found the list of 74 executives who attended my first management conference: Number 53 is one R.J. Topping, Regional Personnel Manager, West!'

Mike Smith was now in charge of William Hill, with Len Cowburn deputy chairman. But Green's departure was viewed by the trade as a portent. Peter Fiddes, the editor of *Betting Office Supplies* magazine, paid tribute to 'one of the most innovative thinkers in bookmaking', musing that 'We can ill afford to lose someone of his calibre,' and noting 'growing City rumours in the summer ... that bookmaking was not quite the image the vast conglomerate Grand Metropolitan wished to portray . . .' This was to be spectacularly confirmed in September 1989. John Brown was having second thoughts about his role at Brent Walker, and went to see George Walker to tell him he was leaving at the end of the month. 'You can't,' Walker told him. 'I've bought William Hill lock, stock and barrel for £705 million.' He had just struck a deal with Grand Met's Allen Sheppard in the back of a taxi.

That seemed a lot of money to Brown, but he was soon in: 'I had a strong emotional desire to run William Hill.' Walker needed to satisfy the banks that he could put a management team in place

to run the business. He invited John Brown to be chief executive and his friend and former finance director at Hills via Sears,
since 1983, Bob Lambert finance director. When Brown asked him
about his business plan, Walker replied, 'Oh, I haven't got one.
You and Bob have to do that … so we can get the money off the
banks.' With the help of the Standard Chartered Bank they duly
produced a ten-year plan, and the banks (Standard Chartered and
Lloyds) signalled their support with a letter of intent. A new en-
tity, the William Hill Group, was set up to acquire the business
from Grand Met, with £350 million of the purchase price coming
from a bank loan, £285 million from Brent Walker in the form of
a high-interest loan note, and the remaining £50 million deferred
for a year, interest-free – although Brent Walker were legally committed to pay it in cash to the William Hill Group to pay on to
Grand Met. It was soon rumoured that the underbidder had been
Bob Green. Walker told Brown he had made an agreement with
Grand Met that if William Hill made less than £51 million profit
in 1989, then, 'for every £1 million less than £55 million, £12.8
million would be knocked off the £705 million purchase price.'
When the two companies met formally to make the deal Grand
Met announced it had sold 40 shops to Ladbrokes, knocking a
further £20 million off the price, and there was also a bizarre dis-
cussion as to whether the purchasers should be prepared to take
on Hill's substantial liabilities should either Elvis Presley or the
Loch Ness Monster prove to be alive! Once everything was agreed,
Mike Smith, the man who had got rid of John Brown, was on his
way, and Brown became chief executive, determined now to make
William Hill the market leader once more.

'I would recommend him for anything, John Brown,' says Jarvis
Astaire. A direct, plain-spoken man who wrote a self-deprecating
autobiography, *Lucky John*, John Brown had grown up in the East
End of London, where his father ran a small newsagents whose
regular customers were too poor to buy more than a single cigarette

or razor blade, and where playing street games all year round against much older boys gave him a competitive spirit. He'd joined Hills at 16 ('What a waste of your life,' his headmaster told him at the time) because, he wrote, 'William Hill had a reputation for not sacking people. He never sacked people in the winter when you lost a lot of racing, whereas most other bookmakers did,' and started out in the Piccadilly office as a tea boy to Ron Pollard. With a very short intermission, he spent his whole working life with the company, taking it over when it was treading water, saving it from going under amidst the chaos progressively engulfing William Hill's new parent company, and eventually presiding over a successful flotation that would propel it into the FTSE 100.

Brown's achievement is striking for its single-minded focus on making William Hill a successful British betting company. He was never tempted to take the company into other parts of the leisure or entertainment business. After the unhappy experience in Belgium he was very reluctant to expand into betting markets overseas. He intervened in the politics of the betting industry by necessity, to safeguard the company's interests, rather than by choice. Although he made William Hill a leader in several key innovations, including debit card betting and numbers betting, he kept the same core strategy: to attract customers by making William Hill, whether in shops, by telephone, or online, the most convenient and efficient way to make the widest possible variety of bets at the most competitive prices. 'Brown was tough, ruthless – knew what he was doing all the way,' says Jarvis Astaire. 'John Brown could write the bible on betting.'

'We finally took over on 13 December 1989,' wrote John Brown. It was like boarding the *Marie Celeste*.

I arrived in what had been Mike Smith's office and opened the desk drawers to find that there wasn't a single piece of paper in any of them. The filing cabinets were empty and the computer had been wiped clean. The business was drifting aimlessly ... The existing management had been uncoopera- tive and obstructive in the run-up to the takeover, and we found a business in turmoil.

Key people were disaffected by enforced relocations or had left already, telephone betting operations were hampered by software problems that would take two years to overcome; even mail was be- ing misdirected and unanswered. Bills were not being paid on time, and already unhappy staff were regularly querying their wages.

Brown and his finance director Bob Lambert set about try- ing to whip the business into shape. 'Bob was the rock,' he would later say of Lambert: 'the solid foundation on which the success of William Hill was built. Without him, we would have failed.' Within a year there was a brand-new management team, giving one person clear overall responsibility for each area of the busi- ness. Internal promotions made Liam McGuigan operations direc- tor for betting shops, David Lowrey telephone betting director and Bryan Robinson property director. Steve Olive, who had started his career at Ford, was brought over from the United States to become personnel director. David Hart moved from Ladbrokes to become development director and Bill Haygarth, once a consultant from KPMG, became IT director. Bill Wilson returned to William Hill as director of Raceline, as did Kevin Hogan, who became the com- pany secretary.

In an echo of how things had been back in the late 1960s when he'd first assumed responsibility for betting shops, Brown found the estate in a mess once again. With little or no cash available for acquisitions, he set out a ten-year plan to transform the presence of William Hill on the high street, based on re-siting and extending 5% of the shops each year, closing loss-making branches, and applying for new licences in better locations. Shops bought 20 years earlier had not been refitted; there were many different frontage styles and colours – blue and white, red and brown, green and red, green and white – so Bryan Robinson was put in charge of a redesign scheme for 5% of the shops each year with a common branding based on the company's colours – 'William Hill is synonymous with blue and white,' observed Brown. 'That's the brand; why change it?' – and convenience, without luxury, for patrons. No wooden writing shelves (because punters scrawled on them); no padded seats (because punters stuck pens in them); lighting trained on newspapers and away from television screens; some carpet, but not too much (because punters put out their cigarettes on the floor); and the cheapest possible ceiling tiles (because punters never looked up at them). He found that there were 45 different types of controls for working the central heating systems in the shops, and 57 different time-switch controls. One standard control was adopted for each. Robinson rolled out a revolutionary new shop design based on a metal framework that could hold newspaper panels, shelves and betting slip dispensers and was easy to fit and replace, which enabled three shops to be fitted out for what it had previously cost for two – and looked much better. By the end of the ten-year period 700 William Hill shops had been re-sited, extended or obtained new licences, with no fewer than 180 of the most profitable shops situated in new developments.

Brown looked at marketing: 'Abstract, waffle-type marketing was not for me. Our theme was price-led advertising.' On telephone betting, he gave overwhelming priority to convenience, and was surprised by the success of a promotion offering free calls to customers. Using its existing system, William Hill improved its service so that it could capture a telephone bet within 19 seconds, and give secret priority to high-stake customers. It took up the offer of an improved system from British Telecom that showed calls waiting and allowed staff to be switched to man the phones at the start of big races.

At David Lowrey's prompting, on Grand National Day 1990 William Hill became the first bookmaker to launch credit card betting by telephone; British Telecom reported that its network had been jammed by calls. Media protests at the provision of gambling on credit led the banks to withdraw the facility after two days, albeit ultimately temporarily, but they were open to the use of Switch, the first debit cards, which William Hill introduced later the same year, though initially they insisted on manual clearance of bets over £10, which threatened excessive delay to customers. It was an innovation of lasting success. In 1995, debit cards accounted for one-third of William Hill's telephone turnover; in 1998, that figure rose to 47%.

Brown also decided to address the persistent problem of illegal betting. With betting tax resulting effectively in a 10% surcharge for punters, there were plenty of opportunist bookies in clubs, pubs and factories happy to take advantage by offering deduction-free betting. Bookies didn't threaten pub business by selling alcoholic drinks: why should Hills allow their business to be threatened? Brown put his head of security Chris Bird on the case, who asked staff to keep their eyes and ears open for any examples of illegal gambling that could be reported. 'These cases were taken to court and the landlords lost their licences,' says John Samuels, author of *Down at the Bookies*, who worked on the project with Bird. 'It was a long, hard slog and an expensive exercise – our action proved invaluable in early 2001 when the betting industry was trying to convince the government it should change the whole betting tax regime.'

The final element of Brown's turn-round strategy was relentless cost-cutting, an initiative whose name, 'Cut the Crap', reflected the character of the man, and at times involved a Gladstonian search for candle-end savings. First-class rail travel was banned for all but exceptional circumstances, saving the annual profit of a mid-range betting shop, and he demanded the use of second-class postage and the end of A4 envelopes, since it was significantly cheaper to fold documents in half and stuff them into an A5.

William Hill were the first to introduce credit card betting in 1990.

All of these efforts were conducted against the background of a long and bitter dispute with Grand Met over the purchase price of William Hill, and a simultaneous battle with the white knight, George Walker, to keep him from using William Hill's healthy cash flow to sustain his increasingly sickly empire. In September 1990

Brent Walker froze a £50 million payment due to Grand Met, the final instalment of the purchase price, on the grounds that William Hill profits for 1989 were well below the £51 million trigger, and demanded a £160 million refund. The William Hill Group's draft accounts had indeed showed a profit of just £44 million, £14 million short of what Grand Met's figure indicated it to be, and suggested shortfalls from Grand Met's accounts under no fewer than 48 separate headings. According to John Brown, Grand Met had used techniques later made infamous by Enron and others, booking anticipated profits and cost savings before they had actually happened. In reply, Grand Met denounced Bob Lambert for being an 'old-fashioned accountant'.

Almost as soon as he had acquired William Hill, financial markets had turned against George Walker and his debt-loaded empire. The bank rate climbed to 15% in 1989, putting high stress on Brent Walker's repayments to its bankers, and fell back by only one percentage point the following year. William Hill was a major cash generator, and not surprisingly Brent Walker sought to borrow from it and even make use of its overdraft. Bob Lambert resisted, and told Brent Walker's finance director, Wilfred Aquilina, that he would charge them interest. Within months of the acquisition, Brent Walker had borrowed £45 million from William Hill, including money due to pay general betting duty to HM Customs and Excise. The banks objected and even threatened legal action against John Brown and Bob Lambert – averted because they had been open about the loans and had charged interest – but henceforward William Hill's cashflow was to be ring-fenced.

Shortly after, John Brown fought off an urgent request from George Walker.

> Even after the bank said Brent Walker could not borrow it he came on the phone one day and said, 'I need £20 million, John, and I need it today.'

I said, 'But, George, you can't have it.'

He said, 'What do you mean I can't have it?'

I said, 'You know the banks have told us we can't give it to you.'

He said, 'That's my fucking business. I bought it and I want it today.'

Walker, Brown would reflect later, 'was the most amoral person I ever met in my life. He didn't know what morals were ... If it was right for William Hill, if it was right for George Walker, or if it was right for Brent Walker, he did it, he didn't care.'

At one point Brent Walker's share price had crashed from 72p to 18p, and in November it tumbled again. The best the company could do was negotiate a standstill on its loan repayments pending discussions of a £1 billion refinancing deal. The fates of both Brent Walker and William Hill were now in the hands of their bankers. William Hill's bankers, led by Hill Samuel, insisted on a new boardroom structure for Brent Walker that included Brown and Lambert joining the board. The banks appointed two independent directors, without whose assent Brent Walker would be unable to make any decisions about William Hill.

George Walker then twice attempted to secure use of a £2 million surplus in William Hill's pension fund to invest in a Cayman Islands company, and was twice frustrated, the first time when Brent Walker's company secretary Keith Dibble voted against it, the second when an article in the *Evening Standard* revealed his plan, which a furious Walker wrongly accused John Brown of leaking. This was less than a year before the Maxwell scandal at the *Daily Mirror*, and years later, according to Brown, Walker thanked Bob Lambert for resisting: 'Thank God you stopped me getting that money ... I'd have been in prison now if it wasn't for that.' At the end of 1990 the banks insisted on the removal of Brent Walker's finance director, Wilfred Aquilina, and George Walker's replacement as chairman (he continued as chief executive) by a City grandee, Lord Kindersley, who would also take that role for William Hill.

Five months later, in May 1991, matters came to a head when Brent Walker's delayed accounts for the previous year revealed a £256 million loss, with a write-down of £600 million in assets. At vital refinancing talks to discuss asset sales, the 60 banks to which Brent Walker reportedly owed £1.5 billion demanded George Walker's resignation, which he refused. Lord Kindersley then said he intended to call a board meeting to oust Walker, failing which the banks would put Brent Walker into liquidation, as should Grand Met win its action to recover the deferred £50 million it would put William Hill in breach of its covenants and the banks could demand payment of their loans. On liquidation William Hill would then be worth far less than its £685 million purchase price. John Brown attended a crucial meeting packed with some 50 lawyers, advisers and potential administrators of William Hill, led by Eric Nasland, the tough-minded Standard Chartered Bank executive responsible for debt recovery. When Nasland saw Nicholas Ward, the Brent Walker chief executive, taking notes he walked out, saying he wasn't prepared to have Ward writing down what he was saying. It left a stunned silence. 'The only sound,' recalled Brown, 'was the lawyers working out their bills.' The banks finally agreed on tighter ring-fencing of William Hill's cash and Brent Walker's decision-making.

The climactic board meeting on Wednesday 29 May was preceded by what must have been a stilted dinner at George Walker's expense in a Brent Walker casino on Park Lane (near where William Hill's head office had once stood), at which Lord Kindersley told John Brown he would have to remove George Walker as chief executive or risk receivership for Brent Walker. The next day at the meeting at Brent Walker's Trocadero offices (another Hill's haunt from earlier days), Walker made a passionate speech for half an hour, dwelling on his personal efforts to save his empire and the high-profile friends, including Michael Smurfit and Tiny Rowland, he had induced to support him. He refuted Kindersley's contention about the threat of receivership. Malcolm Williamson, the head of Standard Chartered, said the threat was not a bluff and put it in writing. Alan Carr, a senior partner at the board's legal advisers, assured the directors that the threat was real and that their duty to shareholders was to save the company from receivership. 'It was getting very late, after midnight,' recalled John Brown. Kindersley insisted on a vote. Six directors voted for Walker's removal, five against, and there were three abstentions. 'I voted against George,' admits Brown.

> It was the worst moment of my business life. I was voting to remove the man who had put me in charge of William Hill and put me on the board of a public company. I considered myself a friend of his, but I couldn't let my liking of George stand in the way of preventing Brent Walker being brought down.

Walker, the 62-year-old chief executive, was out of the company he'd founded.

'I believe after six hours of aggression from the banks,' he said at the time, 'that my board of directors succumbed to their pressure. I was amazed more than surprised. It was a frightening experience.' Ken Scobie became the new chief executive. 'I got on fine with George,' reflected Len Cowburn later – 'but he didn't even let his own right hand know what his left was doing.'

Walker and his wife Jean still owned 27% of Brent Walker – which now had a capital value of £17.5 million while owing, according to John Brown, 'about £1.4 billion' – and remained on the board until December 1991, an obstacle to refinancing negotiations. In August Kindersley called in the Serious Fraud Office to investigate irregularities, mainly in Brent Walker's film and property interests. Finally, in March 1992 a refinancing package of £1.6 billion for

Brent Walker was agreed by its banks. Lord Kindersley stood down as chairman (of Brent Walker and Hills), and it proved hard to find a replacement, but he was succeeded initially by Ken Scobie, who also took on both roles, until eventually Sir Keith Bright, former head of London Transport, was recruited in January 1993, also for both jobs. That year saw the departure from William Hill of Len Cowburn, who had joined the company in 1967; the following year he would re-emerge in the industry as a non-executive director of Stanley Leisure, eventually becoming their deputy chairman in 2000. Len had been happy to continue his interest in industry politics, for which John Brown was grateful: 'I'd never have been able to cope if [they] had been stuffed into my already bulging inbox.'

By March 1994 William Hill was due to repay £350 million in bank loans, and the banks warned that they would not roll over any debt or issue any new loans. Brown observes: 'We were making about £50 million profit a year, but we were only able to pay the interest on the loan.' This left a simple choice: either sell William Hill, or float it on the Stock Exchange. The syndicate of lenders and the company's legal advisers recommended a float, but the major lenders, Standard Chartered and Lloyds, secretly lobbied Bright against it. Lazards advised the Brent Walker board that a flotation would raise a maximum of £500 million – John Brown disputed some of their assumptions – and that the banks would do better to refinance William Hill. Shortly before the flotation prospectus was due for issue, Standard Chartered and Lloyds met the boards of both William Hill and Brent Walker and told them they would guarantee to repay all the other banks. Just before Christmas both boards opted on legal advice for the guarantee of refinancing William Hill rather than the uncertain result of a flotation. The remainder of Brent Walker would be held together, and its assets sold off, while William Hill was rebuilt. 'William Hill was the glue,' wrote John Brown, 'that held Brent Walker together while it built up and sold its other assets.'

In June 1994 George Walker and Brent Walker's former finance director, Wilfred Aquilina, appeared in court on charges of false accounting, theft and conspiracy. In October Walker was cleared, Aquilina convicted on one charge of false accounting. For the first half of 1995 Brent Walker unveiled a loss of £51.4 million; William Hill an operating profit of £22 million, compared to £33 million for the corresponding period a year earlier, clearly showing the impact of the new National Lottery. It would be 1996 before Brent Walker would finally turn the corner and report its first true profit since its near-collapse in 1990, but in the same year the sale of its Pubmaster chain for £171 million – all swallowed up by bank debts – left as its assets only William Hill and a few properties.

In late September 1996 the vital court case on the disputed deal with Grand Met over William Hill's 1989 profits and the discount on Brent Walker's purchase price was at last resolved, the arbitrator ruling that Brent Walker had paid almost £118 million more than it should have done – 'Vindication,' pronounced John Brown, who hastily booked a jazz band to appear at Hill's Wood Green head office to play 'Congratulations!' and 'We're in the Money', along with champagne, balloons and streamers. A surreal moment ensued when a TV crew arrived at the offices to conduct an interview with Graham Sharpe about the potential financial disaster facing the company following Frankie Dettori's 'Magnificent Seven', which had happened a couple of days earlier, costing William Hill alone £8 million plus and the industry over £40 million, but found a building full of happy, cheering staff, who had just heard the news from John Brown over the internal PA. 'We must have looked like wonderfully good losers,' mused Brown.

During 1997 the financial pages reported rumours that first Coral, then even the Tote, were seeking to buy William Hill, but overnight on 9 October the troubled association with Brent Walker finally came to an end as the Japanese bank Nomura International, through its investment arm run by Guy Hands, paid a reported

£700 million to acquire William Hill, complete with its 1,515 UK betting shops and 9,000 staff, a deal that spelled the end of Brent Walker's time on the Stock Exchange (and Sir Brian Goswell's as current Hill's chairman – 'yet another who knew nothing about the business', in John Brown's words). 'I always said William Hill was worth that much,' was George Walker's verdict. 'I fought to keep that company when they were trying to sell it for £430 million so I'm pretty pleased with myself.' Nomura had outbid the brewers Bass, venture capitalists CVC Partners – favoured by Hill's management – and a joint offer from NatWest and the Prudential by at least £20 million, buying the company through the newly created Grand Bookmaking Company. John Brown and Bob Lambert were officially told the news just after midnight – 'All the big City firms are constitutionally incapable of finalising an agreement during normal working hours! At 1am Nomura rustled up a roast chicken dinner and bottle of wine for us.'

The following year Brown invited Nomura's top man Hands to Royal Ascot, and was shocked when he arrived wearing a hired suit that 'seemed to be three sizes too big. His top hat was balanced precariously on his ears and the bottoms of his trousers were in concertina folds … we all had such a laugh.' But as he was used to, star financier and investor Hands had the last laugh, as 'he still managed to back the first three winners.'

CHAPTER 22
SECOND TIME LUCKY

Perhaps it seems less of a surprise now than it did at the time that, just eight months after buying William Hill, Nomura's boss Guy Hands was reported to be preparing to bring William Hill to the stock market. Sure enough, in January 1999 plans were unveiled for a £900 million stock market flotation to take place the following March. 'This business belongs on the stock market,' John Brown was quoted telling the *Daily Mirror*. 'It does not belong within some conglomerate.' It was a very profitable business and very cash-generative, he added, major investments were to be made in its telephone and internet betting arms, and 'there is probably room to buy another 300 to 400 shops over the next three to four years.' Shares were expected to cost between £1.55 and £1.75 and would be subject to a minimum £1,000 investment, it was suggested.

The prospectus for the flotation gives a good snapshot of the business in 1997. Its total turnover in that year was £1.673 billion. Of this, 84% derived from betting shops, 14% from telephone betting and 1% from on-course betting. The core business of the shops – taking bets on sporting events – generated 99% of shop turnover, that is, £1.383 billion, of which over 70% came from horseracing and just under 20% from greyhounds. Other sports, including football in this year with no World Cup or European Nations championship, and betting on special events (such as the Oscars), produced only £79 million (6%).

Clearly, William Hill was still dependent on traditional betting. But revenues from this source had been essentially static: £1.549 billion in 1995, £1.574 billion in 1997. Total revenues had grown by £122 million – but most of this had derived from three new sources.

Numbers betting contributed £52 million in 1997 and amusement-with-prizes machines £20 million. These had been virtually non-existent in 1995. In that year, index betting contributed just £1 million; in 1997 this had risen to £25 million. Taken together, the three new activities had accounted for some 80% of William Hill's growth since 1995.

The figures for telephone betting demonstrated the success of William Hill's pioneering introduction of debit card betting. Total telephone betting revenues had risen from £181 million in 1995 to £237 million in 1997. Debit card betting revenues rose by £40 million to £103 million, overtaking traditional credit account betting, which fell from £108 million to £101 million. As already suggested, index (or spread) betting was the other major source of growth.

A further significant challenge to Hills at the end of 1997 had been headed off in 1998, when the new Trade and Industry Secretary, Peter Mandelson, blocked Ladbrokes' proposed takeover of Coral. It would have made Ladbrokes the nation's biggest bookmaker for good, joining Coral's 833 shops to its own 1,904, against William Hill's 1,515. Ladbrokes were ordered to sell all of their interests in Coral within six months, and subsequently other, less threatening, potential buyers for Coral emerged.

In the final week of the flotation Warburg Dillon Read, the merchant bankers handling the process, told Nomura it would not manage to achieve the target price, and on the last day Nomura disappointed John Brown and Bob Lambert by agreeing to cut the price from 155p a share to 135p, reducing the market valuation of William Hill from £840 million to £780 million.

Reluctantly, the two men continued with a final set of presentations to Barings and Lazards, but before this could happen they took a secret telephone call from Guy Hands, who told them he had no intention of selling the business for £780 million, and wanted to pull the flotation and sell William Hill to Cinven CVC for £825 million. If Brown and Lambert agreed, they would be invited to stay on, and be paid a bonus equivalent to a sale at the original minimum price of £840 million.

On 20 February 1999, therefore, Nomura sold William Hill to Cinven CVC – the same companies who less than two years earlier had been unwilling to pay £650 million for the company. Nomura agreed to compensate the small investors who'd applied for shares – said to be more than 100,000 – by adding a goodwill payment equivalent to two weeks' interest at 5% when cheques were returned, with William Hill adding a £20 betting voucher (for a tricky Lincoln-Grand National double). The *Daily Mirror* estimated that selling instead of floating would have saved Nomura some £4 million and Guy Hands personally £4.5 million. 'We hear that he is holed up in Barbados – and if he has any sense, that's where he'll stay,' fulminated its City Slicker column.

In 2013 Guy Hands, now chairman of private equity firm Terra Firma, assessed William Hill's short period under Nomura's ownership:

After 16 years of sustained success with William Hill going from strength to strength, it is surprising to consider that, back in 1997, its future was seen as hanging in the balance. Its owners, Brent Walker, had been forced by the banks to put it up for sale. The consensus was that the then relatively new National Lottery would cannibalise other forms of betting and that William Hill, as a male-dominated, high-street-focused, horse and greyhound betting establishment, was doomed to decline.

We took a different view. We were attracted by the asset-backed nature of the business, and we saw the upside that William Hill, with new strategic direction, would be able to produce. In particular, we believed that revenue could be grown, most notably through the development of new channels including telephone and online betting, as well as repositioning the business to be less male-dominated, and providing products which appealed both to women and to a younger audience.

We felt that the National Lottery provided the opportunity for the rebirth of the betting industry. It would legitimise gambling and generate pressure to relax the then severe restrictions on the sector. For example, shop windows would no longer need to be blacked out.

Unusually for firms going through a change of ownership, the leadership team, led by John Brown, did not reject change but embraced it – John could soon be seen playing with a laptop in the back of his Bentley (which he bought, appropriately from the proceeds of a bet). Soon he and his colleagues were focusing on bringing William Hill into the 21st century.

In just two years, the equity value of William Hill increased by over £120 million. However, Nomura (our shareholder) wanted to sell, and we reluctantly started plans to float William Hill on the London Stock Exchange. William Hill at the time still had much positive change to implement, and it was not surprising that at the start of 1999 we received an alternative and attractive offer from a private equity consortium which we accepted.

It was with great sadness that we saw William Hill switch ownership. However, it was also with some pride that we watched the company continue to grow under John's leadership and fulfil its potential. Today William Hill is a truly great British institution.

That reference to Brown's Bentley is spot-on. The fulfilment of what had been one of his ambitions was the result of a hefty bet he struck at the 1998 Glorious Goodwood meeting, which cost £1,310 with the Tote and Coral, and involved 25/1, 11/2 and 7/1 winners

– landing him a payout of 'about £75,000'. To celebrate he bought himself the secondhand red Bentley. Not content with that, the next year at the same meeting he hit Coral for 'another £70,000'.

Hands and Brown hit it off as friends and John later revealed that Hands 'told me I was the only chief executive of a company he bought whom he hadn't got rid of. I told him he was the only chairman of William Hill I hadn't got rid of.'

Towards the end of 2000 Cinven CVC in turn planned a flotation of the company, and in October David Harding was brought in as chief executive (the first with no business background in betting) to prepare the company for flotation. John Brown became chairman. Then aged 44, Harding had a family background in betting: his grandfather had been an illegal bookmaker in Lincolnshire, his mother a settler for a small bookmaker in Northern Ireland, and in his own words, 'My dad had always been a punter.' In a varied early career he had been a golf professional, struggled to export cars for a still-nationalised British Leyland and worked in the bush in Papua New Guinea for two years. He then joined PA Consulting as an expert in performance improvement and strategic marketing, next operations director at Mercury One2One telecommunications. At Charles Schwab he had launched their European internet share-trading operation, and then went to the Prudential Group, first as managing director of Life and Pensions (L&P), later becoming deputy chief executive of its subsidiary Scottish Amicable. 'On every single one of them I got down to the ground floor,' says Harding, 'and I understood enough about the business before I started making any changes.' Some of these appointments had mixed fortunes, but they gave him expertise in mathematics, telecommunications and online operations that was highly relevant to William Hill.

The public reason for the flotation was to give William Hill financial muscle. But Harding acknowledges that it also gave Cinven CVC the opportunity to exit from their investment, as all private equity houses will eventually do.

Even before the advent of gross profits tax and deduction-free betting, William Hill's revenues were buoyant in 2001. From £1.65 billion in 1999, total revenues rose by 23% to £2.042 billion in 2000, and then to £2.452 billion in 2001. Allowing for the fact that the financial year for 2001 contained 53 weeks, that represented a further increase of 17.8% – achieved in a year when the racing programme was curtailed by a foot-and-mouth outbreak. Traditional betting shop turnover rose to £1.722 billion, telephone betting turnover by £140 million to £420 million, while online turnover stood at £274 million in 2001.

Cinven CVC chose Schroder Salomon Smith Barney as their advisers on the flotation. Their first advice was that John Brown should stand down as chairman, to ease acceptance of the flotation by major financial institutions, but stay on as deputy chairman or as a non-executive director to continue to deal with political and industry-wide issues. 'I don't think the City was over-enamoured with me telling them they'd fucked it up the first time round,' Brown recalled candidly, 'and I hoped they weren't going to fuck it up this time. They don't like it, do they? Being told they're schoolkids and don't know what they're doing.' He resisted the pressure, suggesting that investors might like to see some continuity in a business with a recently appointed chief executive and finance director, and continued as chairman on the understanding that he would retire at the first AGM after the flotation, since it was contrary to the City's code of governance for public companies to have a former CEO as chairman. By now, William Hill also had a new finance director, Bob Lambert having retired in March 2001. The new man, Tom Singer, was just 39, with a background as a McKinsey management consultant and three years as finance director of Moss Bros.

The flotation prospectus in 2002 had a much stronger message for investors than the one prepared in 1998. It presented William Hill as a market leader in all major betting channels in the UK. It was the second-largest operator of UK betting shops, with a nationwide network of 1,536 shops, all well-sited, with 45% in London and the South East where average stakes per bet were highest. It was the market leader in telephone betting, with 40% of total industry turnover, based on a sustained record of innovation, including freephone and debit card betting. The prospectus noted that William Hill's online operations had generated operating profits of £9.2 million, 3.4% of total online turnover of £274 million. In the directors' view, this was the most profitable online betting operation in the United Kingdom. The prospectus noted William Hill's plans to allow customers to combine telephone and online betting and use of its online casino in a single account. There was also a particularly good growth story. 'William Hill has achieved long-term growth in gross win at a compound annual rate of 9.8%, increasing in every year from 1999 to 2001.' This was attributed to four factors: promoting higher-margin products such as numbers betting and football betting; developing new online product channels with high growth opportunities; longer trading hours; and exit from unprofitable or unpromising businesses.

The flotation was highly successful. The first indicative share prices ranged between 190p and 240p a share, giving a middle valuation of William Hill at £1.42 billion. However, in its final week the share offer was so well received that the ultimate price struck was 225p a share. On the first day's trading, on 20 June 2002, it rose to 241p. Immediately there was speculation that, as the *Daily Express* put it, 'the odds [are] shortening on William Hill going on the acquisition trail.'

At his last AGM in 2003, John Brown as chairman was able to present another strong performance for 2002, his summary of the flotation strategy encapsulating his philosophy throughout his time at William Hill: 'focusing on organic growth in the businesses and markets that we know well ... and taking advantage of product and technical innovation.' Total turnover, in the first full year of deduction-free betting and with a World Cup boost, had risen by no less than 37% over 2001 to reach £3.365 billion. A further 35 betting shops, the H&K Commissions chain, had been purchased for £21 million, taking the total number of shops up to 1,579, as had Sunderland greyhound track (Brough Park, Newcastle, would be added the following year). Gross win had risen by 5% to £528 million, and gross profit by 14% to £416 million. Profit on ordinary activities before finance charges, taxation and exceptional costs had increased by 26% to £141 million; profit after tax and before exceptional costs had risen by 218% to £59 million – the third successive year, Brown noted, of at least double-digit profit growth.

John Brown retired as chairman on the last day of 2003 in his 45th year with the company that had taken him literally from the bottom to the top of the pile. The respected racing writer and broadcaster Alastair Down got it right when he referred to Brown as 'a genuine titan among the major bookmaking figures of the post-war era'. 'Funnily enough, William Hill had a similar reputation to mine,' Brown mused looking back:

> I admit I was never over-generous at patting people on the back. I've never looked for it myself and never really saw why people needed it. As chief executive I'd had to live with several chairmen, and in one way or another all of them were a bleeding nuisance. In my view the chief executive's job is to care about business first and people second. Who ever met a really good man-manager who also produced great results? I certainly haven't met that universal genius yet.

He took a well-earned retirement, much of it still being spent pleasurably, if unprofitably, as a racehorse owner.

CHAPTER 23

NEW WAYS OF BETTING

The National Lottery had been launched in November 1994, the brainchild of the Tory Prime Minister, John Major. With tickets available for £1 a time from newsagents, corner shops and supermarkets, scratchcards for those who wanted an instant flutter, and a weekly prime-time draw on Saturday nights live on the BBC for seven-figure prizes, it started out with huge advantages over the more traditional forms of gambling. The minimum age to 'play', as it was disingenuously couched, was 16, as against 18 to bet with a bookmaker. It was advertised in parts of the media where other forms of betting were not permitted, and to complete the burden it became the only subject on which bookmakers were prohibited by law from taking bets. There was even the added 'appeal' that a significant proportion of the proceeds were to be directed to 'good causes' (not all of which would be universally approved). 'The country will be a lot richer because of the Lottery,' declared Major at the time. 'It is in every sense the people's Lottery.'

It quickly established itself as the world's most successful lottery, and as early as the middle of 1995 its impact on William Hill – as on all bookmakers' business – was as bad as John Brown and other pessimists had feared. For the first half of the year William Hill's operating profits were £22 million, down by a third from £33 million during the corresponding period in 1994. 'All our little punters who had two-quid bets were going to play the Lottery for a pound,' Brown later explained bluntly, 'and we were going to lose it.' A William Hill initiative to profit from the Lottery by selling tickets from kiosks under the name of Norwich Enterprises proved short-lived. Independent research by the Henley Centre suggested that in 1995 the impact of the Lottery was to depress gross revenues in UK bookmaking by approximately 9% and profit-ability by approximately 32%. In an interview with John McCririck on Channel 4 Racing Brown called for a cut in betting tax, and in November the Chancellor of the Exchequer Ken Clarke did make a modest concession, cutting it by 1% to 6.75%, allowing a reduction in total punters' deductions from 10% to 9%.

But a more positive response was needed. Brown pressed for bookmakers to be allowed to take bets on the National Lottery numbers, but the idea never gained traction, even when endorsed in 2001 by the Budd Committee on gambling.

There was nothing to stop them betting on foreign lotteries, however – indeed, to Brown's ire, it *was* legal in Ireland to bet on Britain's lottery! 'They were betting on our lottery, we couldn't … I'm sitting there and I'm thinking we'll bet on the Irish lottery, fuck them. If we can't bet on our own, we'll embarrass the government into allowing betting on ours.' Coral rejected outright his proposal for an industry-wide initiative, as did Ladbrokes after long hesita-tion – both firms had betting shops in the Irish Republic and were nervous of upsetting the Irish government. This was not a factor for William Hill: 'We had no betting shops in Ireland and it was abso-lutely nil downside.' Ian Spearing, who'd joined Hills in 1991, in-tially in a six month consultancy role, after 19 years with Ladbrokes – for whom he'd been MD of their Belgian and Dutch operations – attended an executive board meeting at which the practicalities were discussed:

> I remember John Brown asking Liam McGuigan, our Operations Director, the cost of producing posters and bet-ting slips: £10,000. No one had confidence that the product, named Lucky Choice [by Hill's marketing chief of the time, David Hickling], would work. It involved customers betting on an event that required no skill, and was not televised any-where in the UK. It offered guaranteed odds pay-outs of up

to £100,000 for successfully selecting up to five numbers, or £422 for three exactly. At no stage in our history as book-makers had we launched such a type of bet in our shops.

Lucky Choice launched in November 1995, and in its first week produced new revenues of £400,000 and a gross win of £200,000. Within three months it was making £150,000 profit a week, and £8 million a year in additional gross profit. Characteristically, William Hill kept its success quiet and John Brown told industry inquirers that the new venture was 'poor, ticking over but it's a right struggle'. Eventually, first Coral and then Ladbrokes discovered its success and followed suit.

'Having satisfied ourselves that customers were prepared to bet on "non-skill" products,' says Ian Spearing, 'the question was how to take this forward. The answer was that we developed the first product run by bookmakers for bookmakers.' Lucky Choice had one problem: the Irish Lottery was drawn only twice a week – so John Brown hit on the idea of introducing a draw modelled on the Las Vegas numbers game, Keno. He hesitated for a long time, for fear it would be classed as an unlawful lottery, but eventually, after much legal research and advice, decided that the game had the character of a bet at fixed odds on the result of an event. This time, Coral and Ladbrokes joined the launch of the new game, called 49s, and they approached other bookmakers to have the draw shown on SIS. The big three set up a separate company, 49s Ltd, and the operation was funded by a charge of £5 a week for every betting shop using the facility. Some smaller bookmakers objected to the proposed fee, but William Hill pressed ahead without them. Ian Spearing went to France with Alan Ross of Ladbrokes to ac-quire two Lottery Draw machines, similar to the National Lottery machine, and arranged for a studio to be built at SIS.

The first draw was held on 16 December 1996, offering odds of 11/2 for finding one correct number, up to 99,999/1 for selecting five.

49s was another rapid success, most of the reluctant bookmakers decided to join, and within months it was on offer in 90% of all betting shops. SIS put 49s on their regular package, and staged draws during race meetings as well as before and after. David Costello, a baker from Cheltenham, was 49s' first six-figure winner, his £5 bet on a combination of numbers bringing him £107,128.50. 'As if he kneaded the dough . . .' pondered William Hill's press office. 'The most popular 49s bet was to pick three numbers where bookmakers paid circa £400 [now £601],' recalled Ian Spearing, 'versus the perceived £10 from the National Lottery, albeit on a different basis. This comparison featured strongly in 49s' advertising. Clearly, 49s and the advertising of it was a direct attack on the National Lottery.' Its success was briefly threatened when Camelot challenged it in court as an unlawful lottery, but the judge agreed with William Hill's carefully prepared legal argument, ruling that the fixed-odds payment on winning numbers gave 49s 'predominantly the aspects of betting'. Emboldened, William Hill launched another game, Magic Numbers, in which punters picked four numbers from 20, with a new game every ten minutes. Rapido, a further numbers betting variation, was introduced in January 2000.

Numbers betting made a major contribution to restored profitability. William Hill's revenues from this source rose from £200,000 in 1995 to £18.8 million in 1996 and £52.4 million in 1997, some 3% of William Hill's total turnover, 'but a far bigger percentage of profits', John Brown pointed out. Indeed, at much lower risk than traditional betting, it was far and away William Hill's most profitable activity, with a gross win percentage (total receipts less total payments to winning punters, expressed as a percentage of total receipts) of 47.3% compared to 22.9% for the core business of betting shops. All this, while revenues from traditional betting products were virtually static. Besides its contribution to profitability, numbers betting widened William Hill's customer base, particularly by attracting more women. Today, the numbers betting margin is around 23%.

Mike Quigley ran William Hill Index when it launched in 1995.

Also in 1995, Hills became the first of the big bookmakers to move into another new field, that of spread betting, with the launch in September of William Hill Index. 'Sports spread betting has enjoyed a dramatic growth over the last two years,' explained the company's group racing director, David Lowrey, 'and persistent requests from existing clients prompted us to investigate all aspects of the market.' Spread betting is loosely based on the way stocks and shares are dealt, and to offer it Hills had had to obtain a licence from the Security and Futures Authority. Mike Quigley, Index's 47-year-old general manager, had a favoured way of explaining the concept:

> Suppose England are playing the West Indies in a cricket Test match. We might quote a spread of the England score from 300 to 320 runs. An account holder could place a buy

order for, say £5, if they thought England would do better. This means that for every run above 320 that they scored the punter would win £5. Likewise, for every run below 320, they would lose a fiver. If they thought England was likely to get skittled out cheaply, they could place a 'sell' order, and win the amount staked for every run below 300 England scored, but lose it for each one above that figure.

The new department operated out of offices in Finsbury Park in London alongside the company's international operation for foreign-based clients, though that would later move to the Isle of Man for tax reasons. It had 15 staff: telephonists to trade by taking buy and sell bets, and dealers to set the spreads and calculate liabilities. The traders, selected on the basis of their sporting interests and knowledge, all underwent an intensive training course. The first bet taken – a £200-a-point superiority bet on the American football team, the 49ers – was a loser, netting Hill's £600 profit. 'To be honest,' confessed Quigley, 'from a publicity point of view I'd have preferred it the other way round . . .'

'We were expecting maybe a couple of thousand customers in the first year,' Quigley said, but 'within a couple of months we had signed up our first thousand clients.' As well as Hill's account holders trying it out, the company was attracting customers away from the three existing companies offering this type of betting. Unlike fixed-odds betting, debts from this activity were enforceable by law (other gambling debts have since also become recoverable), and 'for that reason we were required to send a risk warning notice to all potential customers,' explained Quigley, 'to make sure they understood what spread betting is all about.' To those critics who further feared that clients might be tempted into markets with potentially unlimited losses, he pointed out that 'the fact that we had stop-losses on 90% of our markets helped, because people knew the maximum they could be letting themselves in for.'

Quigley opened up a new avenue of spread betting in November 1995, pulling off something of a coup by getting permission from the Football Association to bet on goals superiority on single, non-televised Football League matches. Since fixed-odds singles on such games were not permitted at the time, it hadn't occurred to anyone before him to make such a request in the spread-betting market, 'so we advertised singles on the Premiership, etc., in the *Racing Post*,' recalled Quigley – 'throwing the rest of the industry into disbelief for a few days, until everyone fell into line.'

However, once David Harding had become chief executive he took the decision to end the company's interest in spread betting. 'I think the market turned out to be a lot smaller than senior management had anticipated,' reflects Quigley. 'Plus, there was no expertise within the company to expand it to the much larger financial spread market. One of the biggest problems was retaining dealers and market makers who, generally, we recruited from the shops and trained up – the better ones were then immediately targeted by competitors, who had far superior salary structures at the time.' So Harding bit the bullet: 'I shut it down – it was quite a big decision. Analysts loved it. We tried everything we could to market it but just couldn't create enough interest to justify continuing with it.' In May 2001, therefore, William Hill Index was transferred to the IG Group.

The following year another innovation hit William Hill's shops. On 22 May 2002 a new racecourse opened for business, with the 1.08 the first race from Portman Park, broadcast via SIS for customers to bet on. This was the debut of virtual racing – 'vertical racing', as a cabbie pal once called it, or indeed 'cartoon racing': artificially generated, increasingly realistic images showing events unfolding in real time. Miles Philips of 49s.co.uk explains how virtual works:

A certified RNG (Random Number Generator) provides the result to the machine, but only within a millisecond of the race going 'off'. At the time they leave the gates or line they are moved forward or back 'live' to produce the result at the end of the race. The races are not pre-recorded. Each virtual track has hundreds of horse and dog names that are track-specific. We have made them all up, and regularly check them against real horses and dog names to make sure we don't clash. To understand how it all works, imagine a lotto machine with 100 balls in it. If we take a 10-runner race, with an even-money favourite and a 100/1 outsider, the evens favourite would have 50 balls allocated to it and the 100/1 shot would only have one ball allocated to it. It's actually rather more complicated than that, as it is handled by an algorithm, but it's a good analogy.

Clients soon realised it would not be any easier to find the winners than at any of the real tracks, as 14/1 shot Sweet Woodruff galloped home in the first race. Steepledowns was the next course introduced, in November, followed by Sprint Valley in April 2005. 'The British Horseracing Board head office at the time was in Portman Square,' remembers Miles Philips: 'It's just a coincidence that we called the first Virtual Horse Racing track Portman Park!' Not to be outdone, virtual greyhound racing made its debut in May 2003 when Neath Abbey Blue from trap 5 at 9/2 was the first winner at Millersfield. Brushwood virtual dog stadium followed. Millersfield was named after the famous greyhound Mick the Miller. 'All races are broadcast live over the SIS network,' explains Philips.

The servers are housed in a secure unit with CCTV camera coverage; they are not connected directly to the outside world – i.e. no internet access – and we have had them pen-tested [hackers try and break into the system] and they passed with flying colours.

Astonishingly, in June 2014, a Hill customer backed 25/1, 16/1, 66/1, 25/1, 28/1 and 33/1 winners in a £12.60, 20p unit, bet at Steepledowns and Portman Park – winning £14,279.80.

Meanwhile a further innovation had by now become a significant contributor of revenue. New legislation introduced in June 1996 allowed two so-called amusement-with-prizes or 'fruit' machines to be installed in any betting shop, with a maximum individual payout of £10. By the end of 1997 William Hill had installed no fewer than 2,335, an average of 1.54 per shop. Even in 1996, their first year, they generated £9 million in revenue; in 1997 it was £20 million. In October 1998 maximum cash prizes for these AWPs (Amusement With Prize machines) increased from £10 to £15, and again at the beginning of 2002 from £15 to £25. Kevin Hogan, operations director (Machines) for William Hill discussed the popularity of AWPs with *BOS* magazine.

> In the last six years the perception of AWPs has changed. Whereas in 1996 it was thought the introduction of AWPs into betting shops would detract from revenue that was already about to be stretched by the National Lottery, now there probably isn't an independent or larger chain that would not admit to the increase in business, especially in the early mornings. In some shops it is the only activity early on before racing starts. Young males seem to have a rota of shops and come and play their favourite games.

Hogan said the games were changed 'on average four times a year, keeping up the interest in new games'. But the same year, 2002, saw a yet more significant development.

Steve Frater had been head of customer relations at first Mecca and then William Hill before leaving the company to open betting shops with his business partner Walter Grubmuller. They founded a company called Global Draw and devised the first fixed-odds betting terminals.FOBTs are electromechanical devices that allow players to make bets at fixed odds on a wide range of games and events – some familiar, such as roulette, bingo and simulated horse or greyhound races, others specially invented numbers games. The major attraction to punters is FOBTs' convenience and speed, allied to their simplicity. They demand no expert knowledge, hold an attraction to punters, and also to their operators, with guaranteed returns (in the medium term) of between 2.5% and 5% on the various games.

'The concept didn't start as an FOBT,' recalled Frater, by then managing director of Global Draw, in a 2005 interview with *BOS* magazine (a year later the company would be sold to the US gaming systems giant Scientific Games for a reported £104 million). 'It was about numbers betting. The idea was to produce an automated numbers draw in our shops. In those days you only had 49s, which was a live draw twice a day, and we could do an automated draw every five minutes.' Frater and his partner refined the idea and took legal advice to confirm that, providing the random number generator was offshore and beamed into the shops, the principle would be the same however frequent the draws might be. 'The first games involved sending a number down every ten seconds. That went to five seconds and then to one second. Although games can't be played in one second, it means that when anyone wants to place a bet there's always a number ready for them.' In 1998 Frater and Grubmuller put FOBTs into their own shops, and soon William Hill trialled them, starting with two machines in each of just ten branches, recalled David Steele, group corporate affairs director in 2014, who was asked by David Harding to become involved with FOBTs, despite the boss believing that under the tax regime of the day 'they would never be profitable'. Harding remembers: 'All bookmakers were trialling self-service terminals with the same products as were available over the counter. At this stage the drive was more about cost saving than a new revenue stream and was being done parallel with Electronic Point of Sale (EPOS) trials.'

But when deduction-free betting came in, in October 2001 FOBTs came into their own. 'Gross Profits Tax revolutionised the product,' says David Steele. 'No tax meant that you could run the bets at a lower percentage take-out,' explained Steve Frater, 'so we brought in roulette. That's when the business really took off.' Coral were first to introduce them into their betting shops, with a strong promotion of roulette, and they were followed by Ladbrokes. David Harding thought Coral's roulette facility could be unlawful, because it was being offered on premises which had not been licensed for gaming and he raised his concern with the trade association, BOLA but Coral had a powerful counter-argument: 'If you think about it, every single bet on a roulette table is a fixed-odds bet.' William Hill installed its first terminals in shops in late 2001/ early 2002. 'We were cautious in the early days and it was a while before we moved our machine density up to circa four per shop in line with our main competitors,' said David Steele. The rapid success of Coral and Ladbrokes' roulette facility made it impossible for Hills not to follow suit. 'We were under competitive pressure but we pressed for QC's opinion through the trade association. When it came it was pretty unequivocal in favour of the legality of roulette in FOBTs,' so Harding okayed 'rolling them out across the estate'.

Now, along with Vaughan Ashdown and Chris Bell, the chief executives of Coral and Ladbrokes, David Harding was summoned to a meeting with the Sports Minister, Richard Caborn, and the chairman of the Gaming Board, Peter Dean, at which the industry was threatened with a legal challenge from the Gaming Board. They replied that they would welcome it, to clarify the law, and produced counsel's opinion that roulette could indeed be defended as a form of fixed-odds betting.

They were also armed with the recommendation of the Gambling Review Body's Budd Committee, among whose members was this book's co-author, Mihir Bose, that betting shops should now be allowed four 'jackpot' machines with a payout of £500.

This proved to be the basis of a compromise settlement. The industry would be allowed four FOBTs in each shop, subject to a voluntary code of conduct. They could offer roulette on each terminal but no other casino games. There would be a minimum time interval between bets, and terminals would carry warnings and help pages for problem gamblers. Payouts would be limited to a maximum of £500 with the maximum stake £100. The industry representatives resisted pressure from civil servants for a ceiling on roulette stakes, because that would have made multiple bets impossible; instead, the £500 limit was applied to winnings from bets on any single roulette square.

The industry was aware that the use of FOBTs was, as Steele says the relevant government minister put it, 'under probation' but the deal allowed for a rapid expansion of FOBTs. By the end of 2003 William Hill had installed 3,239, a density of 3.6 per shop. Each one averaged £380 in profit per week. In mid-2014 the company was operating over 9,000 of the machines. Gross win in 2003 from FOBTs and Amusement With Prizes machines (AWPs) was £100.5 million, up £59 million on the prior year.' 'You might think people put their money into the machines instead of making a "normal" bet,' Hill's finance director Tom Singer told the *Express*. 'But in fact, it is quite the reverse. People come in to play the machines and end up putting money over the counter.' David Harding pronounced himself 'gobsmacked' by the success of roulette in FOBTs. He noted that as a traditional game it consistently had far more appeal than the new gambling products which were introduced. He believed that the success of FOBTs annoyed the Blair government, which thought that it had been out-manoeuvred in the negotiations, and he blamed government spin doctors for a crop of media stories describing them as the 'crack cocaine' of gambling. The industry replied by commissioning independent

A familiar sight in current-day betting shops.

research from MORI and Europe Economics. Charles Scott's chairman's statement in William Hill's 2004 accounts drew attention to the gratifying results: 'We are pleased to report that the recent research ... showed no causal link between FOBTs and problem gambling. Accordingly, we believe that the regulatory risk to this part of the business has receded.' David Harding also noted that William Hill's roll-out of FOBTs was demand-led and there was no attempt to target particular areas or classes of customer, and that because FOBTs required cash, they were therefore slower and less dangerous to problem gamblers than online betting using credit or debit cards.

CHAPTER 24

THE MOVE TO THE INTERNET

William Hill had approached the millennium as a traditional, well-managed bookmaker. But almost all its growth prospects seemed to lie outside traditional betting products in betting shops: 80% of its growth since 1995 had come from three new activities: numbers betting, amusement-with-prizes machines and spread betting. The next phase of the company's development, under its new owners Cinven CVC, from early 1999, could therefore be described as an era of migration from traditional betting products. It took two forms. One was voluntary: migration to the internet in a search for a new channel of product delivery and new types of customer. The other was a response to a surprise move by a competitor: migration overseas to escape the impact of betting duty. The speed and success of this response not only protected William Hill's business, but also inspired the government to abolish General Betting Duty (GBD) and replace it with a gross profits tax (GPT) and thus inaugurated a new era for the entire betting industry.

The 1998 World Cup produced a record turnover for William Hill of approximately £40 million (by 2014 it would be over five times greater, despite England's dismal performance), and the company joined the internet revolution when, at the insistence of Nomura, it became the first major bookmaker to take World Cup bets via a website. 'We took £500,000 on it,' said John Brown. 'That convinced me that internet betting was here to stay.' However, it was still very much in its early stages, and the technology was not yet up to all the aspirations for it – 'It wasn't fast enough,' Brown complained. The new medium was not even mentioned in the flotation prospectus later that year, least of all in the description of the forward strategy.

But the new owners pushed John Brown harder. There was not enough public awareness of the new William Hill site, they said, and its customer base was growing too slowly. Brown had launched an advertising campaign on buses in London and Leeds and other major cities, but now, dissatisfied with the site's performance, he pulled them all, and commissioned outside specialists to design a new site. It looked pretty, but its light-blue lettering on a dark-blue background – the work of a 'poncy designer', grumbled Brown – made it hard to read, and it took too long to add new sports to its repertoire. Brown sent the software developers on their way and started over yet again by getting a new site designed in-house. Now dubbed Sportsbook, this was launched in August 1999, but still proved too slow. The addition of more computing power and new equipment brought improvements but exposed new problems. In the run-up to the 2000 Grand National it was promoted with a new advertising campaign: 'No queues on the web' – but on Grand National Day itself it crashed, as links to the Switch debit card system failed. The same problem recurred on another big betting day, the kick-off for the 2000–01 football season. William Hill called in outside help from IBM, Siemens and other specialists in online transactions, and painstakingly implemented hundreds of recommendations for improvements.

Within the company there was much debate over the content of the site. Predictably, John Brown resisted attempts to include extra elements such as horserace form and football league tables: above all he wanted a site that was 'very, very quick', with nothing that would slow it down – and in any case punters could get all this other information from other sources. All that was needed was for the site to work reliably and quickly. Even more strongly, he resisted pressures from Cinven CVC to do 'bounty deals' with new sports content providers, including the websites of leading football clubs. These providers were demanding an upfront payment simply for providing a link to the William Hill site, and a half-share in the gross profits from any customers who had used that link. Brown thought this was a waste of money. Just as with traditional betting, he was convinced that the way to win customers online was to offer them a convenient means of making bets at the best possible prices. 'All we had to do, once our site was right, was to get a customer to visit it once. If the site was good enough, he'd use it, and carry on using it.' For the first time John Brown acquired a personal computer and a laptop and perpetually checked the state of the William Hill site.

Eventually, under the chief executive's relentless prodding, improvements kicked in and the site became fast and reliable. Its business grew rapidly, so much so that the controls could not keep pace. Some customers took to opening accounts with credit cards and then disclaiming any losses by saying that the card was not theirs. Conversely, others would use someone else's card to deposit money, have a small bet, and then ask for the balance to be sent to them by cheque. At one point, William Hill lost hundreds of thousands to an organised online fraud. John Samuels, a security manager for William Hill, writes in his book *Down The Bookies* of an incident that threatened to leave the company with an £800,000 payout, where an online customer appeared to be taking advantage of a fault in the software accounting system to deposit and then withdraw money which would nonetheless continue to show as a credit on his account. Some board members, including Bob Lambert, Brown's long-time associate, wanted him to slow down the online operation until control procedures had been improved, but Brown pressed on, deciding to grow online business no matter what, and sort out problems as they arose. The fault which had led to the fraud was a one-off (much of the loss was later recovered in court), quickly corrected, and Brown pointed out that the loss equated to one or two bad results on a Saturday. In November 2000 William Hill sponsored the live internet broadcast of Celtic's UEFA Cup match versus FC Girondins of Bordeaux, and also supplied a live betting facility during the game – the first time 'in-play' odds had been made available online alongside the live feed of a football match.

Other companies were also throwing money at the race for internet advantage. At the end of 1999 Coral bought Eurobet, an internet betting company, and in March 2000 launched their eurobet.co.uk UK site, spending fortunes on partnerships, deals and high-profile sponsorships. 'Their internet business managed to lose £12 million on Euro 2000,' observed Brown. At the same time, meanwhile, William Hill entered into a deal with CryptoLogic, a leading online casino software provider, which 'made us the first UK bookmaker to have its own casino site,' recalled John Brown. It had a trial as a 'play for fun' operation, and then in January 2000 William Hill made it a 'play for money' casino in US dollars. In April 2001 it added a sterling casino facility. For legal reasons the online casino had to be located outside the United Kingdom, at first in Antigua, then in the Netherlands Antilles. After a slow start, the new venture benefited from improved online marketing, and by the end of 2001 it had around 118,000 registered customers, of whom 35,000 were active.

In May 1999 Victor Chandler, the eponymous head of one of Hill's mid-sized competitors, had stunned the bookmaking industry by moving his telephone operation to Gibraltar to be able to offer tax-free betting. This well-established and respected company was thus able to charge only a 3% service charge compared to the 9% tax and levy deduction by British-based bookmakers. It was a clear threat to all their competitors. In July, Brown was part of an industry delegation to Barbara Roche, the Financial Secretary to the Treasury, urging the government to cut betting duty to 3% or face a general migration of telephone and internet betting operations offshore, with a consequent heavy loss of tax revenue. Roche could promise no immediate action, adding candidly that government did not work like that. Labrokes then announced a major extension of their existing operations in Gibraltar, although Coral stayed put in the United Kingdom as did the Tote, which was under the control of the UK government.

William Hill set about searching for an overseas location for its telephone betting. It could not be the Isle of Man, which for legal reasons could not receive bets from UK customers without subjecting them to a 6% tax. Gibraltar was also ruled out: too far away, flights too infrequent to shuttle the necessary 150 staff, and the telephone system likely to be overloaded as other bookmakers joined Victor Chandler there. The company looked at sites in Malta, Madeira, Liechtenstein and Switzerland and rejected them all. Finally, a chance telephone conversation with a British Airways representative led John Brown to consider the Irish Republic. 'I phoned them and this girl answered with a real Irish accent. I said, "Where are you?" She said, "I'm in a call centre in Kilkenny." I said, "Oh, I'm phoning a London number." Driving to work the next day, the conversation led him to think of siting a call centre in Kilkenny and the computer in Gibraltar. 'Then we'll overcome the problem [of having to charge betting duty]. Nobody's in this country. The person taking the bet ... and the person laying the bet, i.e. the computer, aren't in this country.'

In July 1999 the Irish Republic cut betting duty to 5%, but Brown thought that this could be avoided altogether if bets were struck outside the Republic by non-Irish punters. The Gibraltar government was reluctant to allow the computer operation, fearing that it would make the colony complicit in a tax-avoidance scheme, so he switched his sights to Antigua, which William Hill had explored as the site for its online casino operation. Bill Haygarth, internet operations director, was then on holiday in Canada. Brown told him to fly to Antigua and not leave the island without an agreement to allow William Hill to take bets there.

Meanwhile, Brown struggled to obtain approval for the call centre in the Irish Republic. 'We established that it appeared to be legal for us to set up a call centre there,' says Ian Spearing, who had looked closely at Irish law, 'and provided we accepted no bets from Irish citizens we would not be subject to Irish tax. As the call centre was in "Europe" and offering a "service" we could advertise it in the UK.' The Irish Development Agency continually raised bureaucratic problems, but Brown could afford to ignore them since William Hill intended to finance the venture itself. Much more important was the resistance of the Irish revenue authorities. They were reluctant to accept Hill's argument that bets processed by the call centre were struck overseas and therefore exempt from duty. Ian Spearing remembered he and Brown leaving one meeting with a civil servant who 'gave us a really hard time. It was pouring with rain, neither of us had an umbrella, we were getting drenched, and felt we were going to get the thumbs-down.' Fortunately, the Irish finance minister Charlie McCreevy was a bucolic racing lover who was eager for the 200 new jobs William Hill promised. The company had already committed itself to Ireland by purchasing a site in Athlone, identified and equipped by Hill's David Steele, for the call centre, but John Brown warned the Irish that he might look elsewhere, 'to which the minister said to the civil servant, "We want the jobs. This is all right"'. The last obstacle was the shipyard workers in Antigua who were refusing to unload the computers. Once agreement was reached William Hill installed undersea cables to handle the traffic.

Although in third place behind Victor Chandler and Ladbrokes in setting up an overseas telephone operation, William Hill ended up with the most sophisticated and the most supple system. It linked four locations in separate jurisdictions: odds setting still in Leeds in the United Kingdom; accounts held in the Isle of Man; bets taken in the call centre in the Irish Republic staffed by a mixture of experienced people from Leeds and local recruits; the bookmaking operation in Antigua. 'We needed various service agreements to ensure our actions were legal in each jurisdiction,' says Ian Spearing. It commenced trading in January 2000. Initially,

William Hill followed Victor Chandler in imposing a 3% adminis-
tration charge, but this was removed in January the following year,
making William Hill the first UK bookmaker to offer UK customers
telephone betting, and internet betting via www.willhill.com, with
no deductions whatsoever. Later, as a special offer, the domestic
site also went deduction-free. The whole operation, said Brown,
was 'a great testament to management'.

For all the success of the elaborate offshore operations, William
Hill was still a British bookmaker, and never contemplated permanent migration from its core business of running British betting
shops. In common with its major competitors, it sought to use the
threat of migration to pressure the British government into policy
concessions, although there was no unanimity within the bookmaking and racing industries as to what those concessions should
be. In January 2000, as keynote speaker at the industry seminar
organised by the British Betting Offices Association, John Brown
launched a daring new idea. One which, he admitted, 'I'd first
heard from Bob Green many years before.' General betting duty, he
proposed, which had been in place since November 1966, should
be replaced by a tax on bookmakers' gross profits. There would
then be no deductions for punters. He argued that a short-term
loss of revenue would be more than compensated for by bookmakers returning operations to the United Kingdom (or keeping them
there), thereby undermining illegal betting and growing jobs and
company profits. 'This country,' he concluded, 'with its well-regu-
lated, highly respected betting industry, has a unique opportunity
to protect and grow its core home market, the betting shops, and
emerge as a world leader for sports betting, an exporter of bets and
an earner of foreign currency.'

The speech earned admiring headlines in the *Racing Post*,
but the idea of a gross profits tax at that stage was not even official William Hill policy, let alone the industry's. In the run-up
to the 2000 Budget, most industry representations called for cuts

in general betting duty from its current level of 6.75%, rather than abolition. The British Horseracing Authority asked for a 5% rate, and several bookmakers for 3%. The Chancellor Gordon Brown announced no duty cut in the actual Budget but began a consultation on 'modernising' general betting duty – a characteristic New Labour mantra which could mean everything and nothing. HM Customs & Excise (still at that time an independent department) commissioned an economic study of options for change, as did the Levy Board's Bookmakers Committee.

The idea of gross profits tax now started to gain traction, and it was the preferred solution of the HM Customs study. In his Pre-Budget Report in November 2000 Gordon Brown signalled that the government was looking at 'GPT' and this message was reinforced by the Financial Secretary to the Treasury, Stephen Timms. With an unaccustomed rhetorical flourish, the earnest minister said that the government was ready to 'make a bet' on the bookmaking industry to bring betting back onshore. An informal understanding was reached, as John Brown recalled. 'When William Hill decided to move to Gibraltar we got gross profits tax on the basis we would come back from abroad, an unwritten guarantee that we would come back.'

Just a few days before the 2001 Budget, Frank Tucker, the HM Customs & Excise commissioner responsible, actually asked bookmakers to give their view of the right rate of gross profits tax. John Brown thought that the government would go for a 20% rate and urged the industry to press for 15%, while pointing out that 15% looked larger than 6.75%, the current rate of general betting duty. Still more revealingly, the Treasury press office canvassed bookmakers for their response if the Chancellor were to introduce a gross profits tax. William Hill promised an enthusiastic one, stressing their renewed commitment to betting in the United Kingdom and support for British racing.

Finally on Budget Day itself, 7 March 2001, Gordon Brown announced the replacement of general betting duty with a gross profits tax – at 15%. Gross profits were defined as the difference between gross stakes and gross winnings paid out. Implementation was scheduled for 1 January 2002, but the success of preparatory work led to the change being brought forward to 6 October. John Brown was delighted with the outcome, describing it as 'truly momentous. The significance can't be over-estimated. The new tax changes everything – the basis is now fairer, it is set at a sensible rate, and this enables the bookmaker to stand the tax – without deductions from the punter.' He celebrated with 'a nice cup of tea'. William Hill honoured its unspoken promise by closing down the Antigua operation, returning telephone bookmaking to the UK and offering deduction-free betting to all its customers. The change benefited bookmakers, the racing industry, punters and the Exchequer – a benign scenario for all the parties which lasted for some years, until the arrival of betting exchanges.

Brown and Ralph Topping, then Director of internet development, brought the online business into profit in its second year – 'possibly the only bookmaker in the UK to be doing so,' contended Brown, claiming that Coral Eurobet managed to lose over £19 million that year. The figures showed that in 2001 (with no help from a major soccer tournament), Hill's Sportsbook generated £274 million in turnover, with a gross win of £35.5 million (13% compared to 20% for William Hill's whole business) and operating profits of £9.2 million. That represented 11% of William Hill's total turnover and 8.6% of its total operating profit, and though it could be argued that the online operation depressed William Hill's margins, crucially it attracted a younger and more international set of customers than betting shops and telephone betting. Now the new flotation prospectus for 2002 was blazoning the directors' view that this was the most profitable online betting operation in the United Kingdom.

CHAPTER 25

THE DAVID HARDING YEARS

The 2002 flotation had been particularly well timed. Betting exchanges were not yet a significant phenomenon or a major news story, relations with the racing industry were quieter than usual and William Hill could offer the prospect of an additional £1 billion in revenues returning to legal bookmaking when punters' deductions were abolished after the introduction of gross profits tax. 'It was a wonderful window of opportunity to get that business away,' reflected David Harding, 'and it was tremendously successful as a float – ten times over-subscribed.' Even six months later, he believed, the flotation would have been far less successful, as betting exchanges were by then already gaining traction.

The concept of betting exchanges – originally entitled peer-to-peer betting – was pioneered in the UK by Flutter.com in May 2000, an online business founded by two American university graduates. A month later it was followed by Betfair, co-founded by Andrew Black, a former derivatives trader and the grandson of the right-wing Conservative MP Sir Cyril Black – a notable opponent of gambling – and Ed Wray, an Oxford graduate and highflyer with the financial services firm, JP Morgan, and launched with a rather tasteless stunt in which coffins were paraded around London's Covent Garden to symbolise (somewhat prematurely) the death of traditional bookmaking.

Both Flutter and Betfair had the same basic idea. Instead of offering odds themselves on sporting events, they used the internet to put would-be punters and layers in contact with each other, to create multiple individual betting markets, or 'open-market betting', in which the company, as the 'enabler', would take a commission from winners. A person offering a price on Manchester United to win a soccer match would be matched with one willing to offer the reciprocal price on the team failing to win. Hence the term 'betting exchange', which quickly became established. Flutter's founders, however, made a fatal mistake. They saw their site as a social facility – a kind of sporting version of Facebook – in which, for example, friends would bet on who would win their weekly squash match. Betfair realised that punters wanted to bet seriously on anything and everything. Although Flutter's site was much easier to use than Betfair's and far more popular with customers, it was swallowed by its competitor in January 2002.

For internet-savvy punters, betting exchanges offered several new attractions compared to traditional bookmakers. The biggest of these was empowerment. Users could offer bets at their own prices on as many events as they liked, so long as they could find someone else to accept them. Their potential winnings were therefore almost unlimited, although so too were their potential losses. Even allowing for their commissions, betting exchanges could offer their customers in aggregate slightly more favourable odds than traditional bookmakers. This was because the exchanges were not actually accepting bets themselves on sporting events, and were therefore not compelled to seek an 'over-round' on the same scale as a traditional bookmaker. (The over-round is a measure of a bookmaker's ability to set odds to put him in profit from all the bets taken on all the possible outcomes of an event.) However, the liquidity, or amount available to back or lay on specific outcomes was frequently insufficient to supply all would-be participants. Another advantage of betting exchanges quickly became apparent, although bookies have since matched the facility. This was the facilitation of 'in-play markets', which allowed customers to bet on specific events (for example, the next scorer in a soccer match) after a sporting event had started.

Nonetheless, David Harding had not been worried by the market hysteria around betting exchanges and the fears of City analysts of 'disintermediation' – the prospect that betting exchanges would end punters' need to use a bookmaker to make a bet. 'We saw very quickly that 90% of our business came from cash punters in the shops, betting in £2, £3, £4, £5 stakes. These guys were not going to go online, have to deposit money to the extent of their potential liabilities and act as a bookmaker ... I never saw them as a mass market product.' However, he was concerned that they could undermine the integrity of betting markets in sport – primarily because they offered customers a new and easy way to 'lay' against teams or individual players – that is, to bet on their failure. Soon it also became apparent that betting exchanges had contributed to a new risk of 'spot-fixing', or pre-arranged unlikely outcomes of specific events.

The early years of the century, indeed, saw the cricket match-fixing and other Asian-based betting scandals, even though these were actually products of illegal gambling and logically supported the case for universal legalised and regulated forms of gambling. Match-fixing had not been a significant problem for traditional bookmakers in their core businesses, such as horseracing and football. But 'it came as a shock to William Hill when they discovered that some sporting events were corrupt,' said Harding.

Along with other traditional bookmakers, William Hill had well-established systems for detecting unusual patterns of betting, not least the human interface at betting shops and the customer log system. The problem of corruption in betting was much more acute for betting exchanges, which functioned exclusively online and offered multiple betting choices on specific events that could be fixed by collusion between a small number of participants. 'We found indications of corruption in betting patterns from most of the head-to-head sports,' said David Harding.

However, for all the heat and light generated by match-fixing allegations, very few authenticated cases have emerged compared with the number of sporting events contested: 'Over the past five years we have been offering 50,000 betting events per year in retail – and are now up to 100,000 – yet since September 2007 we have initiated just 19 reports to the UK Gambling Commission, as we are obliged to do should we detect suspicious incidents', said trading director Terry Pattinson in 2014. Online incidents, also extremely rare, will be drawn to the attention of the European Sports Security Association, whose role is to provide an early warning system to deter corruption of betting markets through manipulation of sporting events.

David Harding certainly supported other industry sources in their protests to government about competition from unregulated betting exchanges. 'If you track the over-round per runner over the past 12 months,' he commented in January 2003, 'highlighting the theoretical profit margin in a specific event, in this case horse racing, you can track it from the point where Betfair and Flutter merged. Since then, there has been a steady decline in the theoretical over-round per runner. Some racecourse markets now return over-rounds of only 1.2% to 1.3% per runner. That is not sustainable. I cannot have a price mechanism for 50% of my business being desecrated.'

Harding shared John Brown's scepticism about international ventures. In his case he perceived the debate in the UK and overseas about how to recognise and regulate gambling to be driven by the reluctance of policymakers to make gambling open and legal, as a way of preventing it drifting into criminal hands. This was especially true of the EU, he thought, which made very little effort to harmonise gambling regulations and challenge national systems that were heavily influenced by religious and moral lobbies. Many countries were determined not to give up state monopolies where gambling was concerned, for fear of loss of revenue. Now a serious obstacle arose to the company's Sportsbook operation. Overseas this had been based on a simple premise, that, as Harding explained, 'not unlike Amazon and Google ... the bet was negotiated and struck in Ireland, and we were responsible for it being legal where the bet was struck, but the customer was supposed to ensure that it was lawful for him to place the bet in Ireland.' For the industry, this assumption was threatened by a crackdown in the United States, where Congress (under pressure from domestic special interests) passed the Unlawful Internet Gambling Enforcement Act of 2006. Scarcely read by most legislators and tacked on to a measure to improve security at seaports, the Act effectively outlawed online betting on the great majority of online sporting events. Moreover, several individual states, particularly Missouri and Louisiana, introduced their own provisions against online gambling. Earlier in 2006 David Carruthers, chief executive of BetOnSports, was arrested whilst on a business trip to the US and charged with racketeering, conspiracy and fraud; in the September, Peter Dicks, the British chairman of Sportingbet, was arrested in New York on charges of offences against the new Louisiana legislation. Another leading operator, Party Gaming, entered laborious negotiations with the US Department of Justice which culminated three years later in an out-of-court settlement for $105 million in fines. In David Harding's view all of this new legislation, on top of the already-obscure Wire Act of 1961 (which meant William Hill had not offered sports bets to US residents) – none of it tested in court – made it impossible for William Hill to continue accepting gaming wagers from the United States. The company announced in September 2006 that it was to cease accepting bets from American citizens (identified in the system by their use of a credit card issued by a US bank), a decision which in turn compromised its operations in European countries, since it suggested that the system could also enforce a ban on bets from their citizens.

In any case, Harding remained convinced that, thanks to the introduction of gross profits tax, the UK market still had immense growth potential. 'When we floated, we ... estimated there was up to £1 billion of gross win in illegal bookmakers because of the tax on turnover [and the resulting deductions from punters], and that somehow that would come back into legal channels … Everyone assumes that growth came from the fact that we found more customers. I don't think that we did. I think that illegal money found its way back, regardless of product.'

William Hill's 2004 accounts mentioned reduced margins in horserace betting as more customers bet online. This had little impact on profitability, however, because the introduction of gross profits tax and the end of deductions encouraged customers to recycle bets – that is, re-invest winning bets until they had lost as much as they were prepared to lose. There was no longer any tax penalty for a bookmaker in allowing a customer to make dozens of bets in sequence. 'We didn't mind if people spent all day losing that money,' stated David Harding. 'It didn't matter.' In this way, greater betting volumes compensated for reduced margins. The same logic applied to roulette in FOBTs. Harding constantly had to rebut City analysts who wanted William Hill to 'do more horseracing' – with a margin of 16% – and less roulette, where the margin was only 2.7%. 'I said, "Well, it doesn't work that way. It doesn't matter if it's 2.7% – it just takes them longer to lose it."'

Harding's long-held aspiration was to 'get Ladbrokes' – to overtake them as Britain's biggest bookmaker by once again owning more shops than them. 'I very quickly decided that I would make it my mission to get to be number one for two reasons. One, I got royally pissed off with constantly being described in the press as Britain's number two bookmaker.' But secondly,

having been through various businesses I'd always come to the conclusion that it's far easier to get everyone aligned against the common enemy than it is around the common goal … I think everyone in William Hill thought that our mission was to get Ladbrokes, and I think people were focused on it. You could talk to an individual shop manager and he knew exactly what was happening at the Ladbrokes down the road. There was a real desire to win and massive pride when we did get ahead of them.

In particular, both he and John Brown had resented Ladbrokes' claim to be the voice of the bookmaking industry, sustained by a heavy PR and lobbying effort – a point which would not have been lost on Len Cowburn. At that time Ladbrokes had around 2,200 shops compared to William Hill's 1,600, while Coral had around 1,100. Combining with Coral by merger or acquisition would raise monopoly issues, so the likeliest route to outstrip Ladbrokes would be to acquire one of the middle-ranking chains, Stanley, Betfred or the Tote. The 2002 acquisition of Essex-based H&K Commissions, which had 35 shops, was a signal of intent. Eighty per cent of Hill's shops were also now trading on Sundays, which had been legalised in 1995.

Meanwhile, David Harding had to resist a proposal to open a call centre in India, where he had understandable concerns about the integrity of the betting market. But the City constantly pushed him to adopt an international strategy for William Hill and mimic Ladbrokes' move into the Chinese market. To placate it, Harding announced plans to link up with European rival Codere to launch a betting business in Spain in which football betting would be prominent. Just as he had been quick to follow Coral and Ladbrokes into FOBTs, so he was ready to follow competitors in setting up an online casino based on Java software. 'If somebody comes up with an innovation in bookmaking, everyone else can copy it within five minutes. There's nothing [where] you can get intellectual property and a sustained competitive advantage.'

Once William Hill had gone public, Harding soon discovered that he needed messages for three different audiences. 'You've got to say what the analysts want to hear, thinking about the share price and their comfort; you've got to make sure you don't say anything that messes up your negotiations with government who are look-ing at regulation; and, given that you've got ongoing litigation with horseracing, you're always sending messages to them.' Because the William Hill flotation had attracted a high number of small retail investors, Harding also found himself having to maintain a higher profile in the media. 'There was a little bit of the story that was "cheeky chappie bookmaker", anecdotes, little stories' – one exam-ple was William Hill's public thanks, in the 2004 accounts, to the unfancied Greece football team for winning Euro 2004.

While City analysts were concerned about the age profile of betting-shop customers and urging him to search for younger mar-kets, Harding was anxious to diversify William Hill away from horseracing anyway. When he arrived at the company horserac-ing was generating 59% of its gross win, but he had inherited an ongoing row with the horseracing industry over the levy, which was claiming 10% of William Hill's gross profit from horserace betting. Moreover, horseracing was inherently volatile, which was especially inconvenient for William Hill after it became a public company. 'I discovered, every time you'd have to do a profits warn-ing because of horseracing results or bad weather, you got a kicking because they didn't believe you.'

Elaborated Harding:

BAGS (Bookmakers Afternoon Greyhound Services) which had also been providing evening meetings to the shops since they were permitted to open in the evening from April 1993, wasn't the lead product, but we were very keen to increase the number of betting opportunities, and we did try to pro-mote greyhound racing more. That helped to ensure that betting shop punters had a new outlet for a bet every ten minutes, and pushed greyhound share of turnover to 19%.

The change in philosophy came about partly because of a natural desire to reduce dependence on horseracing, which was our most expensive product, given we paid away 10% of gross win in Levy.

Under GPT, as long as the 'bet to extinction/recycling' theory held, by offering lower margin bets on BAGS and virtual racing between horseraces, the greater the proportion of gross win the bookmaker kept.

I always felt that GPT enabled the betting experience to become more like the gaming experience, whereby the punter got better value by being able to have more, and more frequent, bets for his money – so the 'dwell time' grew for the bookmaker.

At the end of the day, horse racing was some 60% of group gross win when I started and less than 30% when I finished – so, overall, I reckon the diversification strategy worked.

However, particularly during the World Cup year of 2002, Harding recognised that a growth strategy had to rely on football to attract young punters. 'I didn't totally believe that, but you had to send the signal that you were doing it. I was also trying to send an aggressive signal to horseracing. Work with us to grow your share of the pie, but stop trying to steal a bigger share, because that comes straight off our bottom line and we will diversify away from horseracing.' Betting shops were not a major outlet for football betting, because of the legacy of the football pools and its influence on older customers, for whom betting was a once-weekly event through the coupon. To attract rapid betting, and from younger customers, William Hill therefore had to turn to the internet. Sure enough, betting on the Euro 2004 football tournament turned a profit of around £11 million, double what had been expected.

Indeed, 2004 was a landmark year for the company, with its share price rising in April to over £5, making its market valuation £2.3 billion – sufficient to propel William Hill into the FTSE 100.

It was an achievement that seemed to amply justify the £2.84 million bonus paid to Harding the previous year, which had made him the UK's fifth highest-paid company director. The chief executive then blotted his copybook temporarily in June by selling £5.2 million-worth of shares to fund his divorce from his wife of 23 years, Lucia: the consequent crash in the share price wiped a reported £75 million, or some 3%, off the value of the company!

By the beginning of 2005 William Hill's shares were still higher, at 555p, and had been higher still. Another year of excellent results in 2004, with profits before tax up by £36 million to over £205 million, was giving Harding the opportunity to return serious money to shareholders: a total of £453 million, indeed, as a one-off payment worth 115p per share, on top of the regular 16.5p dividend. 'If you add up dividends, share buybacks and this latest return of capital,' wrote the *Daily Express*'s City Editor Stephen Kahn, 'William Hill's shareholders have received a total of £752 million since the bookies came to market in 2002.' 'When you consider we only raised about £950 million from new equity,' added Harding, 'this means that we've given investors around 80% of their money back.' Now was the time, he went on, to be looking to expand the estate of shops: 'I think we can grow up to about 2,200 if we can find the right shops in the right place at the right price.'

He duly found them, and before the shareholders could receive their windfall, the *Daily Mirror* broke the news in April that William Hill were in 'exclusive discussions' with Stanley Leisure, the fourth largest bookmaking chain. 'I had a phone call from Stanley's CEO,' Harding later recalled,

> telling me that there was going to be an auction process between Coral, Betfred and the Tote to buy them, and did we want to be in? I told him, 'I can't, as I have to give back £450 million to shareholders.' My mind was racing. What the fuck

can I do? 'Give me a period of exclusivity,' I asked. 'I've got the cash. None of the others have.'

He came back to me a day or two later. 'If your offer begins with a "5" you're OK.' We entered a two-week period of exclusivity during which I pondered how best to do the deal. It was finally clinched ... after having to go back to the City to tell them, 'We're going to buy Stanley Leisure instead of giving the money back to shareholders.' I have to say the non-executive directors were very supportive.

On 16 May it was confirmed that the company had agreed to buy the 624 betting shops for £504 million, strengthening William Hill's presence in the north of the country, and taking it to 2,184 shops and once again past Ladbrokes. The deal included Stanley Leisure's 51 Irish outlets, prompting David Harding to tell City analysts that he had just 'parked a tank on Paddy Power's front lawn' – a remark he possibly later regretted. As a condition of the takeover more than 70 shops were sold off to the Tote for a figure variously reported as between £35 million and £48 million. Eighteen months after the acquisition, the average annual profit of Stanley shops had risen from £38,000 to £80,000, compared to an average £108,000 for William Hill's existing shops. A year later, the Stanley shops actually overtook William Hill's in profitability. Harding had fulfilled his ambition of overtaking Ladbrokes. William Hill had once again become Britain's biggest bookmaker.

A poignant event in September 2005 was the last reunion of the extended Hill family. The first having taken place in the mid-1990s to celebrate 100 years since the marriage of Grandpa William and Grandma Lavinia Hill on 26 December 1896.

'By coincidence, it was my mother's 97th birthday,' recalled William's nephew Neil Hill, son of William's older

brother Edward (known as Dick), who had helped to arrange the gathering in a village hall in Sutton Coldfield –
there was even a bouncy castle. 'There were approximately
110 people there if I remember correctly,' Neil recalled,
'embracing four generations of the family. Unfortunately Joe
Ward Hill [William's brother, and the last survivor of that
generation] was unable to attend.'

The Stanley acquisition might be viewed as opportunistic, but
David Harding went on to pursue a bigger target: a merger with the
Rank Group. For most people Rank was still better known under its
previous name of the Rank Organisation, as a film maker and cinema chain. Its iconic image of a muscled man (featuring, amongst
others, the boxer Bombardier Billy Wells) striking a vast gong was
fondly remembered even if the subsequent films had foundered at
the box office. However, since 1995 the Rank Group had progressively divested itself of nearly all its predecessor's interests in cinemas and film making, holidays, leisure attractions, photocopying
and amusement machines. By the end of 2004 it had refocused
itself almost entirely as a gaming and bingo business, as the operator of Top Rank casinos and Mecca clubs, with a presence in online
gaming as a result of its 2003 acquisition of the Blue Square gaming
business. Deluxe Film (once Rank Film Laboratories) survived as
Rank Group's last link with the movie business.

David Harding was on good personal terms with the Rank
Group's chief executive, Mike Smith, who, during his time at
Grand Metropolitan, had actually been briefly head of William
Hill at one stage. In 2005, a merger seemed to make good business
sense to both of them. At the time the two groups had an almost
identical market value: £1.92 billion for William Hill and £1.97
billion for the Rank Group. It would create a betting and gaming
giant with a market value of around £4 billion, joining William
Hill's strengths as a bookmaker to Rank's as a casino operator,

while enhancing their presence on the internet. A merged group could better confront the new challenge set by Gala's takeover of Coral, which had created a gaming, bingo and betting group with a comparable market value.

In December 2005 Harding proposed an all-share merger, but this was rejected by the William Hill board. According to the *Sunday Times*, his colleagues thought that Rank's share price had been inflated by market expectations of an imminent bid, and they noted that Rank's most recent six-month profit performance was far inferior: £71 million compared to £124 million for William Hill. The Rank board never put the proposal to a vote. The idea of a merger refused to go away, however, and received a new stimulus only weeks later when Rank sold off Deluxe Film – seen for years as a 'poison pill' to prospective bidders. It was only killed off for good in March 2007 when Harding, presenting William Hill's results for 2006, announced that a Rank merger was 'not on the agenda'.

The 2006 results were again impressive, with operating profits of £292.2 million despite a 'challenging' second half of the year. Harding also confirmed that 14,000 staff would be in line for a bonus, having missed out the year before, while the dividend was up 19%. A major contributor was the World Cup, which brought Hill's a profit of £17.5 million – £4.5 million more than the previous tournament in 2002 – working out as £273,000 profit per game, even though the early stages of the tournament had seen the company 'like a boxer on the ropes', according to Harding, with favourites winning 20 of the first 24 games. Hills had estimated that the month of June could be the biggest betting month of all time, with £1.3 million per hour being gambled, and an overall total of £1 billion.

In June 2007, only months after presenting these results, David Harding, whose contract was indefinite and would only end automatically on reaching 63, dropped a bombshell with the announcement of his intention to step down as chief executive. Money was clearly not a reason for his going, as his salary had just been increased again to £530,000, and in the previous two years he had also received a substantial number of shares. Rather, what seems to have happened is that the non-executive members of the board's opposition to the Rank merger had led him to decide it was time to go. Without such a major initiative, he hinted in looking back on his decision, he could not see the opportunity to build on his achievements.

But Harding also confirmed the accuracy of the official reason given – that he was 51, wanted a new challenge, and more time with his young son. 'There was an element of seven-year-itch involved,' he reflected. 'You start off full of zeal … I had a plan, I had things to do, it was exciting. I used to go to work and I used to feel like every day we'd moved the business forward. Then towards the end I felt like I was swimming in treacle. There was just so much bureaucracy, so much that held you back, and I didn't feel the same zing.' William Hill had exploited all the growth possibilities that had arisen from deregulation and the switch to gross profits tax. Now, he anticipated a new phase of intrusive supervision: 'I was thinking … over the next two years the new regulator's going to be all over us, it's going to be very bureaucratic. I don't want to spend my time in maintenance mode, getting chipped away at.'

Harding was leaving a company transformed during his tenure. William Hill had successfully floated on the stock market; it had risen in value to join the FTSE 100 Index of leading shares. It had built the most profitable e-commerce business in the sector, and been early to introduce the phenomenally profitable FOBTs. Its gross win and net profits had more than doubled, and its share price had risen from 225p at the 2002 flotation to 650p. 'The biggest failure of my tenure,' as Harding saw it? 'Our failure to get Betfair properly regulated.'

But above all, under Harding's leadership, William Hill had become the industry leader. 'The biggest highlight for me was finally overtaking Ladbrokes on turnover, number of shops, size of web business and profitability in 2006,' was his verdict on his time as chief executive. 'I always saw getting to be the number-one bookmaker as our primary "mission" during my tenure.'

The question was who would succeed him? It could not be Tom Singer, who had left in November 2006, to be replaced as group finance director by Simon Lane, a chartered accountant. Three months before Harding's surprise announcement, two new executive directors had been appointed: Ralph Topping, who had been group director, operations since 2002, and Ian Spearing, corporate strategy and development director. But, having broken the mould last time round and decided to head hunt for its chief executive, would the company follow the same process that had secured David Harding? Or could it go back and strike lucky with an internal candidate as it had done with John Brown? It was this dilemma that preoccupied the board for the next few months.

CHAPTER 26

A SMALL STEP FOR A MAN, A LARGE PAYOUT FOR WILLIAM HILL

In 1964, a young man called David Threlfall had asked for odds that man would set foot on the Moon before the end of the decade. Astonishingly, he was offered 1,000/1 – who created or quoted those odds is, unsurprisingly, unknown, although what evidence there is points towards it being William himself – which he took, to a bet of £10, equivalent in those days to twice the average weekly wage. In July 1969 the *Eagle* landed on the Sea of Tranquility, Neil Armstrong climbed down the ladder to take one small step, and the personnel officer from Preston had won £10,000 (over £140,000 today). The following month he was pictured in the *Daily Mirror* lying on a sun lounger on a beach in Nassau with two waiters hovering over him. As recently as May that year he had been offering his betting slip for sale for £8,000, and found no takers. Legend has it that Mr Threlfall, who became for a while something of a media darling, then purchased a fast sports car with his winnings, and subsequently died in an accident in it.

William Hill, interviewed later that same year, estimated that the Moon landing had altogether cost his company about £50,000. 'We try to serve a demand, whatever that demand may be,' he explained simply. 'I remember once bumping into a bridegroom's stag party, and he made six or seven bets with me on the children he'd have – evens a boy, evens a girl, up to 500/1 for triplets. I had the voucher delivered to his wedding reception and it was read out with the telegrams. They did have a child, so he won.'

William's realisation of the long-term publicity value of such wagers is demonstrated by the tiny percentage margin in his favour of those baby odds. There was – and is – little downside in such bets. If they lose, the bookie pockets the stake. If they win they guarantee a publicity dividend usually worth more than the payout.

In 1974 journalist Graham Sharpe, who had joined Hills two years earlier, working in the shops, arrived in the company's publicity department with the brief to recreate the demand its founder had seen, by introducing and publicising a wider range of novelty bets and quirky sponsorships.

Soon William Hill was renowned as the place to go for punters looking for a bet a little out of the ordinary, and for journalists looking for a gambling-related story to come. Over the next forty years Hills have taken tens of thousands of bets from parents that their new-born will grow up to achieve sporting greatness by playing for their country, winning Wimbledon, or scoring a World Cup-winning goal.

Parents have bet on what sex their children will be, and whether there will be one, two, three or more of them; on the date their children will be born and, when they are, on their passing exams, achieving university degrees, or appearing on the front cover of fashion magazines.

Darlington doctor David Wright won £1,000 in 1990 with the first exam-related bet, on son Andrew achieving 11 'A' grade GCSE passes – Hills knew he was on a winner when the lad's headmaster also backed him!

People bet on themselves losing weight, passing driving tests, living to be a hundred, recording hit singles, and writing bestselling novels.

Even though in Britain discussing the weather is a national pastime, the only weather-related bet any bookmakers used to take was on whether there would be a white Christmas, and to satisfy the Met Office and trigger a pay-out the snow had to be falling not only in London, but also at midday. Hills therefore teamed up

Both *The Sun* and, here, the *Daily Mirror*, led the paper on the news that William Hill had opened a book asking punters to bet on when the 1978 summer downpours would end.

with the London Weather Centre to expand the range of 'white Christmas' locations available for betting on, and then set about exploiting every opening for a weather-related wager. At the height of the scorching summer of 1976, William Hill offered the rare opportunity to bet on when it would next rain in London – at odds of 10/1. The media coverage was instant and widespread. When the British weather had returned to its default position in the summer of 1978, Hills were betting on when it would *stop* raining, which prompted a *Daily Mirror* front page headline of 'SODDEN AWFUL' above their story about the odds while *The Sun* also made it their main story of the day – 'BETCHA IT WON'T RAIN!'

In 1985 the company was offering 100/1 that rain would fall in London every day of August, and by the 20th of the month had cut the odds to 10/1, even though there had never, since records began, been a month in which rain had fallen every day in the same location. As the summer of 2003 got hotter and hotter Hills cut the odds on temperatures hitting 100°F (37.8°C) anywhere in the UK from 33/1 to 16/1, and eventually down to 6/4 as it reached 95°F in Jersey. Then on 10 August the barrier was finally breached, and the industry-wide payout was probably in excess of £250,000.

Another classic topic for water cooler conversations (assuming we had them then) around the country was the prime-time television of the day, so in March 1980, when a record numbers of viewers watched the dastardly oil baron JR Ewing sensationally gunned down in the final episode of the Texas soap opera *Dallas* on the BBC, William Hill opened a book on 'Who Shot JR?' It was the first time a bookmaker had ever created a betting market on the outcome of a television programme's plot-line, and it attracted worldwide headlines. When Sharpe took the idea to Hill's director Roy Sutterlin (who had himself invented one of the most popular wagers, the 'ITV 7' on the seven races the station televised on a Saturday afternoon) he vetoed it out of hand – quite properly assuming that the scriptwriters would already know who had shot Larry Hagman's character. But that episode had come at the end of one series, well before the cast had been signed up for the next, or the script even been written. After securing a double-page spread in the *Sunday Mirror* should Hills put odds in place, Sharpe again braved Sutterlin's wrath, to be told, 'We'll do it. If it costs us, you're out on your ear. If it works, I'll take all the credit!'

The media immediately saw a story in the betting angle, the BBC even publicising the odds on its flagship sports programme *Grandstand*. No fewer than 20 million people watched the fateful episode; then, a few minutes later, BBC TV News showed the moment again, along with William Hill's odds on each suspect. By the time the new series aired and Kristin, the 5/2 second favourite was revealed to be the guilty party, Hills had taken around a quarter of a million pounds in bets, and paid out £160,000 on her. At the end of the year Hills followed up by becoming the first bookmakers to bet on what would be the most-watched television programme on Christmas Day (the all-channel Queen's Message was excluded). In 1997 a man from Hertfordshire who had changed his name by deed poll to Santa Claus backed himself to have the Christmas number one hit single. He didn't, but the Spice Girls, backed from 16/1 to 1/8, did, which cost Hills £92,000 – and to make things worse, enough snowflakes fell in London, Manchester, Newcastle and Norwich to trigger a payout at 7/1 to punters who had bet on a white Christmas.

A third national obsession was the Royal Family, and in 1982 the company broke new ground by starting to take bets on the activities of its members – something so unthinkable even a couple of years earlier that a Sunday tabloid had carried a front-page story about bookies turning down bets on the sex of Princess Anne's forthcoming baby. The arrival of Princess Diana changed the media's and the public's attitude to the Royals completely, however, and William Hill offered odds of 12/1 on the imminent Royal baby being christened William (subsequently shortening them to 7/2 amidst tabloid speculation only gently encouraged by Hill's press office, about a 'Palace coup'), with George favourite at even money. Ladbrokes excluded themselves from such vulgar speculation on the grounds that they were 'bookmakers to the establishment', only to change their minds once the bet's popularity became evident.

" I REMEMBER HE HAD BIG EARS AND A BEARD... "

Sun cartoonist Franklin speculates that Hills were royally fleeced when Charles and Diana named their first-born William in 1982.

In June 2005 punters plunged cash on the surely unlikely event of the Queen wearing a brown hat to Royal Ascot. The colour had been a 10/1 outsider, but a leak of information was suspected as one punter in a Windsor betting shop had tried to stake £1,000. When Her Majesty did indeed arrive in brown Hills were out of pocket to the tune of £5,000.

After the Royal Family, the next Pope and the next Archbishop of Canterbury have also, thanks to Hills, become popular betting topics over the last 30 years. In 2012 a flurry of bets for the Bishop of Durham, Justin Welby, to be appointed Archbishop of Canterbury saw him backed to favouritism, having at one stage been a 10/1 shot, and he proved himself rather more of a man of the world than some of his predecessors by tweeting about the move in odds

Uniquely a communion service was held in Hill's Camden branch to celebrate 125 years since St Michael's was established on the current betting shop site.

and suggesting that successful punters might wish to make a donation to their local churches. When Lord Runcie, Archbishop from 1980–91, met Hill's managing director, John Brown at a charity dinner in York and told him he fancied a flutter on a horse he'd seen with an 'ecclesiastical name' the company opened probably the only account for an Archbishop of Canterbury. Unfortunately there was no divine intervention and the horse lost. In 2002 a London vicar even conducted a communion service in a William Hill betting shop. The Camden branch stood on the site of the original St Michael with All Saints and St Thomas, and to commemorate the church's 125th anniversary the Revd Nicholas Wheeler took the service amidst the shop's usual business of the day, though he did turn down the offer of a £125 free bet with proceeds to the church.

Not yeti, Chris! Mountaineer Bonington found evidence of the existence of the Abominable Snowman – but it was destroyed and the bet was lost.

Extra-terrestrial intervention and the discovery of mythical beings have proved perfect territory for speculative bets and endless PR. In 1983 William Hill cut the odds on the existence of the Loch Ness Monster being definitively proved within a year to their shortest ever price of 25/1 as reports from the Scottish Highlands suggested that sophisticated sonar equipment had picked up strong contacts. Of course, the odds soon retreated to 250/1 when no further evidence was forthcoming, but Hills would go on to sponsor a number of 'Monster Hunt weekends' at Loch Ness, offering punters the chance to bet on whether Nessie would ever be proved to exist, and also win up to £250,000 ('what's the matter with you, make it a million,' urged John Brown) by producing the evidence that it did.

In 1988 the renowned mountaineer Chris Bonington went into a William Hill shop to place a bet that his forthcoming Himalayan expedition, later sponsored by Hills, would return with proof of the existence of the Yeti. He returned bearing what he was convinced was conclusive evidence, only for it to be confiscated by officials from the Department of Agriculture, and burnt. In 2010 a man placed £1,000 at 1000/1 at a Hill's branch in Wiltshire (probably not coincidentally the county with the greatest number of UFO sightings to its credit, not least with the celebrated 'Warminster mystery' of the 1950s) that the existence of intelligent extra-terrestrial life would be confirmed by the serving Prime Minister or US President within a year, and in July 2012 the company revealed it had taken bets at 1,000/1 for a UFO to appear over the Olympic stadium during the London Games. It would later reject calls to pay out on the basis of some extremely unconvincing footage on YouTube.

In reality, of course, our political leaders are far too busy canvassing for election to spend time confirming the existence of extra-terrestrials. In 1991 a New York client staked £25,000 with William Hill at odds of 9/4 for Bill Clinton to win the US Presidential Election, thus collecting a profit of £56,250 when he defeated George Bush senior in November 1992. At one time you could have had odds of 50/1 from Hills that Hillary Clinton would become the first female President of the USA; they were slashed to 5/1 when she won a place in the Senate, and many punters are still hoping to collect on the bet. The leadership of the Conservative party is a subject that has consistently attracted bold stakes: in June 2001 Michael Portillo attracted a bet of £10,000 as the odds-on favourite – but didn't win – and in 2005 David Cameron was backed down from 10/1 to 11/10 and eventually 1/25 to defeat David Davis, with one William Hill client so convinced this was a racing certainty that he risked an amazing £200,000 to make £8,000 profit, a record amount for a political wager, until a man walked into a Hill's shop in Surrey in June 2014, and bet £400,000 at odds of 1/4 that the

Scots would vote against independence in that September's referendum. He returned later to bet an extra £200,000 at 1/6.

William Hill also turned their attention to the other end of the ballot paper, laying the former rock and roll star and eccentric self-publicist Screaming Lord Sutch, leader of the newly formed Monster Raving Loony Party, a bet to collect 200 or more votes at the Darlington by-election in 1983. He did so comfortably, his winnings covering his deposit, and it was the start of a long-lasting relationship that would result in the company sponsoring the party's General Election campaigns and, when it changed its name to the Monster Raving Loony William Hill Party, even appearing on the ballot paper. And when the popular comedy actor Bill Maynard stood as an independent at the Chesterfield by-election in 1984 he struck a bold bet of £2,000 at 5/2 that he would poll 1,500 or more votes. He finished a very respectable fourth to Tony Benn, and had he claimed the 178 votes that went to Screaming Lord Sutch, he'd have collected on his bet. In 1978 Patrick Wholey struck possibly the most pointless bet of all time, a £1 accumulator from which he stood to collect £5 million – when the Loch Ness Monster was discovered, UFOs landed, there was a dry weekend in London, and a 100/1 shot won at Newbury!

One of the most delightfully eccentric books William Hill ever opened was down to one of its own shop managers. In 1994 Paul Batchelor, manager of the Bartley Green branch in Birmingham, offered odds on how long it would take the men from BT to repaint the local phone box. What he dubbed 'The BT Handicap' quoted

6/4 Finished by Wednesday
7/2 More than 50 tea breaks
8/1 Paint dry in three days
12/1 Phone doesn't work
50/1 'Wet Paint' sign stays for weeks
100/1 Painted wrong colour

Local punters estimated a few hours, but in the end it took four days, with an embarrassed BT official muttering about 'a very time-consuming process'.

Other inspired eccentricity generated in-house included the sponsorship of the World Snuff-Taking Contest in 1979 in Somerset, followed by the Man versus Horse Marathon in mid-Wales, leading to a payout of £25,000 when a runner defeated a mounted horse over 22 miles; books on which breed would become Supreme Champion at Cruft's and offering every customer who brought in an old £1 note a free £10 bet, to publicise the launch in 1987 of live satellite racing broadcasts in Hill's London shops. That promotion proved almost too successful, with the company giving away £188,130 in bets, and handing over £18,813 in pound notes to Children in Need. 2001 saw the idea for goldfish racing, with a large aquarium equipped with the obligatory half-submerged arch, and the first out of half a dozen readily-identifiable goldfish to swim through it the winner, all broadcast live on the internet and in Hill's branches as a unique gambling opportunity. Health and Safety regulations, er, sank the idea.

Sometimes, however, a proposition is just too outlandish or unsavoury to take on. In 1992 a New York professor wrote asking to place a series of bets with Hills that within two years the British Army would accidentally bomb France; Toulouse in France would be devastated by flooding; a nuclear accident would occur in the Rocky Mountains in Colorado; a major earthquake would hit New York; and a new dictator would take control of Iran. In 2001 the company turned down a car park attendant from Norwich who wanted odds of 1000/1 that before 2007 someone in Britain would be eaten or otherwise killed by a big cat.

Not to be sniffed at – a unique sponsorship: the 1979 World Snuff Championship. Who nose who won!

An Isle of Wight man, Geoff Sartin, was philosophical when advised that should he prove correct in predicting the date on which his wife would die the local constabulary might declare an interest. 'She said she doesn't mind me placing the bet,' he maintained. But Hills did. The company did, however, accept a very interesting bet from a 91-year-old man, Arthur Robinson, a retired solicitor in Crediton in Devon, who staked £500 that he would die by 6 December 2005. At odds of 6/1 the bet would pay out £3,000 if he passed away – which, under the arrangement whereby he had transferred his assets over to his wife in 1998 and was required to survive a further seven years in order to discharge any tax liability for her on them, was the precise amount of tax she would face if he didn't! In the event, Arthur was still alive on 7 December 2005.

Another man died just a couple of weeks before he was set to win a further £10,000 by staying alive until 1 June 2010. Jon Matthews, who patronised the William Hill branch in Fenny Stratford near Milton Keynes, had been diagnosed in his late fifties with terminal mesothelioma in early 2007, and told he was unlikely to survive until the end of the year. So, that October, he asked William Hill if they would be prepared to take a bet from him that he would still be alive on 1 June 2008, 1 June 2009 and 1 June 2010, staking £100 at 50/1 each time on the first two, and at 100/1 on the third. He won the first two bets, collecting winnings of £5,000 each time, but died in early May within sight of a third win. However, the company donated the winnings he would have collected to Harefield Hospital where he had been treated, to buy an important piece of equipment in his memory. Lawrence Tout, for reasons best known to himself, bet £5 at odds of 1000/1 that he would be struck by lightning.

A Hill customer's death benefited Oxfam in one of the company's strangest pay-outs, when Roger Federer won the Wimbledon singles title in 2012 for a record-breaking seventh time. Back in 2003 Nick Newlife had placed a series of bets with William Hill, including one of £1,520 at odds of 66/1 that Federer would ultimately win at least seven titles. But Mr Newlife died in 2009, bequeathing the bet to Oxfam, which collected £101,840, enough, their spokesman calculated, to enable the charity to bring food to 10,000 families for a month.

Others bet on longevity rather than mortality. On 2 January 2005 Arthur Best from Shrewsbury won £7,000 from Hills for turning 100, which ten years earlier he'd backed himself to do to the tune of £110 at 66/1, and his winnings paid for a party for 43 friends and relatives. Two years later Alec Holden from Epsom collected £25,000 on 24 April 2007 for reaching his centenary, having staked £100 on himself at 250/1. And in 1995 Graham Sharpe laid one of the company's more bizarre bets to John W. Richardson, a Londoner now living in California, who will win £500,000 if he fathers a child in the year 2040. Since he was 55 at the time, Sharpe gave him odds of 10,000/1, because in 2040 he will turn 100. Mr

Richardson says he will offer half of his winnings to any woman who will bear that child. In 2002 Donna Munn from Portslade in East Sussex, meanwhile, won £1,000 for having her first child on 9 June. This made her new daughter the fourth member of her family to celebrate their birthday on that date, for which Hills had given Donna odds of 20/1 for a £50 stake.

In 2000 Pete Edwards took a long-range gamble on his grandson's sporting future by betting £50 at 2,500/1 that he would one day play for Wales at football. Harry Wilson was then just three, but 13 years later he became the youngest player to win a senior cap for Wales when he came on for the final few minutes of their match against Belgium, and his grandfather became £125,000 richer and was able to quit his job. An air stewardess from Surrey, Melissa Dockray, won £750 in 2008 for marrying her boyfriend in Las Vegas, having bet on Valentine's Day 2007 that they would wed within two years, and her winnings will double if they are still married in 2018. In 2004 Brett Allen, a 21-year-old student, lost his bet of £25 at 100/1 that he'd date Kylie Minogue some time that year.

William Hill was founded as, and continues to be, a company that primarily takes bets on sport, and has done so with clients the world over – for example, bets on the London 2012 Olympics came from some 180 countries, from Austria to Zambia.

Over the years it has taken, and paid out on, some remarkable sporting wagers. In April 2012 the company accepted a bet of £500,000 on Big Buck's to win a race at Aintree. But at odds of 1/5 the customer only won a further £100,000. In 2006, though, a client in Tyne and Wear lost his £374,000 bet that the USA would win that year's Ryder Cup: they were thrashed 18-9. With Spurs 3-0 up at half-time against Manchester United in September 2001, a Blackpool-based internet punter decided to splash out £10,000 in the hope of collecting an easy £625 profit by backing them at 1/16 to clinch victory. They lost 3-5. When the businessman Michael Knighton attempted to buy Manchester United, William Hill faced a liability of up to £1 million on his requested bet that one day he would play for a top-division football club. Knighton did become a director, and one afternoon in 1989 even ran out on to the pitch in a team shirt kicking a football. He later confirmed that, had his takeover bid succeeded, he would have insisted on Alex Ferguson picking him as a substitute and bringing him on for the final seconds of a match.

In 1994 Adrian Fitzpatrick staked £8,000 with William Hill that Manchester United would retain the Premier League title, Crystal Palace would be champions of the First Division, and Brazil would win the World Cup by beating Italy. When Roberto Baggio missed a vital penalty in the Final, Fitzpatrick picked up £400,000. (When Diego Maradona put England out of the 1986 World Cup with his disputed 'hand of God' goal, William Hill had refunded the stakes of punters who had bet on a draw. This was the first time any bookmaker had ever offered such a concession to punters, costing a five-figure sum, and rivals Ladbrokes and Coral refused to follow. It didn't, of course, change the result of the game, which Hill's also paid out on!) In 2001 Mick Gibbs from Staffordshire won half a million pounds for a mere 30p stake on a 15-event accumulator. The 'big one' included all four English and three Scottish football divisions, plus the Conference; the Rugby Union Premiership; cricket's County Championship and NatWest Trophy, and his win was sealed at odds of 1,666,667/1 when Bayern Munich defeated Valencia in the final of the 2000–1 Champions League.

George Rhodes from Aldershot made the *Guinness Book of Records* when his 1984 ITV7 for 5p beat odds of 1,670,000/1, but Fred Craggs defied even longer odds of 2,000,000/1 by landing the biggest-ever betting shop accumulator bet in 2008, on his 60th birthday, at William Hill's branch in Thirsk. He selected eight horses to win at various courses, portentously starting with Isn't That Lucky and finishing with A Dream Come True, and duly placed his 50p bet. But it wasn't until Mr Craggs visited another Hill's shop in

The *Daily Mirror* leads its news agenda with the story that William Hill 'ruled out' Maradona's hand-ball goal in the England v Argentina game and compensated clients who bet on a 1-1 scoreline. Reporter Alastair Campbell later became Tony Blair's spin doctor.

Bedale that he was told the betting slip he hadn't bothered to check had actually made him a millionaire. Barry Tomlinson visited his local Hill's shop in early 1997 to tell the manager he hadn't had time to bring in a few bets he had placed some time ago. He then placed

1,840 betting slips on the counter going back up to four years, and it emerged that he had a total of £11,122.22 winnings to collect. The only punter on record as turning down winnings had also placed his bet at a Hill's in Twickenham in 1997, but managed to lose his betting slip. When it was explained that he just had to write a copy to be paid his £512 he stunned staff by declaring, 'It is my fault that I lost the betting slip, therefore I do not deserve the winnings.'

In recent years Hill's internet clients have made some extraordinary wins, too, and perhaps none more than Paul Gwilym from Cardiff, who in the early hours of one morning of April 2009 decided to have a 30p flutter on one of William Hill's online casino games to allay his insomnia. Very soon he had won £114,561.16. 'I'm so excited,' he said, 'I haven't slept since.' In 2011 an online punter from Malta needed Liverpool to score an 87th-minute winner to beat Chelsea 2-1 to clinch his 683,738/1 accumulator on 19 English and Scottish league games and win £585,143.24 for his stake of just one euro, or 86p. Another client won £1,426,000 on williamhillcasino.com betting on his lucky number 23 at roulette. At one point, as his winnings continued to grow, he called the company to ask whether his computer was playing up!

A 29-year-old Newmarket stable girl, Olesia Kuzmychova, won £238,155 from a 20p spin on the William Hill Vegas slot game in January 2014. 'I can now visit my mother in Ukraine for the first time in seven years,' she said. Amazingly, just seven months later, she won another substantial six figure sum.

But the bet to end them all, and nearly bookmakers with it, was on 28 September 1996. On that day Frankie Dettori created racing and betting history by riding his Magnificent Seven winners at Ascot at odds of 25,095/1. His fans won almost £50 million backing all of his mounts in almost every possible combination. The day's biggest winner was William Hill customer Darren Yates from Morecambe, who collected £550,823 from the £60 he'd staked, despite his wife telling him that morning, 'Don't waste any more of our money on that Dettori.' Ironically, Shooting Light, a horse owned by Hill's managing director John Brown, might have saved the company much of that pay-out had it managed to win the last race of the seven, but finished only 17th of 18. In total, William Hill lost a barely believable £8 million that day. 'I spent that Saturday night working out how we were going to arrange for £8 million to be ready and waiting on Monday morning, in cash, to pay out winning betting shop customers,' said Brown.

Perhaps the most enduring and effective non-racing sponsorship the company instigated has never impacted directly on its turnover, but 2013 saw William Hill celebrate the 25th anniversary of its annual William Hill Sports Book of the Year award, with the prize going, appropriately, to the horseracing writer Jamie Reid for his dramatic and compelling book, *Doped*. The high-profile award ceremony at the Hospital Club in London, broadcast live on BBC Radio 4's *Front Row*, at which the winner received a cheque for £25,000 and a specially commissioned hand-bound copy of his book, symbolised how far both the award, and indeed the genre of sports writing, had come over the course of a quarter-century.

Back in the 1980s sports books were very much the poor relations of the literary world: apart perhaps from cricket, which had always inspired a distinguished literature, sports writing in the UK was not considered a literary genre. One man, however, was convinced of its enormous potential – that with the right encouragement and promotion publishers would take a chance and commission more adventurous and insightful writing about sport. So John Gaustad, an exiled Kiwi who had been working at the university booksellers Heffers in Cambridge, risked opening a shop, Sportspages, in central London, stocking just sport-themed books, fanzines and memorabilia.

In 1988, Graham Sharpe, who set the odds for the Hill betting markets on the literary heavyweight awards such as the Booker and Whitbread Prizes, spotted a gap in the market where a sporting equivalent might fit. Gaustad and Sharpe met to compare notes, and soon agreed that the crucial element of any award for sports books would be the make-up and quality of the judging panel. They approached a selection of potential judges, therefore, offering them no money, a slap-up dinner and the chore of reading dozens of sports books to determine which was the best. Not one of those approached turned down the offer, and in 1989 the first ever William Hill Sports Book of the Year was judged by the BBC broadcaster Harry Carpenter, rugby legend Cliff Morgan, experienced and respected sports journalists Hugh McIlvanney of the *Sunday Times* and Ian Wooldridge of the *Daily Mail*, with John Gaustad chairing. For many years the prize was awarded amidst a tight scrum of guests in the cramped confines of the Sportspages shop.

Twenty-five years on, and the William Hill Sports Book of the Year is now the richest and most prestigious award of its kind in the world. Publishers' sales directors lurk at the back of the room as the winner is announced, ready to order instant reprints of tens of thousands of copies for a book now guaranteed to join the Christmas bestsellers. Shortlisted Hill authors have also been shortlisted for the Booker and other major literary awards; difficult, obscure, controversial sporting topics which might otherwise never have seen the light of day have been published, celebrated and become bestsellers as a result. The sports pages of the broadsheet newspapers devote substantial features to appraising each year's shortlist. For an author such as Nick Hornby, receiving the award for his first book *Fever Pitch*, a wry and self-deprecating account of his dogged support for an Arsenal team yet to embrace the free-flowing football of the Wenger era, it led not only to his swift acceptance as a major British writer – *Fever Pitch* is now accorded the status of a Penguin Modern Classic – but confirmed the emergence of a new, genuinely literary kind of sports book: personal, maverick, moving, and above all not just for sports fans. Winning the award twice has since confirmed both Donald McRae and Duncan Hamilton with similar reputations. Amongst other winners, sportsmen such as Marcus Trescothick and Brian Moore took readers into uncomfortable depths of their characters and psyche few sporting superstars had ever contemplated revealing in public; together with *Fever Pitch*, Laura Hillenbrand's *Seabiscuit* and Daniel Topolski and Patrick Robinson's inaugural winner *True Blue* were made into worthy movies.

The current judging panel still includes McIlvanney, doyen of British sportswriters, along with broadcasters John Inverdale and Danny Kelly, *Times* writer Alyson Rudd, and the recently retired footballer and former chairman of the Professional Footballers Association, Clarke Carlisle – and judges still serve on an unpaid basis.

They do get the occasional free bet, though, as do the short-listed and winning writers – with mixed fortunes. Daniel Topolski confessed at the 2013 awards that after 25 years he had still to de-cide what to stake his wager on; when controversial cyclist Lance Armstrong's *It's All About The Bike* won he put his bet on himself to win the Tour de France; one author who must remain nameless deliberately put his on a non-runner in a horse race – so that he would receive the stake money back; another found a four-horse race and put a quarter of his stake money on each, hoping for an outsider to win.

The Australian cricket writer Gideon Haigh wanted to put his bet on the greyhound he part-owned in Melbourne. But Paul Kimmage, the former Tour de France cyclist-turned-journalist who won in 1990 with *Rough Ride* – and was twice since shortlisted – which exposed many of the dubious habits of his co-riders, had the most to own up to. Covering a Five Nations rugby match between Ireland and England at Lansdowne Road in Dublin, he put his bet on the visitors to win. With time running out, Ireland were still ahead, to the joy of every Irishman in the ground except one: 'I was the only Irishman there hoping England would get over the try line for victory.' They did, leaving him uncertain whether to laugh or cry.

CHAPTER 27

TURNING ROUND THE TANKER

David Harding's unexpected announcement that he was to leave was, not surprisingly, seen by the City as a huge blow. William Hill was regarded as a well-run company, and to follow him, the general feeling was that the company would once again have to head-hunt. But eight months later, with the headhunters having come up with no candidate to capture the board's attention, the focus changed to an appointment from within the ranks. The failure to find a replacement before Harding departed in September 2007 meant Charles Scott had to combine the role of chairman and chief executive until February 2008, which contravened the Code on Corporate Governance. For the first time in years there was no chief executive's review of the accounts.

Ralph Topping was one of the three internal candidates rumoured to have been approached, and he came close to not applying. Even five and a half years later the 'cock-up' Hill's had made of the whole process was still obviously a raw subject:

> I don't know if you have heard of the term 'thrawn Scot', who absolutely takes umbrage at anyone insulting them. We never forgive ... When you're asked to throw your hat in the ring, being the kind of guy that I am, I never throw my hat in the ring. I've always been approached for jobs and I kind of took umbrage at that.

Nevertheless, in February 2008 'he was finally handed the keys to the chief executive's office,' wrote Nathalie Thomas in that 2013 *Telegraph* interview, 'but only after William Hill's board wasted eight months looking everywhere else other than its own backyard.'

In opting for Topping, however tortuous the process might have been, the board was of course going back to the John Brown model, as Topping, like Brown, was a one-company man. Topping acknowledges Brown as 'a huge influence ... he was sharp ... tough but fair', but there were important differences. Brown was a Londoner, and Topping a very proud Scot from a Presbyterian background who had always felt a deep sense of attachment to his homeland. Born in 1951, a policeman's son from near Linlithgow, an historic lochside town in West Lothian, some 20 miles from Edinburgh, he had started working for Mecca Bookmakers in Glasgow one day a week while a law student at Strathclyde, to fund his petrol bill for driving from home to university, having been driven out of his lodgings by an almost constant diet of smoked haddock for breakfast.

> The Mecca betting shop was actually near Hampden Park, so I ended up near the home of Scottish football as a Saturday boy. The betting shop also had mainly women working in it which was very unusual at that time. I was only about 19, 20, years of age and I liked it a lot.

This was despite the shop having no toilet facilities, and employees having to go to the garage next door! He also recalls taking bets from a certain Alex Ferguson back in the 1970s. Quitting his degree course without graduating to follow a career in bookmaking was, however, a decision he would ultimately call his 'biggest regret', but

> The bottom line is, after spending some time abroad I started [in 1973] working full-time. I was around 21 years of age ... and always thought I would do something else in life, but didn't. I have always remained within the industry, and the pay was absolutely fantastic compared with a teacher at that time, which is probably what I would have ended up being.

It was as he started in the industry that he received some advice that, more than 40 years later, he still considers the best he has ever received:

> This came from a man who is now dead, Kevin, when I was a trainee manager. He said, 'It looks like you will go far in this organisation. The higher up you go, do not forget where you came from. You come in with an unblemished reputation: make sure you leave with one.' I have never forgotten that advice.

Topping soon worked his way up the company ladder, and when Mecca and William Hill merged he stayed around, and from 1998–2002 was internet development director, pioneering Hill's online presence and helping to make the company a market leader; from 2002 he became retail operations director, then in 2007, group director, operations.

Even before Topping took over as chief executive he had been an instrument of change at William Hill, introducing Sportsbook in 1999 to mark the company's move into online business. His arrival as chief executive was to see further, more wide-ranging changes. Some of this related to how the company presented itself to the world, and the 2008 accounts, the first since he'd taken over, were characterised by a new openness. 2009 marked the 75th birthday of the company, and now there was a full-page group photo of the entire board, assembled much like a sports team. His chief executive's report included a two-page Q&A spread accompanied by a picture of Topping in the sort of pose David Dimbleby might adopt. It is clear from his answers that when he took over as chief executive he realised William Hill was a huge tanker that was listing and urgently needed turning round. In the process, various things that had been essential for his predecessor had to be thrown overboard.

The first to go was the much-talked-about IT project. By 2006 it had become clear that Hill's Sportsbook internet platform was no longer fit for purpose, and under David Harding the development of a new technology programme called NextGen was 'designed to rectify these issues and deliver systems clearly superior to anything currently available to our major competitors'. Topping was just as keen on technological improvement, but it was very quickly clear to him that NextGen was not the answer. In November 2007 the board decided that the NextGen programme had to be consigned to history. In January 2008 the *Guardian* reported that chairman Charlie Scott 'is to call in an outside technology firm to rescue its under-performing internet betting division in a move that will lead to a £26m write-off in its in-house software development programme'.

However, Scott emphasised that this had nothing to do with David Harding's recent departure. Ralph inherited this issue when he became chief executive.

Scrapping it meant an impairment charge of £20.9 million – £20.5 million of internally developed software and £400,000 of computer hardware equipment. 2008 was to see further expenses of £4 million, resulting in a total cost of £24.9 million. But that, as far as Topping and his board were concerned, was a price worth paying to get shot of something that was not going to work.

But while IT had proved costly, Topping soon realised it was easier to get rid of an internal project than deal with the mess in the overseas business Harding had ventured into with such high hopes, as this could not be a simple executive decision for the board, but would involve working with foreign partners. To understand what Topping was up against we need to go back to 2006, when the group had signed up with the Spanish gaming group Codere, a company dedicated to the private gaming sector in Europe and Latin America, for a joint venture to develop a sports betting business in Spain, and another relating to the Italian gambling sector. On paper Codere had a lot going for it, with more than 25 years' experience operating slot machines, bingo halls, sports betting outlets, racetracks and casinos in Spain, Italy, Central and South America.

In 2006 Spain looked a very inviting prospect. The country was one of the largest gambling markets in Europe and had plans for the liberalisation of its gambling industry. Indeed, the Madrid region had already published legislation allowing for the establishment of land-based businesses and regulating sports betting, and other regions were following in Madrid's wake. The William Hill-Codere plan was to apply jointly for a licence in Madrid and other regions once the regulations were passed. In Italy, they were jointly awarded 20 concessions to operate horseracing betting shops, seven concessions to operate sports betting shops, and 28 concessions relating to sports betting facilities. Remote licences relating to horseracing and sports betting were also applied for and granted, and other opportunities for growth were anticipated. Altogether William Hill planned to invest at least £25 million.

Topping had been chief executive for only seven days by the time the 2007 accounts were approved, so had no hand in crafting the optimistic noises made in them about Spain and Italy. But now, as he settled into Harding's office, he was faced with the reality of the 2008 situation and how badly the world economic crash had affected Spain. It was clear drastic action was necessary if the company was not to bleed more money overseas. In July 2008, therefore, William Hill sold its Italian joint venture company, resulting in a loss of £1.2 million. That left a huge problem in Spain, where, under the name Victoria Apuestas, the joint venture had 98 branches and, after a review of its value, an impairment charge of £5.4 million had already been implemented. It could be argued that between 2008 and 2009 the Spanish business was recovering: in 2008 the total revenue of three joint ventures in Spain had been £1 million, and the overall loss £11.6 million; in 2009 revenue had jumped to £6.4 million and the total loss reduced to £9.3 million.

But such an argument was dancing on the head of a pin: the simple fact was, Hills needed to get out of Spain. However a decision to leave was one thing; to actually leave, quite another, and as events demonstrated, it took time and would not prove easy. Not until January 2010 did Codere complete the purchase of William Hill's 50% stake in the last joint venture, for the sum of just one euro.

At last Topping and the board could claim the nightmare was over. 'Historically the Group's business has proved to be less exposed to the economic cycle than many other consumer facing industries,' the 2007 Operating and Financial Review had maintained: Spain had shown this was no longer true, and now there was another overseas venture where Hills had to cope with the consequences of a dramatic economic downturn. Following the 2008 economic crash the age of the Celtic Tigers had come to an end, the Irish economy was in meltdown, and the board was busy making provision for losses there. The value of the goodwill in its betting offices in the Republic was written down by £6.8 million, and their fixed assets by a further £1.4 million. During 2009 the company closed 14 of its shops in the Republic. In 2010 a review of branches there was announced, followed in December of that year by confirmation that those trading unprofitably were to close. In December 2011, Hill's remaining shops there were sold.

Foreign forays were not the only problem for Hills. Telephone betting, long a mainstay of the business, was also in trouble. In 2009 there were 113,700 active telephone customers, who tended to be sophisticated horseracing punters betting more on average than customers in the shops or online. But despite this, in 2009 telephone betting had slipped from an operating profit of £5.9 million the previous year to a loss of £1.8 million, reflecting, moreover, a steep downward fall in net revenue, from £53 million in 2007 to £39.8 million in 2008 and £29.7 million in 2009 – a drop of 25%. Though the reason given was the impact of the adverse economic climate in reducing the number of runners per race and increasing price competition at the racetracks, Topping argued that the real reason was the handicap imposed by an uneven tax and regulatory playing field on operators based in the UK. While William Hill paid 15% gross profits tax on gross wins and a 10% statutory levy on any UK horseracing bets, offshore operators paid neither. Betting exchanges paid 15% gross profits tax, but not on gross win, rather on the amount they took from customers, which typically worked out as 2%–5%. 'Telephone is our most expensive channel for taking a bet,' Topping pointed out, 'and we have call centres in Sheffield and Leeds that at peak can take 600 calls simultaneously.' He revealed the entire telephone system was being reviewed, which meant optimising the customer base and looking at where the operations should be located, and aimed to return telephone betting to profitability in 2010.

Topping knew that to really turn the tanker round and get it moving in the right direction he needed a bold new initiative. In October 2008, therefore, eight months after he took charge, a deal was struck after some hard negotiations with Playtech, a leading gaming software company founded in 1999 and floated on the Stock Exchange in 2006, that was still 40% owned by Teddy Sagi, an Israeli entrepreneur. With over 1,500 employees, not only in Israel but also in Eastern Europe and in the Philippines, Playtech offered a range of online casinos, poker rooms, bingo games, fixed-odds arcade games and mobile gaming. The deal involved creating a new business, William Hill Online, and Hills acquiring certain assets, business and contracts from Playtech, including 30 gaming sites and a customer services and online marketing organisation. Playtech had 29% of William Hill Online in return for the acquired assets, and William Hill had call options to reacquire that 29% stake in 2013 and 2015. 160 marketing employees based in Israel and around 110 customer services employees in Bulgaria joined William Hill Online. Hills also had a five-year licensing agreement for Playtech's casino and poker software, which was considered the market leader. The deal had to be done, Topping argued, because Hill's previous online strategy was not working. In essence it was the old story of the penalty paid by those who start off first and then find the competition has not only caught up but streaked ahead.

The transaction was actually completed on 30 December 2008. It was calculated that in selling a stake of 29% of William Hill Online to Playtech William Hill had made a gain of £86.4 million, which enabled the losses from scrapping the IT project and the joint ventures to be turned into an overall profit on exceptional items of £77.2 million. All the more important given there had been a loss of £14.2 million the previous year.

Topping could not have been more bullish about the deal, declaring that it combined two 'highly complementary businesses'. He added: 'Our e-gaming capacity was marginal and we were weak internationally. The assets we acquired from Playtech have given us websites, terrific online marketing and customer relations expertise, a vast affiliate network that will drive customers to our websites and an established European customer base and profit stream.'

In the 2008 accounts Ralph made a significant point: 'We are no longer just a bookmaker. Between our internet sites and the machines in our shops, gaming accounts for 38% of our net revenue in 2008.'

Even as he executed the Playtech deal – undoubtedly a major change for the company – Topping knew that it faced a huge problem: cash. This may seem ironic in a business largely dealing with cash, but in terms of having cash to make acquisitions William Hill was not exactly flush. In the past William Hill's acquisitions had caused problems, and back in December 2005, with the City fearing that David Harding had overpaid for the Stanley shops, the company had been relegated from the FTSE 100 Index. However, this was a time when boom and bust was supposed to have been eliminated and when the company made much of the fact that it gave back money to shareholders by buying back shares. At the annual general meeting in May 2006 the company had secured shareholders' permission to buy back up to 10% of the share capital, and bought back 7%, at a total cost of £178.4 million. This meant that since its flotation in June 2002 William Hill had bought back 17% of its issued share capital, returning £402.5 million to shareholders, and ensuring that the company's earnings per share improved.

But now, in the vastly different world of 2008, all those thoughts had to be quickly forgotten. Even as Topping was negotiating the Playtech deal, in November 2008 analysts from UBS (Switzerland's biggest bank, one of those dominating corporate banking) had voiced concern about the level of the company's debt, then at around £1 billion. At the end of 2008 its debt facilities totalled £1.45 billion, with two maturities, £1.2 billion repayable on 1 March 2010 and £250 million on 30 July 2011. Within two months of the Playtech deal, therefore, the reordering of the bank debt and the refinancing of the company had begun. On 27 February 2009, £250 million of the committed but undrawn facilities were cancelled, reducing the available facilities to £950 million. On the same day, new Forward Start Facilities, totalling £588.5 million, which could be drawn from 17 January 2010, were entered into.

All this, of course, created a funding gap and, as Charles Scott admitted, 'the current credit market conditions have not made it possible for William Hill to refinance the Group's existing bank facilities in full in the bank market.' The company decided it would not pay a final dividend in 2008, and instead of giving money back to its shareholders, it would ask them for money. A one-for-one rights issue was announced, to raise £350 million, priced at 105 pence per share, a 57% discount to the closing middle market share price, and in April 2009 the proceeds were used to repay bank borrowings, halving the amount available under the first facility to £700 million. In November 2009 the company also launched its first corporate bond, a £300 million seven-year bond with a coupon rate of 7.125%, again to pay down debt, in effect cancelling the £50 million and £250 million facilities due in 2011. Ultimately, by the end of 2009 the net debt had been reduced by £419.5 million to £602.6 million.

However, the 2009 accounts could hardly be said to provide much of a platform for a strategy for the next couple of years, let alone further ahead. Group revenues had increased by 4% to £997.9 million, but operating profit was down 6% to £258.5 million. Earnings per share were down 35%, the third successive year it had fallen, and net operating expenses had also risen by 14% to £586.4 million.

Topping continued to stress the lack of a level playing field between William Hill and its offshore competitors. In 2009, with the news that the company's online revenues were up by 63%, he confirmed plans to move William Hill Online's operations to Gibraltar. Amongst other reasons, Topping noted, 'we are paying 17 times more tax in the UK than we will be in Gibraltar. The Government blew a big chance to make the UK a centre for online gambling,' he went on, noting that William Hill had paid £300 million in UK taxes in the previous year. 'If it had made this an attractive place to do business, then this would never have happened.' It was estimated that the move could save the company some £10 million, and that 75 staff would move to work in Gibraltar. Though the 2010 World Cup, held in South Africa, was the best for bookmakers in 40 years, according to the chief executive, thanks to 'results that not even an octopus could have predicted', (a reference to a so-called 'psychic octopus' that had become a media personality during the tournament), the bulk of Hill's telephone operation followed the online operation to Gibraltar in February 2011, meaning the closure of its call centre in Leeds and the outsourcing of the one in Sheffield, affecting altogether some 400 jobs. A further saving of from £4 million to £7 million per year was expected.

By the time the 2010 figures were published William Hill had a new chairman, Gareth Davis, who had recently retired as CEO of Imperial Tobacco, and Topping had some justification for feeling that the corner had been properly turned. Net revenues were up 7% for the first time, passing the thousand million mark at £1.07 billion. Overall the operating profit of the business was up 7% to £276.8 million, and earnings per share rose by 5% to 21.7p. What was encouraging was that the growth was across all three channels, online delivering a 24% net revenue increase with Sportsbook up 95%. Retail benefited from 11% growth on gaming machines staking and telephone from an improved net revenue margin offsetting lower amounts wagered. After losing £1.8 million in 2009 the telephone business made a small operating profit of £900,000. The exceptional items were £6.1 million, down from £34.8 million the year before with all those write-downs of goodwill.

Topping reiterated that the UK, which provided 75% of the revenue, would remain the bedrock of the business, not least the betting shops, which he bullishly defended from the charge that they were now past their 'best-by' date:

> In the UK almost 7 million people bet with a bookmaker. Of those, the majority used high street bookmakers only – almost 4.4 million of them. Retail is still the channel of choice for most customers because of its convenience, the ability to bet with cash and community experience.

The international expansion strategy led by William Hill Online was going well: Online had seen 800,000 new accounts in 2010, a 22% increase on 2009.

But even as the accounts were with the printers a Stop Press announcement had to be inserted:

On 22nd February 2011 the group secured an interim injunction against Playtech Ltd to ensure the group's legal rights under the William Hill Online joint venture agreements are maintained. Playtech recently initiated discussions with William Hill seeking possible significant amendments to the current William Hill Online joint venture agreement. There's also been press speculation regarding discussions between Playtech and Ladbrokes Plc. The group remains committed to the success of the William Hill Online joint venture. Further announcements will be made as appropriate.

Though that injunction was ultimately discharged after months of discussions with Playtech, leading to changes in the agreement, other, more dramatic, problems would follow with Hill's partner in its crucial Online venture. This, it could be said, marked the moment when the company needed to think hard about reacquiring Playtech's 29% stake in 2013.

CHAPTER 28

BACK INTO THE FTSE

In August 2011, there was something of a harbinger of trouble when a William Hill branch in Tottenham, North London, was burned to the ground by rioters as unrest swept the country.

A month later, William Hill suddenly pulled out of negotiations to buy the mobile betting operator Probability, which specialised in low-value, high-margin games of chance.

The word was that the potential acquisition was not well received by its Israeli partner Playtech who, rumours suggested, feared such a deal might adversely impact on its own interests.

Within weeks, though, there was a more serious problem.

Suspicions were aroused in late September, when the chief marketing officer of William Hill Online, Eyal Sanoff – a close friend of Playtech's 40% shareholder Teddy Sagi – would not give William Hill access to the computer systems at its Tel Aviv office.

William Hill set a deadline of 30 September for the Tel Aviv office to comply with its demand; three days before, Sanoff quit. The Tel Aviv office had refused to co-operate with an internal audit instigated by Hill's head office. According to *The Daily Telegraph,* 'plans for a rival business' were discovered.

Ralph Topping was also less than happy to uncover what was alleged to be a string of payments from the Tel Aviv business to pay for managers to have table-tennis coaching, while there were also reportedly a rabbi, a fish feeder and a hairdresser on the books.

His response was to sack seven senior managers and several junior staff. According to reports, the severance payments ran to some £2 million and depended on fired staff agreeing to 'non-compete' clauses.

These departures, and that of Sanoff, who had resigned, but was reportedly planning to sue the company for alleged breach of contract and making his work impossible, destabilised the remaining workforce in Tel Aviv – thanks to the success of William Hill Online, 185-strong – who were now fearing for their own jobs, with rumours spreading that William Hill planned to close down Playtech's marketing support centre and move operations to Gibraltar. *The Times* reported that William Hill managers in Tel Aviv had attempted to undermine the company by encouraging staff to walk out. 'We received an e-mail when this all started,' an anonymous employee was quoted as saying. 'It convinced me, and I think all of us, that if we stuck by [local managers] and the rest of the team we would keep a job here.' On Sunday 16 October none of the Tel Aviv employees showed up for work, and fewer than 20 appeared on the two subsequent days. An e-mail from William Hill Online's CEO Henry Birch assuring them that their jobs were safe failed to convince them.

Walk-outs followed by staff at William Hill Online offices in Bulgaria and a Playtech business in Manila where William Hill Online was a major customer. Sagi had owned all three businesses.

Straight away Topping got on a plane to Tel Aviv, accompanied by Birch and William Hill Online's chief operating officer Jim Mullen, and spent four days there. The plan was for Mullen and Birch temporarily to take over Sanoff's responsibilities and set about changing the culture of the business. According to the *Daily Telegraph*, when Mullen arrived at the Tel Aviv offices he was locked out, the e-mail and telephone systems were taken down, and he and Birch were directed to a local beach. The paper quoted a source as alleging that Sanoff had earlier told Mullen he was only at William Hill Online to protect Teddy Sagi's interests. The paper also quoted Topping, who had met with Playtech CEO Mor Weizer, as saying, 'If there's one guy who could put an end to this with one phone call, it's Teddy Sagi.'

The air was now filled with contradictory stories. William Hill kept trying to reassure the staff, saying it had no intention of closing the Tel Aviv operations. Birch was said to have offered incentives to staff that came into work. Other sources reported that William Hill Online was taking away the authority of Israeli managers ahead of the transfer of operations to Gibraltar. William Hill had to keep the London Stock Exchange informed, and on 18 October announced that 'Senior William Hill Online management are currently on the ground in Tel Aviv working through these issues.'

It also issued a statement disclosing that, 'Several other senior managers in Tel Aviv are now subject to disciplinary actions in relation to the disruption this week within the marketing business in Tel Aviv, and in the customer service and back office operations in Manila and Bulgaria.' 'I'm absolutely furious,' Topping was quoted by the *Daily Telegraph* as saying on departing Tel Aviv for London, 'but cannot comment further.' By early November he was no happier, and venting in his blog his frustrations with Mor Weizer, the young CEO of Playtech – a company, after all, that William Hill had tied up with primarily to access its state-of-the-art technology: 'He always seems to have just had BlackBerry problems and laptop malfunctions when you call him or email him and he fails to respond by return. The current period of Trappist-like silence from Mor with me is nearly a week!'

The Times spoke for many in the media, where the story was extensively reported, in seeing all this as a classic clash of cultures: 'You had this clash between the British way of doing things – by the book, dotted i's and all – and the Israeli way of doing things.' 'The real combatants in this relationship are Mr Topping and the Israeli Teddy Sagi, the 40% owner of Playtech,' wrote Roger Blitz of the *Financial Times*:

'It's like Ali versus Frazier,' said one person who knows both men. 'They are two individuals who aren't scared of each other.' Mr Topping's blog alludes to a wider problem William Hill has had with its partner. WHO [William Hill Online] employs almost 1,000 people in Tel Aviv, Manila and Sofia. Manila is a WHO facility owned and run by Playtech. But William Hill insiders say they have had continual battles with members of WHO's management to gain access to information and data. Playtech's argument is the dispute was a WHO matter that did not involve Playtech staff nor Mr Sagi. But William Hill insiders believe the Tel Aviv personnel – who are critical to the operation because of their knowledge of online media buying and Playtech software – were more loyal to Mr Sagi than to the company that employed them. The short-term resolution is that up to 40 Tel Aviv-based WHO staff have left, as has Eyal Sanoff, the operation's chief marketing officer. But the long-term issues remain. William Hill has an option to buy out Playtech's 29% stake in WHO, either in 2013 or 2015. Given William Hill's problems in trying to find out information about its WHO asset, there are two salient questions: what exactly would William Hill be buying; and what guarantee would the group have that the Tel Aviv staff would stay with WHO?

When the Playtech 'uprising' began, Ralph had been sitting on a beach in Zanzibar, relaxing after returning from a safari. He remembers taking a call from one of his security men, telling him: 'I'm in Tel Aviv. We can't get in the offices, we're locked out. The staff are on the beach holding a meeting.'

'I pay you a hefty sum,' Topping replied. 'Don't you think you might have worked out you should be on the beach – get down there now!'

Staff had been deliberately and wrongly told that Hills were planning to close the offices down, and they were in fear of losing their jobs. 'We had to work around the management, and as the situation escalated we used social media – Facebook and Twitter – to communicate with staff.'

Amongst the team Ralph sent out were senior executives Thomas Murphy, David Russell, Marcella Meechan and Phil Moyes – the latter even climbed through a bomb shelter to gain access to one building.

'The management was clearly trying to use delaying tactics, and every time we seemed to be getting somewhere, they changed their minds. Thomas would negotiate with their lawyers for ages. The next day they'd come back and move the goal posts again.'

Ralph arrived to take over the negotiations. 'I told their lead lawyer, "You're a terrific lawyer but if I asked a lawyer in Glasgow about the weather and he told me it was raining, I'd get an umbrella. If you told me it was raining I'd have to look for myself."'

Then Ralph began to play hardball. '"You've got five hours, or I'm going. We'll pull the plug. Our business may suffer but I only care about our reputation." Within two and a half hours they said they were ready to sign a deal. I wouldn't go in there – but sent a colleague. We called their bluff.'

Did the business suffer? 'It was slightly impacted but we were then able to mould the business in the William Hill culture.'

Had the bluff not worked? 'We would have had to close it down. We would have suffered but I would have been prepared to do it.'

The next year saw more positive developments, both home and abroad.

With football vital to the company's success, in January 2012 Hills were unveiled by the FA as their 'official betting partner' to the England team and the FA Cup.

The company was also sponsoring the Scottish Cup Final (since the 2011/12 season), while Ralph Topping had been non-executive chairman of the Scottish Premier League since 2009, and remained so until late 2012. Ralph came from a family of Hearts and Rangers supporters, but as a 'contrary boy', opted to follow Hibs. His football involvement resulted in an invitation for him and wife Elizabeth to the Royal Box at Wembley for an England v Scotland international. When his countrymen took the lead, 'I erupted out of my seat – Go on, Scotland, get intae them!' Ralph looked around the box: 'Those around me were silent, remembering the rules for the Royal Box. Polite applause only.'

Ralph Topping announced his ambitious and long-term Project Africa in May 2012, designed to build a school and accompanying facilities in a remote area of Kenya, whilst incorporating a subtle undercurrent of helping to develop the talents and personal growth of staff who visit the community and take part in the work. Hill's 'ambassador', footballer Robbie Savage also joined in, suffering a badly damaged wrist after being thrown from the camel he was riding.

Overseas, the company's renewed appetite for a strategy of international expansion took a major step forward with the establishment of its first-ever operation in the US, when in June 2012 the company was granted licences by the Nevada Gaming Commission that enabled it to complete the $55 million (£35 million) acquisition of three US sports betting businesses, American Wagering, Inc., Brandywine Bookmaking LLC, and the racing and sports book assets of Sierra Development Company. Further international footholds had previously been secured with approvals for licensing in both Spain and Italy for William Hill Online, and now William Hill became the first British bookmaking company to be licensed in Nevada. The deal brought the company 159 locations state-wide, including 83 wagering kiosks, amounting to 55% of Nevada's sports book locations, though only 11% of an annual state-wide sports betting market, reported to reach $2.7billion. Nevada was the only state in the country with legal wagering on sporting events, but race and sports books, while popular with a loyal clientele of sports bettors, generate less than 5% of the state's gross gaming revenue and usually partner with resorts to run a casino's sports wagering.

Being licensed in Nevada 'was a tough party to get into', Topping said, though eased by the regulators' business-friendly attitude: 'I started filling out the application form on the day of the royal wedding [between Prince William and Kate Middleton],' he added, 'and didn't finish it until well after it was over.' But American commentators had no doubt he had played a crucial role in persuading the commissioners: 'It was hard to tell whether it was Ralph Topping's witty personality, his brogue or the quality of his team's presentation,' reported one. Topping had told them that the NFL was fun to watch, but from a betting perspective 'it's boring'.

Even here William Hill could not escape Playtech, however. The only tension during the hearing occurred when regulators asked about the two company's links, mindful that Teddy Sagi had been questioned by gaming regulators in Gibraltar about his financial dealings and whether his company had illegally accepted wagers from American customers – and also that he had spent nine months in jail in 1996 on bribery and fraud charges. 'My concern is not with the people in front of me, 'was how Commissioner John Moran Jr put it, 'but with those that are not in front of me.' Ultimately they noted that William Hill was being licensed for land-based sports books in Nevada and not an interactive gaming licence: when its application for an online licence was reviewed, Playtech and its leading investors would be summoned to answer questions.

American Wagering, Inc. operated the Leroy's Horse and Sports Place franchise; Brandywine Bookmaking had the Lucky's sports book brand; and Sierra Development Co. operated as Cal Neva Satellite Race and Sports in Northern Nevada. William Hill obtained non-restricted gaming licences from the Nevada Gaming Commission for five senior personnel and set about integrating the businesses and rebranding them as William Hill US, with American Wagering's Vic Salerno as its chairman, Brandywine Bookmaking's Joe Asher as CEO and Club Cal Neva's Jeff Siri as chief operating officer. Topping said William Hill would invest about $3 million in technology at its properties and offer 'in-play' wagering on sporting events.

The figures for 2012 showed Hills would have to be in for the long haul in the States, as William Hill US made an operating loss of £600,000, not helped by weak sporting results, particularly in the NFL in November, but by February 2013 Hills operated in 190 locations in Nevada, both in casino-based sportsbooks and in bar locations. It was providing hardware and software to many of the major Nevada sports books, and could also claim to have one of the leading mobile wagering applications available in the US. In addition Hills had become the exclusive risk manager for the State of Delaware sports lottery and the Marriott hotel in St Kitts. In July 2013 William Hill marked the fact that it had become the exclusive sports betting provider at Monmouth Park racecourse in New Jersey by becoming the title sponsor of the $1 million Haskell Invitational, the flagship Group 1 race run at the track. The longer-term aspiration, should sports betting become legal in the state, was for William Hill to develop a full sports book at the course.

The company had also turned its attentions to 'one of the largest licensed betting markets in the world where William Hill does not have a footprint,' as Ralph Topping put it: Australia. In December 2012, together with the European gaming firm GVC, it had finalised a takeover of its online rival, Sportingbet. It was a complicated transaction, as Ralph Topping explained to staff: 'In effect, GVC buys the whole business, and William Hill pays to acquire the Australian business from GVC and to take a call option over the Spanish business. Australia is a standalone business which will make it easy to bolt on.'

On 19 March 2013, William Hill completed the acquisition of Sportingbet's Australian business and was granted a call option over Sportingbet's Spanish business for a cash consideration of £459.4 million.

The option was duly exercised in Autumn 2013.

In Australia there were regulations limiting what a company could do, and indeed the 2001 Interactive Gambling Act had banned what the Australians called 'in the run betting', on racing and sporting events, and online gaming services such as online poker, online casino games and virtual poker machines. But pre-match betting on racing at sporting events was not prohibited, or on other contingencies such as elections and weather. Topping saw Australia as 'a well-established gambling culture, the fixed-odds bookmakers have been reshaping the market, and there's scope for the regulatory regime to liberalise over time, particularly in relation to in-play betting and gaming'.

William Hill was now operating across nine countries: Australia, Bulgaria, Gibraltar, Israel, Italy, the Philippines, Spain, UK, USA. In August 2013 William Hill swooped to acquire one of Australia's fastest growing online betting businesses, tomwaterhouse.com, for A\$34 million (£21.25 million), with Topping hailing the deal as further developing Australia as 'William Hill's second home territory'.

But the Sportingbet acquisition once more showed what a difficult partner Hills had chosen in Playtech, a frustration increased for Topping by having to deal with Mor Weizer again. In December 2012 – as Hills launched industry innovation Cash In My Bet, enabling online football clients to elect to take a profit while the bet was still 'live' – Weizer issued a statement declaring that under the terms of the joint venture agreement William Hill would be 'bound to conduct its remote gambling business through the William Hill Online business, in which Playtech is a 29% shareholder'. He went on to say that if the joint acquisition with GVC was completed, William Hill would be obliged to offer to sell the remote gambling activities of Sportingbet to William Hill Online within six months of completion of the acquisition and Playtech's rights gave it the absolute discretion to determine whether William Hill Online accepted such an acquisition. 'Playtech believes that it is likely,' Weizer's statement concluded, 'that the acquisition of the Sportingbet activities would add considerable value to William Hill Online.' Within hours a Hill's spokesman was quick to rubbish any such idea. 'Playtech have no rights to a business that is not part of William Hill Online, and therefore this has absolutely no effect on any valuation.'

The City interpreted this as an attempt by Weizer to push up the purchase price of Playtech's own 29% interest in William Hill Online. The Hill's board had already decided that William Hill Online was strong enough to do without a minority interest that was proving such an irritant, and the three investment banks employed as required under the Framework Agreement came up with a value of approximately £424 million for the minority interest on a debt-free and cash-free basis. Towards the end of February 2013 the investment banks' figures were notified to Playtech, and seven days later the board resolved to exercise the call option. Ralph called it a 'major milestone' for the company.

The board now had to decide whether it would borrow to pay Playtech or essentially use money raised from shareholders through a rights issue. The decision was to go for a 2 for 9 rights issue to raise approximately £375 million after providing for expenses, with £50 million from part of the 2012 Bridge Credit Facility to make up the required amount.

Nor was the Sportingbet acquisition without problems in Australia itself. During 2012 Ralph Topping had gone there six times. 'The truthful answer is there's a lot of work to be done,' he told the *Telegraph*. 'The user experience of the [Sportingbet] website is awful. The quality of some of the management was below European standards so some of them had to go, we had to look at marketing very closely and we had to look at the telephone business and digital business. There's plenty to go for but we are under no illusions … I am fairly calm and relaxed about it – we will sort it.'

With the share price in August 2012 at £3.14, it was reported that 700 staff who had saved the maximum £250 a month over the past three years were in line for an extra £10,000, thanks to its increase from £1.83 when the Sharesave scheme had started back in 2009. Hill's 2,370 shops saw a modest 1% increase in revenue to £789.7 million, though profits dipped 4% to £196.8 million. Online revenues, on the other hand, were up 28% to £321.3 million, and profits up 17% to £106.8 million.

A significant contribution to the online business was now coming through mobile phone betting. William Hill's mobile Sportsbook app had been launched in Apple's App store in February 2012, and in just ten months to the end of the year exceeded 500,000 downloads. With the iPhone app followed up by one for the iPad, *Marketing Week* magazine was reporting that in-app betting was now making up 30% of all online wagers. Ralph Topping waxed lyrical about the use of mobile phones: 'You can bet when you're on the move, out at dinner, at a game with your friends or sitting at home on the sofa. It's a transformation. No-one could have imagined this 30 years ago.' Mobile punters, he said, were betting in their 'pyjamas and evening wear'. By the middle of 2014 the Sportsbook app had been downloaded over two million times.

Smartphones were increasingly dominating the world of betting, and with William Hill boasting the most-downloaded betting app available, the 2013 Cheltenham Festival marked a further advance for mobile betting, doubling compared to 2012. The opening day of the Festival saw William Hill app downloads match the levels of Grand National day, and over one million bets were placed via mobile devices during the four-day Festival, constituting 43% of the company's total online business. Gold Cup day alone saw a 142% rise in betting numbers, and double the stakes of the previous year.

Two further online innovations towards the end of 2012 were Priority Prices, an industry first in offering customers – via Twitter, Facebook or text – the chance to gain advance notice of stand-out odds on the biggest sporting events, and what was described as 'the world's finest online casino', with Mayfair-trained table hosts catering for every type of player with stakes from £3 to £500. 'The dealers are an actual, real person, and the games are played in real time', boasted the website.

Despite William Hill's impressively steady growth and profitability, Ralph Topping's pay came under attack at the 2012 AGM when more than half of investors failed to back the company's remuneration report, with 48% voting against, and a further 3% withholding their votes. The controversial aspects of his package were a £1.2 million retention bonus, which Topping, now 60, would get if he stayed with the company until the end of the following year, and an 8.3% pay rise. The company's chairman, Gareth Davis, insisted the chief executive was worth every penny and that it was crucial to keep him, noting that Ralph had been 'instrumental in revitalising the fortunes of William Hill since taking the job in difficult circumstances four years ago', and pointing out that the shares had risen in value by 18% over the last year and the dividend 16%.

The implicit rebuke from some of the shareholders certainly did not induce Topping to adopt a lower profile. On the contrary: a year later he was again raising eyebrows in the industry with an outspoken attack on Ladbrokes. Contrasting William Hill's first-quarter performance in 2013 – an 8% rise in operating profits – with the 13% fall at Ladbrokes over the same period, he said he couldn't understand how a £6 million drop in Ladbrokes' income at Cheltenham could trigger a profits alert when it was followed by what for the bookmaking industry was a stunningly profitable Grand National, with the victory of the 66/1 Auroras Encore making it Hill's 'best ever' with profits estimated at around £19 million over the three-day Aintree meeting. 'I'm thinking of going to a Buddhist retreat for three weeks to figure it all out,' was Topping's robust verdict.

Topping's bullishness was fully justified on 1 May 2013 – the 52nd anniversary of the legalisation of betting shops – when William Hill rejoined the FTSE 100 Index of the leading shares on the London Stock Exchange. Staff at the London headquarters, Greenside House, were treated to tea and cake as the share price rose to 425p. Shareholders were pointedly offered Irn Bru and haggis at that year's AGM.

The following month, on 14 June, Ralph was voted Number One Chief Executive in the leisure, entertainment and hotel sector of the prestigious annual Extel Survey.

CHAPTER 29
EIGHTY YEARS OLD

Joe Ward Hill, William Hill's younger brother and perhaps the relative who had most in common with him over the years, died in 2010 at the age of 88. His older brother had wanted Joe to join him in business but, perhaps keen to establish himself in his own right, he had created his own chain of 50 betting shops, which ultimately he'd sold to Ladbrokes rather than William Hill. It has been suggested that this was something of a betrayal of his brother – also that having agreed a deal to sell to William Hill, the sale was hijacked.

He'd also taken a leaf out of his brother's book by developing Ward Hill Stud in Hertfordshire. As chairman of the Betting Office Licensees' Association, and a member of the Tattersalls Committee for a record 45 years, he'd become a major figure in the bookmaking world. But above all he was the last direct family link with the time when William had put the foundations of the William Hill Organization in place back in 1934 – a time when the Sabini gang terrorised racecourses, pony racing attracted huge crowds to Northolt, even a fledgling bookmaker like William Hill would have his first offices in grand Jermyn Street – and when the easiest and most common way to place a bet was to go to the races and hand it to the man stood on his stool with a satchel.

By 2014 it was over 40 years since William's death, the company he founded was celebrating its 80th anniversary, and this was a completely different William Hill Organization for a completely different world. It had businesses in nine countries, and currently took bets from customers in over 120. Where its founder had been an implacable opponent of betting shops, it now owned almost 2,400, more than anyone else in the UK – at the end of 2013 Gerry Connor, in the company's Group Services department, had calculated that during the course of a year they used 34,929 miles of till rolls and tickets. For all that, their most consistently profitable activity was no longer taking bets on horse races but customers playing roulette on computerised terminals. William Hill now took more money on football than horseracing online. To William Hill the word 'app' would have meant absolutely nothing, but now a significant percentage of his company's customers were placing their bets (using credit cards) on their mobile phones or tablet computers.

'I never saw a bookmaker to equal him,' respected *Sporting Life* journalist Geoffrey Hamlyn had said of William Hill in his pomp. 'His true ability was in actually making a book, in thinking faster than anyone else. Hill's mind worked at the speed of light,' added Ron Pollard.

Such byzantine and bewildering computations of odds had all been done inside his head, standing on a stool by the rails.

In July 2013 the group trading director, Terry Pattinson, gave an insight into the methods currently in use to ensure the company was pricing up the maximum number of events with the maximum number of odds – now up to some 100,000 betting events per year:

> We've created a mix of old-school bookmaking and the new breed of trading.
>
> Old-school bookmaking is where our horseracing and football compilers know what a price should be on a horse or a football game weeks or months in advance. Most of the compilers have been with the company for 10 to 20 years – their experience is invaluable to headline key prices. The new breed of trading is all about embracing technology, creating hundreds of betting options using feeds and algorithms.

The company's In Play department, revealed Pattinson, where they were now trading 40,000 football matches and 30,000 tennis matches a year and 'our profits are soaring', already had 85 colleagues working in it, with more being recruited, and 'their job is to gather every piece of statistical data and then run their mathematical techniques. The reason we are number one in product depth and number of markets is purely down to them getting the right algorithms and data feeds in.'

In February 2014, with the announcement of William Hill's results for 2013, Ralph Topping spelled out the scale of the transformation into 'one of the world's leading multi-channel betting and gaming businesses'. Already William Hill Online and the Australian businesses were accounting for around half the company's operating profit, and international markets 15% of net revenue. The online performance of Sportsbook saw staking levels up around 400% over the last five years, with 39% of its wagering coming through mobiles. Mobile gaming net revenue had grown by 166% over the course of the last year. In 2013 the group's revenue was up 16% to £1.49 billion, with operating profit up 1% to £335 million.

One thing was for sure: William Hill had conclusively outgrown its traditional rival. 'For almost 80 years they have gone head-to-head in the battle to be called Britain's biggest bookmaker,' wrote Dominic Walsh in *The Times*. 'But, according to the chief executive of William Hill, the traditional rivalry with Ladbrokes is now consigned to history and he regards some of the internet-based betting groups as his closest competitors.' Somewhere, the shades of William Hill and Cyril Stein would have exchanged meaningful glances. Ladbrokes' 2013 results were a measure of the disparity in performance: pre-tax profits down by two-thirds to £67.6 million, and operating profit down by 33% to £138.3 million. Ironically, in the week William Hill bought out Playtech, Ladbrokes did a deal with them to take over its online business. 'Ladbrokes perhaps is confronting the same strategic problems that William Hill was confronting in 2008,' reflected analyst Ivor Jones. 'What is different is time, of course. The online gaming market has transformed from 2008. William Hill has its leadership position.' 'The outspoken

Scot [Ralph] cites Bet365, owned by the Coates family, and Paddy Power, the Irish bookmaker,' noted Walsh, 'as more worthy rivals.'

The anniversary year was only 11 days old, however, when it brought a reminder that the traditional business – and risks – of being a bookie never change. That Saturday eight odds-on Premier League teams won their games, along with a number of other well-fancied sides, and the result was possibly the worst weekend of football results ever for the bookmakers. William Hill was hardest hit of all, with losses estimated at £13 million. But Ralph Topping was not downcast about the hit: 'These are the kind of results, just like "Dettori day", that change customer behaviour,' he maintained. '50,000 customers online won at least £50, and retail saw the same thing. That's great because it is the sort of win that gives customers confidence. Now they know accumulators can, and do, pay off.'

For the future, however, William Hill, with the rest of the industry, faced serious challenges. Over the last two years unease had been brewing at parliamentary level about what was seen as the undesirable spread of opportunities to gamble excessively. MPs such as Diane Abbott and David Lammy deplored what seemed to them an inexorable proliferation of betting shops on the high street, and indeed a 'clustering' of such premises apparently in the most impoverished neighbourhoods – this despite Ralph Topping pointing out to Ms Abbott that 'actually the number of betting shops in Hackney had dropped in her time as an MP.' The spread of FOBTs in betting shops had led to fears that they encouraged irresponsible spending, and might even be highly addictive. The MP for Bath, Don Foster, argued that the maximum stake should be reduced from £100 to £2. In a phrase borrowed and much used – many believe misused – by the media, they were dubbed the 'crack cocaine of gambling' despite little or no conclusive evidence linking them to an increase in problem gambling.

Ralph Topping declared himself 'against betting shop clustering on social grounds'.

I can see for myself some pretty stark examples and I can understand why people might raise localised objections. Betting shops have always been part of the community, but when the situation starts to alienate communities, then the industry needs to listen. We think a 'cumulative impact' test would be lawful and sensible and could be sensibly applied by licensing authorities.

In a letter to the *Sunday Telegraph* on 23 February 2013 he joined the heads of Gala Coral, Ladbrokes, Paddy Power and Betfred bookmakers in defending the industry's practice on fixed-odds gaming machines. 'The overwhelming majority of our machine customers gamble responsibly,' they wrote. 'Problem gambling levels in the UK are low by international standards ... and have not increased since the introduction of gaming machines in betting shops or the inception of online gambling.' But the letter acknowledged the 'concern' around the machines, which now accounted for about half of industry profits, and previewed, as 'a first step', a new code of practice that allowed players to set a maximum amount they were prepared to lose during a single session. Making above all a request that any proposed restrictions on FOBTs be based on solid evidence, they announced an independent review on FOBTs to be carried out by the Responsible Gambling Trust.

In September 2013, the Association of British Bookmakers, with the approval of William Hill and the majority of bookmakers, stressing that 'we consider one problem gambler to be one too many', issued the Code for Responsible Gambling and Player Protection. It promoted measures that included staff training to detect the signs of potential problem gambling more quickly; central analysis of data to identify abnormal activity both in specific shops and, where possible, in regard to individual customers; and mandatory time, and stake money-based reminders to customers using gaming machines, together with the ability to set spending and time limits on them. This was followed up in March 2014 by the introduction of technical changes to FOBTs to back up the measures introduced in the Code. 'I'm confident it is going to assist,' said Ralph Topping. 'More interventions with our customers will occur. Coupled with technology changes, customers will be better able to stay in control.'

But the industry was concerned to hear from political insiders that even displaying posters in their windows bearing these messages, alongside those popping up automatically on the machines, might not be enough to placate critics. Sure enough, even as the 2014 Grand National was being won by a relative longshot, the 25/1 Pineau De Re, bookmakers were finding it difficult to raise much of a smile, after the Budget a few weeks earlier had increased the tax on the fixed-odds betting machines from 20% to 25%, barely a year after it had been introduced. Had the new level, due to take effect from 1 March 2015, applied in 2013, the company estimated it would have cost it an additional £22 million. Shares in all the leading bookmaking companies had tumbled. In the *Racing Post* Graham Green described the British Horseracing Authority chief executive Paul Bittar as 'already fearing the worst':

He knew that hints that the Prime Minister, David Cameron, was to demand an even tougher clamp down on the rules governing machine playing in the shops 'could have dire consequences for racing's finances, bringing with it the threat of job losses, cuts to the fixture list and racecourse closures'.

However, Bittar's pessimism was tempered by confirmation from the government that it intended to extend the horseracing levy to offshore betting operators, although not before April 2016 at the earliest.

Ralph Topping caught the gloomy mood, predicting the closure of a significant number of betting shops, perhaps over 100. 'The funding of racing directly correlates to the number of betting shops that trade,' he argued. 'The government has failed to understand base economics and the importance of retail betting shops to the racing industry.' Older bookmakers thought back to the way in which a Chancellor chasing a tax windfall had instead effectively killed off the football fixed-odds industry. 'The effectiveness of the betting industry's lobbying and its supposed influence over government policy has declined,' wrote Bill Barber, the *Racing Post*'s industry editor: and it 'did not notice the Treasury sneaking up behind to deliver the fiscal equivalent of a snooker ball in a sock to the back of the head.'

There would be more to come at the end of the year, with a fundamental change in how betting tax was levied, from 'place of supply' to 'place of consumption'. Hitherto, if you were supplying gaming from the UK, you paid tax on all your gross gambling profits, but if you were supplying UK customers from outside the UK you paid no UK gambling taxes. Now, if you offered remote gambling to a person who usually lived in the UK – no matter where in the world you were based, as long as the gambling could be accessed from the UK – you would become liable to one or more betting taxes. (The only positive consequence was that UK-based operators supplying remote gambling to customers outside the UK would no longer be liable to gambling taxes.)

Ralph Topping remained confident that William Hill's expanded product range, its formidable online operation and a plan for £15–20 million of cost savings would enable it to weather the storm of the anticipated Point of Consumption Tax and indeed attract more market share. But in an interview with the *Sunday Telegraph* he set out the consequences of a draconian crackdown on betting duty – by abstracting more profit from an industry that was already paying the levy – in characteristic terms. 'What funds greyhound racing and horseracing?' he asked simply. 'Retail betting.' The more retail betting was taxed, the greater the threat to the ultimate survival of these two long-established sports.

Topping then had to respond to a *Sunday Times* article by the then Culture Secretary Maria Miller in which she asked whether 'the seemingly constant gambling adverts on television are appropriate' and called on the sector to 'put social responsibility at the heart of their businesses'. In his blog Topping was concerned to 'dispel a myth that gaming machines have driven an increase in problem gambling', citing expert research showing problem gamblers typically use six to seven different products. 'The issue is, therefore, about player "behaviour", and it is not, as some of you will believe, product-centric. A problem gambler is a problem gambler. It's a person thing, and it is not a product thing.' He also pointed out that the already low level of problem gambling in the UK had actually reduced from 0.9% to 0.5% of the population.

> Therefore, as it is not product-centric, I believe other sectors should also consider a similar Code-based approach as problem gamblers are not confined to the betting shop sector. They are of course to be found using National Lottery products and 16-year-olds are allowed to gamble in premises where question marks exist in my mind about sufficient scrutiny.

On the question of gambling adverts, he pointed out that while advertising spots associated with gambling across all commercial TV channels had increased from 0.7% in 2006 to 4.1% in 2012, only 6.6% of them related to sports betting – bingo took 38.8%, online casino and poker 29.6%, 25.6% lotteries and scratch cards.

The issue of 'social responsibility' Miller raised seems unlikely to go away, and is one that Ralph Topping's successor will have to deal with.

CHAPTER 30

RALPH'S REIGN COMES TO AN END

David Russell joined William Hill before its successful flotation, almost fifteen years ago, via textiles and airline catering. He'd never previously given bookmaking much thought, but was head-hunted for the human resources role within the company, and was excited by the challenge.

In 2014, David was Hill's human resources director.

He met Ralph Topping at the time his rise through the ranks was beginning, and the two connected. 'We both have an instinctive feel for people, and have a natural understanding of the importance of giving them recognition and respect. We may have occasionally been wrong in our initial judgement, but when we needed to make difficult decisions we acted. That's why a number of senior people passed in and out of various positions very quickly.

But Ralph saw the importance of bringing in new talent with different skill sets which hadn't been represented in the company before.'

Russell continues: 'Ralph, whose leadership potential was spotted by David Harding, who thought he'd been under-utilised, had seen the strength of the potential online opportunity, but knew he needed to act quickly to change the wrong technology direction we had initially been taking by attempting to build our own bespoke platform. He saw that here was an opportunity to catch and pass Ladbrokes – for years we had been as good as them but had never got the credit we deserved. Duff leadership was partially responsible for their own downfall, but we were the architects our of own success.'

However, David and Ralph are also firm believers in the long-term survival of betting shops. 'They will remain integral to us for the foreseeable future, but,' warns Russell, 'serving forty years in retail, whilst credible and important is not the thing that will propel us forward competitively into the future'.

The two worked well together, and once Ralph became CEO – 'he had the breadth of knowledge to take the role on, and suddenly he got the train set, and was able to move the parts about without interference' – they were able to introduce and implement the HOME strategy and, after being offered a number of possible opportunities, opted for Ol Maisor, and thus Project Africa was born.

Explains David: 'HOME represents the principles at the heart of our business. HOME binds our people together with a shared vision of the William Hill spirit and culture. Far from being a set of unattainable company values, HOME principles are an extension of a great working culture, easy to express because they are "the way we do things around here". That's because the HOME principles came from our William Hill colleagues, based on feedback from focus groups on what William Hill means to them.

H is for Hungry for success
O is for Outstanding service
M is for Making it happen
E is for Everyone matters

HOME has proved invaluable in helping to make employees feel part of one overall organisation wherever in the world they are based, and although the aim has been to encourage local management of the acquisitions in the various countries, partly to reduce the strain on senior management of continuous international travel, with the help of HOME they are all becoming integral elements of the company as a whole. Customer benefits accrue through positive feedback towards the attitude of staff.

Project Africa came out of Ralph thinking: 'What can we do to help bind the organisation behind a social responsibility project which it would buy into, even though some might regard it as a cynical exercise in corporate responsibility? But people across the company have raised money, supported and shown empathy for PA.'

For example, a committed group of colleagues in Tel Aviv jumped at the opportunity to be part of a 2014 William Hill initiative to benefit Project Africa, Hike for Health: 'After seeing the proud postings of my Gibraltar colleagues, I instantly felt inspired to do the extra mile for that and went out to run,' said Meir Deutsch, Head of Marketing Planning, Operations & Mobile, and Gadi Shoshani, SEO Sports and Project Lead commented: 'I was thinking about Project Africa every step of the way. I'm glad to be part of a company that offers opportunities such as Hike for Health.'

James Henderson was one of the first senior people to take a hands-on role by taking part in the first employee trip out there.

David believes that 'in earlier days there was far more of a staff and management "us and them" mentality. Now it is much more collaborative, with people working collectively as colleagues. It is partly a cultural shift, partly a business expertise shift. However, there are younger and brighter, more junior people that have greater expertise and knowledge to help develop a multi-channel, international and digital business.

'I think Ralph would like to remain connected to PA even after he has retired and I'm confident it will continue to run and develop in different ways. It is one of Ralph's legacies.

'Another big one is the appreciation of committed staff and their long service – and also of their partners, who are always bowled over by the experience when they take part in events to recognise their contributions.'

David feels a big part of Ralph's success was to run the company as 'a benevolent autocracy' and believes he will cope well in retirement – 'He's had to wrestle with coming to terms with it, but he has plenty of outside interests – photography, wildlife and much more.

He accepted that there is a need to recognise when the right time has come to move on ... '

That time was 1 August 2014, when Ralph's successor, James Henderson, stepped into the role, announcing an operating profit of £176.9 million for the 26 week period to 1 July 2014, from net revenues of £805.2 million.

'You're not going to get another Ralph Topping,' Ralph had declared in 2013. 'I'm the last of a dying breed.'

By February 2014 *The Times* was reporting that: 'William Hill is poised to fire the starting gun in its search for its new chief executive.'

As the 2014 AGM took place in May, Ralph himself seemed unsure how long he would remain at the helm, telling his audience: 'It is slightly odds-on that I'll be here for the 2015 AGM.' He also suggested that his successor 'will inherit a better side than [the recently dismissed] David Moyes did at Manchester United', with which to tackle 'an industry now far more complex than when I began.'

For the challenge of constant change he'd seen during his time in charge, Ralph found an appropriate racing analogy: 'Becher's Brook [was] put in our way so many times that I felt like Red Rum.'

'Rummy' did, of course, win the Grand National three times.

Perhaps what gave him most satisfaction in looking back was, how nowadays 'betting has become really mainstream. I don't think people look down their nose if you have a bet.'

'I hope I've dispelled the illusion depicted by cartoonists,' William Hill had declared, to laughter, at a speech in 1958, 'that a bookmaker is a fat man with a big cigar and a bulging satchel, and who spends the whole of his winter in the sunshine.' In fact, William had indeed been a big man who smoked cigars, was unmatched on the Rails at filling his bag with profits, and only came back from the Caribbean just in time for Cheltenham.

But he was also, in Geoffrey Hamlyn's memorable tribute, 'the monarch of the ring, a leviathan ... the greatest bookmaker who ever lived', and had built an eponymous company that had become the biggest and best in its field.

Posterity's verdict on the man who saw William Hill through to its 80th anniversary, in a form William in many respects would not recognise, seemed likely to be comprehensively favourable, perhaps above all because it remained a company cast in the mould of its founder.

'Ralph saw the market earlier than his rivals,' wrote analyst Ivor Jones. 'When you look back at Ralph's period of control, probably what you will say is that he continued a trend for William Hill being pretty far-sighted.'

Ralph had certainly moved the company forward into the bright new areas of gambling which opened up in recent years – but he also remained aware of the business's long-established roots.

After 16/1 outsider Salad Dodger won the 2014 William Hill Greyhound Derby, worth £200,000 to the winner, Ralph announced that the event would become the richest dog race ever run, worldwide, by raising the first prize to £250,000 for 2015.

William Hill began his rise at London's greyhound tracks, and another managing director, Sam Burns, was well aware of the sport's often under-estimated value to the company's well-being: 'I went so many times I was beginning to bark.'

As the end of the reign of the man who says his own, most admired figure is 'the Dalai Lama', approached, Ralph spoke of feeling emotional, just as the founder, who had even decided to quit earlier only to renege, had done: 'The hardest part after forty four years with a company,' reflected Ralph, 'is getting into your head that you are leaving. I feel part of a family here.'

The 2014 World Cup, for which Ralph was still firmly in charge, produced a record £227 million turnover for the company (Ladbrokes took a mere £115.3m according to their own website). Over 22 million bets were placed from Hill's clients in 115 countries. The biggest single bet was a $350,000 stake from a US customer, which won $30,000. The biggest single winner received £514,500 after staking £147,000 on Germany lifting the trophy at 5/2. Over 462,000 bets were placed via mobile devices on the Final alone. In 2010 it had been 6,899.

During the tournament, the company's £1 million, state of the art studios in Leeds were on air broadcasting to the betting shops until 10pm, with contributions from Robbie Savage and Hill's own Lee Phelps, out in Brazil. Launched for the Cheltenham Festival by racing figures Jim McGrath and John Francome, the facility took three months to create, and boasted three studios, one for retail, two for online radio, with some 50 freelance broadcasters and 25 full-time staff involved. Hill's Head of Broadcast, Mike Grenham, hailed the facility as 'the best in the industry'.

Decades earlier William had plugged the company via Radio Luxembourg.

William Hill had become an official Supporter of the England team in 2012. Before their dismal early World Cup exit at the Group Stage, the company had faced a potential £2 million plus liability should they have won the tournament.

When they did win the World Cup in 1966, it had cost William Hill, then with no betting shops, a mere £8,000 – yet a spokesman had still bemoaned the loss.

Using a modern day method to reinforce a traditional message, Ralph observed wryly on his Twitter feed: 'Some old grey haired bookmakers still moan about all losses. May it always be thus – or we're truly done for!'

In an interview for this book just after news broke of his departure date, Ralph reflected:

'Any business needs the right man in charge at the right moment.

'The first example I had of dealing with the pressure of being CEO demonstrated that it is the loneliest job when you are left to make the decisions. They have to be based on believing you're doing the right thing, when you've got good guys saying "do it", bad ones saying "don't" and you can't be sure you've made the right choice until afterwards.

'At one board meeting before I was CEO, a lot of money was asked for to buy more bricks and mortar businesses in Italy. In my view this was wrong and I spoke up saying so.

'When I became CEO we were still saddled with Italy and Spain – I went to the chairman, then Charlie Scott, and he was terrific to talk to about business politics. He would always come up with an insight. "This is your first decision," he told me. "You will need to be brave enough to tell them what you plan on doing, that you want to come away from bricks and mortar. Think about this. Then we'll see what reception you get." In the event I got a good one.'

He had realised very quickly that 'There is no CEO school – you're chucked into the deep end of the swimming pool. You're on your own – you can't imitate any other CEO. I've only ever asked one question – "What's the right thing to do for the best interests of William Hill?"'

As Ralph's time as CEO came to an end he was able to boast that 'I never lost a guy I wasn't happy to lose. William Hill needs an extremely strong CEO – all the successful ones have been very strong minded, didn't tolerate fools and didn't like people interfering in the business.

'It would be wrong to say I enjoyed every minute of my six and a half years – there are always lows and indifferent periods. People don't quite understand the pressures on a chief executive. But I was fortunate to work with a very good team – I picked and developed it. It is a job in which to get things done you must be obsessed and obsessive. I had worked for the best obsessive of them all – John Brown.

'I have also never forgotten where I came from – a wee coal mining village called Bridgend, where horizons were usually defined by nearby Linlithgow or, sometimes, Edinburgh – I never believed I would get the opportunity to run a company like William Hill.

'I think I made a difference – I'm proud to have introduced Project Africa, company conferences, the HOME programme, to have done more for people with long service, introduced little treats for people – made a fuss of the partners of staff: I think it is very important that families get acknowledged, as they effectively end up working for William Hill as well. It all makes our company culture different.'

As well as the company's and his personal support for Project Africa, Ralph and wife Elizabeth have sponsored two Masai children through their education at St Thomas Nursery and Primary School in Arusha, Tanzania. The boys, Msurupei Maya and Longorwa Nairuti, are both approaching ten years old. 'I'm also keen to get involved in water provision for the Masai in Tanzania.'

Ralph has plenty to catch up on in retirement: 'As CEO you always get invited to social functions and events, but I rarely accepted – I felt this is William Hill time, I should be doing William Hill things. Now, amongst other things, I'll visit Art museums. We're going to visit Alaska for a few weeks. I like peace and quiet.

'But unlike JB, you will very rarely see me on a racecourse. And, take it from me, there will be no autobiography.

'I'll leave not unhappy with what I achieved, but not completely happy – still feeling there is more I could have done. I have left a company with a good, strong culture.

'I have made a commitment never to do anything to damage or act against William Hill's interests. I will still be involved with football. I will travel. I will continue to add to my extensive collection of natural history books. I'll be able to attend the Edinburgh Book Festival and the Wigtown Book Festival. Then I'll sit on my balcony in Scotland – with the midge machine blasting away – and catch up with my reading.'

Whether that reading will include any newspapers is yet to be decided. Ralph recalls receiving advice about retirement from John Brown: 'He told me: "Let Elizabeth read the newspapers first – and tell her to make sure to remove or otherwise not let you see anything in them about William Hill – because although you'll feel you want to, you won't be able to do anything about it. Just remember what you've done for the company – and console yourself with the thought that they're going to fuck it up, anyway … "'

Ralph also recalls JB once telling him: "We're two different characters. I don't understand what makes you tick – but you get results, and you are one hard bastard.' When I protested, John added 'You are, you just don't know it!"

Whether the same description is applied to James Henderson remains to be seen, but there is little doubt that he is hewn from much the same sturdy material as his retiring, but far from shy, former boss, of whom he says: 'He's been my mentor. He provided strong leadership and direction and at the same time transformed the business.'

James, 52-year-old father of two, was born in London, but lived in the Ashdown Forest area of Sussex until his late teens. In an echo of the founder, who started out with no greater ambition than becoming a farmer, James regards himself as a country boy. His brother is a trainer in France and his nephew was a champion apprentice there.

After 'boring' himself in a number of jobs, including estate agency, James began working for the company in 1985 as a trainee betting shop manager, and had risen by his 30th year at William Hill to group director of operations.

James moved through the ranks, becoming retail operations director in 2006. He moved to Gibraltar as operations director for William Hill Online in 2009, then became retail director UK in 2011. He also oversaw the establishment of William Hill US, and recently took responsibility for William Hill Australia.

Like Len Cowburn, John Brown and Ralph Topping before him, James is predominantly a one-company man.

Like his illustrious predecessors he's been there, seen it, done it, on the shop floor.

Like them – and in the image of the company's founder – James Henderson is, in the words of Gareth Davis, his chairman:

'A natural bookie.'

POSTSCRIPT

I have been asked about where the image of William Hill used on the front cover of the hardback version of this book came from, and when it was taken.

Here is the story behind the photograph. On the front page of the *Daily Express* on 21 May 1963 the headline shouted: 'Shock for bookies – William Hill (Park Lane) refused betting permit.'

The story revealed that Hills were to appeal against the Newington Licensing Committee's refusal to grant a bookmaker's permit for the company's new £2 million, nine-storey London headquarters at the top of Blackfriars Road in Southwark, near the Elephant and Castle. The company had recently moved from Piccadilly in London, where they had been granted a licence by Westminster authorities until 1 June – but their new offices fell within Newington's remit.

The committee's decision had been taken after a bizarre objection from a female professional punter, Mrs Mary Martin, from Nottingham – who had been refused a claimed payout of some £1,280 from Hills for bets placed in January – that they were 'not fit and proper persons'.

William Hill was in determined mood, though: 'Under no circumstances shall we pay Mrs Martin,' he was quoted as saying. Company spokesman Ray Whiteway had told the committee: 'We are not going to pay this account because it is not bona fide. It was rigged betting.' Mrs Martin had struck 256 15/- (75p) five-dog accumulator place bets at Tote odds for a Nottingham greyhound meeting. However, at the track itself Mrs Martin, together with two other people, 'a friend and a student', had initially placed bets worth hundreds of pounds on other dogs, thus inflating the payout on one of her chosen dogs, Persistent Mover.

Mr Whiteway said that 'so many £5 notes were pouring in' that the racetrack manager had called the police. After being questioned, Mrs Martin and her companions were permitted to continue, and they bet in a similar way on subsequent races. 'We would gladly pay any legitimate claim but not in circumstances such as these,' insisted Whiteway.

A spokesman for Mrs Martin, Mr James Burge, responded: 'There was no question of any prosecution for any dishonest conduct by this lady – no suggestion of cheating or fraud.'

On behalf of the Licensing Committee, chairman, Mr Basil Aldous, remarked: 'The committee has a very heavy task to come to a decision in this important matter.'

Despite the lack of a permit potentially preventing the company from trading, a spokesman for Hills was quoted as saying: 'If we should lose the appeal, we will appeal again and again.'

The appeal was set for 31 May and in the meantime the company's operations would continue as normal. William Hill added: 'This whole case emphasises the weakness in betting legislation. The select committee – on which I served – that advised and co-operated with the Government in framing the Betting Act strongly warned the Home Office of the grave danger of vesting power in lay magistrates to issue and renew bookmakers' permits.'

On 11 June 1963 – the day the front cover photograph was taken, outside the London Sessions Appeals Committee venue – 'STILL IN BUSINESS' were the words chalked up on a blackboard in Hill House, the centre of the William Hill betting empire, then 'capable of taking 400 phoned bets every 12 seconds'. William Hill, according to contemporary reports, was sitting in his 8th floor office, where he 'clasped a large whisky' and 'puffed at his cigar' while aides handed round sandwiches, drinks and 'good tips for the dogs tonight'.

These scenes were taking place in the wake of the news that the company had been victorious in its appeal against Newington Licensing Committee's refusal to renew the company's betting permit. William spoke of the 'great embarrassment' this 'piffling' amount had caused him, but had insisted he would not pay 'on a matter of principle'.

However, it had now been agreed that the greyhound bet should be referred to arbitrators appointed by the Law Society.

Despite granting the permit, chairman of the London Sessions, Reginald Seaton commented: 'It appears to be a genuine dispute between the backer and the bookmaker. It is a very good thing that bookmakers should realise they are scrutinised by licensing committees, who do their work, generally speaking, well.' Mr Hill had offered to pay the costs of arbitration 'so that the matter can be thrashed out thoroughly.'

'If I had lost the appeal,' went on Mr Hill, 'it would have meant losing half a million (pounds) turnover a week. There are 2,500 people (working) in this building, but now we can go on.'

Another version of this story was told to Graham Sharpe, whilst this book was being written, by Tim Williams: 'I worked for the Martin Brothers when they owned LSD bookmakers in Nottingham. I was 17 at the time, in 1971. They were teaching me the ins and outs of bookmaking, with a view to me becoming a settler in one of their shops, of which they probably had about ten or so, mainly in, and around Nottingham.

'I believe the Martin brothers had both been officers in the Guards, they certainly dressed the part and had that type of demeanour. I found them to be very kind although outwardly they seemed very tough and hard nosed.

'They taught me in the mornings for a couple of hours in a classroom they had at their offices, then in the afternoon I would help out at the head office or in one of the shops, chalking the boards.

'Paddy Martin told me the story during a quiet time in his office. He ended it by producing a copy of the *Sporting Life* with the headline: "Mrs Martin Loses Case". They chose Nottingham Dogs as it was local, they knew the form, they needed a small crowd (low turnover on the tote). The time of year was chosen because a cold night would also keep the crowd numbers down.

'One dog was selected that they considered could not be placed, in each race.

'At the track they then punted that dog on the tote to be placed (thus artificially boosting the payout for other dogs to be placed). Prior to this they had bet on other dogs in accumulators with William Hill.

'Paddy Martin claimed to me that before it went to arbitration that William Hill had paid him his legal fees and had settled the bet. He added that William Hill offered no evidence to the arbitrator, and also claimed that a couple of weeks after the decision was announced in favour of William Hill, the arbitrator had committed suicide.'

The precise relationship between Mary Martin and the Martin brothers is unclear.

Confirmation that William Hill was firmly embedded in the country's consciousness, during the 1960s, was forthcoming when the owner of Queen magazine gathered together a group of luminaries to be photographed on 12 July 1967. Amongst them was Formula 1 ace Graham Hill; comedian Ronnie Corbett; authors John 'Rumpole' Mortimer and Anthony 'Clockwork Orange' Burgess, deputy leader of the Conservative Party, Reginald Maudling; business tycoon Charles Clore; Jonathan Miller, director, actor, author, television presenter, humourist, sculptor and medical doctor; photographer Cecil Beaton; the Bishop of London; actress Joan Plowright; Princess Margaret's lady-in-waiting, Lady Anne Tennant; and Daily Express cartoonist Osbert Lancaster. And placed almost in the middle of this group of worthies, was William Hill. The photograph was taken by (Patrick) Lichfield.

The *Daily Express* reported on 1 September 1967 that William Hill had been at the races in Deauville, France, 'as a respite from meeting breeders seeking nominations to his stallion, Celtic Ash, the 1960 Belmont Stakes winner, one of the US's leading three year old races. The paper also reported that William was sending 20 of his yearlings to Newmarket for the sales.

There would be an odd link between this apparently unremarkable story and one of the most celebrated attempted coups in racing history.

On Bank Holiday Monday 26 August 1974 I remember being in the William Hill trade room when we became aware of a stream of bets involving three horses. Normally such wagers would raise little in the way of concern – but something odd seemed to be going on, as two of the three horses were apparently now non runners and only one, Gay Future, was still expected to contest his race – and he was predicted to be an outsider at the tiny Cartmel racecourse in the Lake District, where we did not have a representative.

All of a sudden we had hefty potential liabilities on this one horse – and no way of contacting the course to check on the price the horse was likely to return, and if necessary to hedge some money into the market. There were, of course, no mobiles then and there was neither telephone nor blower connection to the course.

Desperate efforts were made to try to get someone to the course before the race, but that was always a futile attempt. Permit-holder Anthony Collins was the trainer of all three horses. An estimated £30,000 of doubles and trebles, all involving Gay Future, with either Opera Cloak at Southwell and/or Ankerwyke at Plumpton, were placed in £5, £10 and £15 units.

Collins was at Plumpton, ostensibly to look after Ankerwyke. His wife was at Cartmel with Gay Future – but also to place on-course bets on his other runner in the race, Racionzer, thus giving on-course punters and bookies the impression that this was the better fancied of the two.

An unknown amateur, declared to ride Gay Future, was suddenly replaced by leading Irish amateur Mr T A Jones, who had already won on the horse in Ireland. Gay Future's odds had drifted to 10/1 at the track, and he looked as though he was sweating up badly – possibly something to do with the soap flakes it later became known he had been lathered with! Gay Future duly won the race by some 15 lengths.

With huge liabilities amounting to an estimated £300,000 or more amongst all of the leading bookies including ourselves, there was relief when the Betting Office Licensees' Association advised members to withhold payment, pending the outcome of enquiries.

Scotland Yard was called in to investigate, and it was decided to prosecute Collins, together with an acquaintance, with conspiracy to defraud bookmakers.

After a seven day trial, both were found guilty, with the judge commenting: 'The degree of dishonesty is in my assessment, although a conspiracy to defraud, very much at the bottom end of the scale.

BOLA (the Betting Office Licensees' Association) then advised members to hand back stake money bet on Gay Future – but to pay none of the winnings. The prosecution had alleged that neither Opera Cloak nor Ankerwyke had ever been intended to run in their races, as it appeared they had never left their stables, and there was much discussion about whether Gay Future had actually been in the care of Collins in England for long enough to be qualified to race.

Given this incident, it was more than a surprise for me to receive a phone call from Mr Collins while this book was being written, proferring a story involving William Hill.

Mr Collins explained that he had been on a trip to Deauville, the French town famed for its up-market lifestyle, its beach, its racing and its casino. Although he couldn't recall precisely the date, it was back in the days when it was not permitted to take more than a token amount of sterling out of the country – quite possibly the very trip recorded in 1967 by the *Daily Express*. But Mr Collins had taken advantage of the suggestion of an acquaintance, who had offered to help get round the currency rules by concealing a number of Scottish £50 notes down the shaft of the golf clubs he had brought with him.

'Once I retrieved the notes I headed for the casino and queued up to exchange them for chips to gamble with' explained Mr Collins. 'But the cashier had never seen Scottish notes before, and was not convinced they were genuine currency, so refused to accept them from me.

'I argued the toss with her, but to no avail, and just as I was turning away I heard a voice behind me, saying "I'll give you thirty quid each for them!" I told the owner of the voice to get stuffed – although maybe not using that polite a phrase – because I thought he was trying to take advantage of my plight. And I then suddenly realised it was William Hill – who, as it happened, I had an account with!'

Perhaps, I suggested to Mr Collins, this was the point at which his mind had turned to how to get revenge on a bookie for trying to make a profit from his situation. Mr Collins, who also revealed that next time he went to Deauville he hid currency for gambling in the heels of his Gucci shoes, laughed heartily at the very idea.

Here is one more fascinating William Hill anecdote which didn't make the original cut for the first edition of the book.

The actor Patrick Macnee achieved great popularity by starring alongside Honor Blackman in the original 1960s TV series 'The Avengers'. Born in 1922, always impeccably turned out in traditional English gentleman-about-town style, complete with trilby hat and rolled umbrella, he was also very fond of a bet. In his 1988 autobiography, *Blind In One Ear*, Macnee, the son of shrewd Lambourn-based racing trainer, 'Shrimp' Macnee, who clearly 'knew the time of day', revealed that 'one day I opened an account with a new bookie named William Hill. Having backed a stream of winners, I was collecting my winnings when a skeletal gentleman with broken nose and cauliflower ears sidled up:

'You' he rasped, 'Git out the back. The Guv wants yer.'

'William Hill was a gentleman. With great courtesy, he explained that given my father's reputation, my patronage was no longer acceptable.

'I do so enjoy doing business with you, Mr Hill.'

'Yes son, but I can't afford you."

Graham Sharpe
April 2015.

APPENDIX: WILLIAM HILL ACCOUNTS OVER THE YEARS

(Some early years are no longer available)

Company Name	Financial year	Takings	Gross profit	Operating profit / trading profit	Profit before tax	Profit for the period after tax
		£000	£000	£000	£000	£000
Holders Investment Trust	1955			252	221	119
Holders Investment Trust	1959			1,345	1,299	732
Holders Investment Trust	1960			1,907	1,908	979
Holders Investment Trust	1961			1,552	1,571	780
Holders Investment Trust	1962			537	454	228
Holders Investment Trust	1963			(163)	(296)	(312)
Holders Investment Trust	1964			1,384	1,231	683
Holders Investment Trust	1965			(2,519)	(2,669)	(2,386)
Holders Investment Trust	1966				556	424
Holders Investment Trust	1967	42,436			203	179
Holders Investment Trust	1968	60,856		287	287	256
Holders Investment Trust	1969	45,367		467	467	313
William Hill Organization Ltd	1970	55,362		1,421	1,421	966
William Hill Organization Ltd	1971	81,719		2,505	2,505	1,552
William Hill Organization Ltd	1972	135,015		2,934	2,639	1,618
William Hill Organization Ltd	1973	146,161		3,915	3,361	1,792
William Hill Organization Ltd	1974	161,570		3,111	2,423	1,297
William Hill Organization Ltd	1978	266,260		8,172	8,320	4,135
William Hill Organization Ltd	1979	310,166		6,720	6,830	3,761
William Hill Organization Ltd	1980	357,458		8,360	8,645	4,232
William Hill Organization Ltd	1981	362,674		5,995	6,328	3,218
William Hill Organization Ltd	1982	389,632	13,360	6,310	2,914	51
William Hill Organization Ltd	1983	427,752	19,333	11,005	6,438	634
William Hill Organization plc	1984	479,098	19,663	11,456	5,892	85

William Hill Organization plc	**1985**	540,255	26,016	16,344	13,534	5,747
Various	**1986**	555,940	32,785	22,530	21,157	13,374
Various	**1987**	602,320	28,038	17,518	17,157	11,022
Various	**1988**	628,222	30,672	20,419	20,167	13,283
William Hill Organization Ltd	**1989**	635,484	90,721	25,358	(2,979)	10,221
William Hill Group Limited	**1990**	1,483,640		57,074		
William Hill Group Limited	**1991**	1,384,810		45,445		
William Hill Group Limited	**1992**	1,415,803		41,037	41,037	
William Hill Group Limited	**1993**	1,542,588		47,452	47,452	
William Hill Group Limited	**1994**	1,582,900		57,500	57,500	
William Hill Group Limited	**1995**	1,551,300	215,700	39,300	(121,200)	(137,300)
William Hill Limited	**1996**	1,647,500	227,700	49,500	59,900	32,200
William Hill Limited	**1997**	1,672,700	265,700	69,900	58,500	44,900
William Hill Limited	**1998**	1,805,838	278,627	90,572	17,724	16,283
William Hill Holdings Limited	**1999**	1,653,200	242,800	70,761	(48,296)	(49,556)
William Hill Holdings Limited	**2000**	2,042,400	313,100	84,600	3,000	900
William Hill Holdings Limited	**2001**	2,452,200	365,000	112,000	27,300	18,400
William Hill plc	**2002**	3,365,300	416,000	139,000	32,400	21,200
William Hill plc	**2003**	5,945,800	511,100	197,500	169,500	124,300
William Hill plc	**2004**	8,287,700	561,400	234,100	207,400	149,800
William Hill plc	**2005**	10,746,100	631,200	218,100	174,600	113,100
William Hill plc	**2006**	13,235,900	733,900	292,200	235,400	166,800
William Hill plc	**2007**	14,797,100	763,200	286,700	209,200	157,400
William Hill plc	**2008**	15,553,900	797,500	276,100	293,300	234,000
William Hill plc	**2009**	15,070,000	839,700	258,500	120,900	81,200
William Hill plc	**2010**	16,519,800	923,100	276,800	193,300	156,000
William Hill plc	**2011**	17,911,400	973,100	275,700	187,400	146,500
William Hill plc	**2012**	18,879,100	1,104,700	330,600	277,700	231,000
William Hill plc	**2013**	20,436,900	1,214,300	335,000	257,000	226,500
William Hill plc	**2014**	21,893,400	1,305,100	372,200	233,900	206,300

These figures are extracted from the statutory accounts, and other public reports of the William Hill PLC group and its predecessors. Due to the evolution of companies' law and accounting practice, the method of calculation or presentation will have varied over time, and the table should be used as an indication of trends, rather than a precise comparison.

The requirements for accounts to be audited have changed in UK law from time to time and, as a result, some of the values in the table do not represent audited results.

In some years the values may reflect a later restatement of results following a change in accounting practice or framework.

Audited annual accounts of William Hill PLC are available at www.williamhillplc.com.

The above extracts are not intended to provide a complete assessment of the current or historical financial position or performance of William Hill PLC.

ACKNOWLEDGEMENTS

This is a desperately difficult, yet totally essential, piece of the book to write.

So many people have helped me during the writing of this book, that it is inevitable I will somehow forget or omit someone's name, and they will henceforth hold a huge grudge and always refer to me as 'that ungrateful *******'.

In an effort to include as near as dammit everyone without whose assistance this would be far less of the comprehensive story I very much hope it is, I am going to list the names in alphabetical order . . .

So, many genuine thanks to:

Geoff Banks, probably as good a bookie as he believes he is; Bob Betts (helped me go to the dogs); Philip Blacker, jockey turned master sculptor; Mark Blandford; Charles Blanning; staff at the now sadly defunct British Newspaper Library in Colindale; Anita Brown (for her brilliant family tree and related info); Gerry Blum; Audrey Bolus; Mihir Bose, my co-author, who contributed much I would have struggled to discover on my own; centenarian jockey, Edgar Britt; Sandy Brown (and his wife Mel), for invaluable personal memories of William and inviting me into their home; Don Butler, Birmingham bookie; Victor Chandler; Professor Carl Chinn, whose knowledge of the Brummie bookie scene was priceless; James Collins; Tony Collins, for an entertaining and indiscreet phone call; Mario Cortesi; Graham Coster – quite simply the most talented and patient editor anyone could wish for, who chipped and chopped at the original, unwieldy mass of material, eventually prising out the book hidden within it; Angus Dalrymple, bookmaking veteran who worked for William, Jack Swift and *The Sporting*

Four members of the Hill family closely related to William, whose help was invaluable to the authors. From left to right: nephew, Neil Hill; Mel Brown, wife of nephew Sandy Brown; niece Jackie Foott.

Life and currently contributes regularly to *BOS* magazine; Berjis Daver; Steve Dennis; William Derby for digging out useful York information; Lucy-Ann Dodd, for her efforts to trace the details of William's cuff-links; Tris Dixon, editor of *Boxing News*, who happily unearthed obscure material about boxing friends of William; Caroline Donald; Andrew Dowler; Claude Duval, always entertaining and knowledgeable; Peggy Evans; Chris Foott, the Hill family unofficial archivist, and mum, Jackie, who not only helped with info but gave me lifts to and from stations; Ian Fry, of Horse Racing Abroad; Marilyn Gowler, who won't rest until she knows for sure; the late former jockey Rex Hamey; Guy Hands; Chris Harper (the nephew who lived with and worked for William (and Ivy) at Whitsbury, not forgetting his wife Nicky and son, Edward; Eddie Hide, still delighted to have ridden William's Cantelo to a controversial St Leger triumph; Emma Higgin; Neil Hill, another of William's nephews, who never ducked a question and was hugely helpful and patient on too many occasions to record; William Hill (a different one, but related); Francis Hyland; Tom Kelly; Paull Khan and Sarah Prest, who delved into the records to help determine when William first sponsored races; Jon Lees, deservedly award-winning racing journo, who pointed me towards some helpful sources; former Press Association chief racing reporter, Willie Lefebve; bookie Stephen Little; Sue Lord; Rupert Mackeson; Peter MacMurray; Sean Magee, 'The Fat Controller' for a demented band of 'Sedgefielders' to which I am proud to belong; betting/newspaper veteran, Charlie Maskey; Paul Mathieu, a brilliant racing writer, who helped fill in the gaps in my collection of Racing Reviews; Heather Meyer, for insight into everyday life at William and Ivy's Whitsbury home; Benno Miller, a veteran of the bookmaking business, but still pin-sharp; Lee Mottershead, a fellow 'Sedgefielder'; staff at The National Archive in Kew; Ben Newton; Jane Newton; bookie/author Simon Nott; Nigel Pemberton's Jamaican insight was much appreciated; Chris Pitt; Ron Pollard, who not only sparked my own interest in the odder side of bookmaking public relations but worked with and for William in the early days; Sir Mark Prescott for supplying details of William's days as a coursing bookmaker at the Waterloo Cup; Sarah Prymer, Archivist at the Library of Birmingham; former stable lad, Trevor Reeves; Jamie Reid, author of the brilliant *Doped* and fount of racing knowledge; Edward Rice; author Meda Ryan who kindly granted permission to quote from her book about Tom Barry; Caroline and Sarah St George, for sharing childhood memories of their parents and grandparents and more; Graham Sims, for telling me about his parents' experiences working for the Hills at their Whitsbury home; Graham Snelling at the National Horseracing Museum in Newmarket; Jackie Sullivan; Bob Urquhart for memories of Whitsbury; Douglas Ventress, who worked for William at Sezincote; Tim Williams; Malcolm Willstrop; Howard Wright, who forensically subbed and critiqued the early version of the manuscript.

All those who worked for, or with, the company and were happy to share information and experiences ancient and modern, amongst them: Bert Arnold; Jarvis Astaire; John Brown; Ian Chuter; Frankie and Peter Connor; Neil Cooper; Len Cowburn; Gareth Davis; David Farmer; Steve Frater; Ken Gillie; Bob Green; David Harding; James Henderson; Kevin Hogan; Bill Hogwood; Bob Lambert; Dave Lowrey; James McClea; Keith Morgan; Thomas Murphy; Terry Pattinson; Mike Quigley; Brian Rayson; Bryan Robinson; Mike Raper; Dennis Read; David Russell; John Santer; John Smurthwaite; Romaine Snijder, without whom I'd actually have had to be nice to people myself, who knows how I work better than I do, yet is still prepared to work with me; Bill South; Ian Spearing; Nigel Spencer; Ralph Topping for announcing to the world that I was writing this book before bothering to tell me!; Lyndsay Wright and Alan Wyborn.

BIBLIOGRAPHY

ABELSON, Edward & TYRREL, John. *Breedon Book of Horse Racing Records* (Breedon Books, 1993)

ARMFIELD, Julian & LANGAN, Fred. *You Win Some, You Lose Some: The Biography of Bill Marshall DFC* (Bill and Pamela Marshall, 2003)

BAERLEIN, Richard. *Joe Mercer: Pictorial Biography* (Macdonald Queen Anne Press, 1994)

BIRD, Alex (with Terry Manners). *Alex Bird: Life and Secrets of a Professional Punter* (Queen Anne Press, 1985)

BLANNING, Charles & PRESCOTT, Sir Mark. *The Waterloo Cup: The First 150 Years* (Heath House, 1987)

BRITT, Edgar. *Post Haste* (Frederick Muller Ltd, 1967)

BROWN, John. *Lucky John* (Highdown, 2004)

CHURCH, Michael. *The Derby Stakes: The Complete History 1780-2006* (Raceform, 2006)

CHINN, Carl. *Better Betting With a Decent Feller* (Harvester Wheatsheaf, 1991)

CLAPSON, Mark. *A Bit of a Flutter* (Manchester University Press, 1992)

CLUTTERBUCK, David & DEVINE, Marion. *Clore: The Man & His Millions* (Weidenfeld & Nicholson, 1987)

COE, Sebastian. *Seb Coe: Running My Life* (Hodder & Stoughton, 2013)

CONNORS, Jimmy. *The Outsider* (Bantam Press, 2013)

COSGROVE, Tom. *William Hill Racing Yearbook, 1973/4/5/6* (Queen Anne Press)

DAWSON, Elizabeth. *Mother Made A Book* (Geoffrey Bles Ltd, 1962)

DESMOND, Florence. *Florence Desmond by Herself* (George G Harrap & Co Ltd, 1953)

DIXON, David. *From Prohibition to Regulation* (Clarendon Press, 1991)

FAIRFAX-BLAKEBOROUGH, Noel. *J.F.B.: Memoirs of Jack Fairfax-Blakeborough OBE, MC* (J A Allen, 1978)

GILBEY, Quintin. *Queen of the Turf* (Arthur Barker, 1973)

GOODERSON, Philip. *The Gangs of Birmingham* (Milo, 2010)

GRIFFITH, Kenneth & O'GRADY, Timothy E. *Curious Journey* (Hutchinson, 1982)

HAMLYN, Geoffrey. *My Sixty Years in the Ring* (Sporting Garland Press, 1994)

HERBERT, Ivor. *Six at the Top* (Heinemann, 1977)

HERBERT, Ivor (Advisory Editor). *Horse Racing: The complete guide to the world of the Turf* (Collins, 1980)

HEY, Stan. *An Arm & Four Legs* (Yellow Jersey Press, 1998)

HIDE, Edward (with Mike Cattermole). *Nothing to Hide* (Macdonald Queen Anne Press, 1989)

HILL, Christopher R. *Horse Power: The Politics of the Turf* (Manchester University Press, 1988)

HUGGINS, Mike. *Horseracing and the British 1919–39* (Manchester University Press, 2003)

JAYNE, Leonard. *Pony-Racing* (Hutchinson, date unknown)

KAYE, Richard. *The Ladbrokes Story* (Pelham, 1969)

LAIRD, Dorothy. *Royal Ascot* (Hodder & Stoughton, 1995)

LAMBIE, James. *Story of Your Life* (Matador, 2010)

LING, Arthur. *Farmers' Breakfast* (Michael Joseph, 1963)

LINNANE, Fergus. *London's Underworld* (Robson Books, 2003)

McCRIRICK, John. *World of Betting* (Stanley Paul, 1988)

McDONALD, Brian. *Gangs of London* (Milo, 2010)

MAGEE, Sean (with Sally Aird). *Ascot: The History* (Methuen, 2002)

MARSHALL, Michael W. *The Art & Science of Racehorse Training: the Bill Marshall Guide* (Keepdate Publishing, 1994)

MESTON, The Rt Hon Lord. *Shaw's Guide to the Betting and Gaming Act, 1960* (Shaw and Sons Ltd, 1960)

MILTON, James. *The Secrets of Pricewise* (Racing Post Books, 2012)

MORTIMER, Roger, ONSLOW, Richard & WILLETT, Peter. *Biographical Encyclopaedia of British Flat Racing* (Macdonald and Janes, 1978)

MORTIMER, Roger. *History of the Derby Stakes* (Michael Joseph, 1973)

MORTON, James. *East End Gangland* (Time Warner Books, 2006)

MUNTING, Roger. *Economic and Social History of Gambling in Britain and USA* (Manchester University Press, 1996)

MURPHY, Robert. *Smash and Grab* (Faber and Faber, 1993)

NOTT, Simon. *Skint Mob* (SNP, 2013)

OAKLEY, Robin. *Frankincense and More* (Racing Post, 2010)

O'BRIEN, Jacqueline & HERBERT, Ivor. *Vincent O'Brien: The Official Biography* (Bantam Press, 2005)

ONSLOW, Richard. *Great Racing Gambles & Frauds Vol. 3* (Marlborough Books, 1993)

ONSLOW, Richard. *Royal Ascot* (Crowood, 1990)

ORCHARD, Vincent. *The Derby Stakes* (Hutchinson, 1954)

O'SULLEVAN, Peter. *Calling the Horses* (Stanley Paul, 1989)

O'SULLEVAN, Peter. *Peter O'Sullevan's Horse Racing Heroes* (Highdown, 2004

PALEY, Henry D & GLENDINNING, John A. *Report On Off Track Betting In England* (New York State Assembly, 1963)

PARKER, Tim Fitzgeorge. *The Spoilsports* (Andre Deutsch, 1968)

PEGG, Norman. *Focus on Racing* (Robert Hale, 1963)

PITT, Chris & HAMMOND, Chris. *When Birmingham Went Racing* (C C Publishing, 2005)

POLLARD, Ron. *Odds And Sods* (Hodder and Stoughton, 1991)

REID, Jamie. *A Licence to Print Money* (Macmillan, 1992)

REID, Jamie. *Doped* (Racing Post, 2013)

RETIRED S.P. BOOKMAKER. *How To Make A Book* (Morrison & Gibb Ltd, 1945)

RODRIGO, R. *Paddock Book* (Macdonald, 1967)

ROYAL COMMISSION ON GAMBLING VOLS 1 & 2 (1978)

RUBNER, Alex. *The Economics of Gambling* (Macmillan, 1966)

RYAN, Meda. *Tom Barry: IRA Freedom Fighter* (Mercier Press, 2005)

SAMUELS, John. *Down the Bookies* (Racing Post, 2011)

SASULY, Richard. *Bookies & Bettors* (Holt Rinehart & Winston 1982)

SETH-SMITH, Michael. *International Stallions and Studs* (Dial Press, New York, 1974)

SIDNEY, Charles. *The Art of Legging* (Maxline International, 1976)

SLATTERY, Finbarr. *Horse Racing* (K, 1985)

SLATTERY, Finbarr. *Following the Horses* (Kerryman, 1996)

SMITH, Raymond. *Vincent O'Brien: The Master of Ballydoyle* (Virgin, 1990)

STEVENS, John. *Knavesmire* (Pelham Books, 1984)

THOMPSON, Douglas. *The Hustler* (Sidgwick & Jackson, 2007)

VAMPLEW, Wray & KAY, Joyce. *Encyclopedia of British Horseracing* (Routledge, 2005)

VARIOUS. *Faber Book of the Turf* (Faber and Faber, 1990)

WALKER, Alan Yuill. *Thoroughbred Studs of Great Britain* (Weidenfeld & Nicholson, 1991)

WARD HILL, Joe. *The Betting Man* (Elcott, 1993)

WARNER, Gerry. *Who's Who in Racing 1947* (Warner's Racing Agency, 1947)

WELCH, Ned. *Who's Who in Thoroughbred Racing* (Vantage Press USA, 1962)

WRIGHT, Howard. *Bull: The Biography* (Timeform, 1995)

INDEX